MODERN HUMANITIES RESEARCH ASSOCIATION

TEXTS AND DISSERTATIONS
(formerly Dissertation Series)

VOLUME 12

Editor
H. B. NISBET
(Germanic)

D1826631

The Significance of Locality
in the Poetry
of Friedrich Hölderlin

THE SIGNIFICANCE OF LOCALITY
IN THE POETRY
OF FRIEDRICH HÖLDERLIN

by

DAVID J. CONSTANTINE

LONDON
THE MODERN HUMANITIES RESEARCH ASSOCIATION
1979

Published by

The Modern Humanities Research Association

Honorary Treasurer, MHRA

KING'S COLLEGE, STRAND
LONDON WC2R 2LS
ENGLAND

ISBN 0 900547 53 7

Printed in England by
W. S. MANEY & SON LIMITED
HUDSON ROAD LEEDS

CONTENTS

ACKNOWLEDGEMENTS

My thanks are due to Sir Maurice Bowra for his generous encouragement of my interest in Greece; to my supervisors, Professor E. L. Stahl and Mr. G. W. McKay, for many helpful criticisms and suggestions; to Fräulein Maria Kohler, of the Hölderlin-Archiv, Stuttgart, and to the D.A.A.D. (German Academic Exchange Service).

PREFACE

Unless otherwise stated Hölderlin's works and letters are referred to by a volume, page and, where necessary, line number in the *Große Stuttgarter Ausgabe* (GStA): e.g. vi, 39, lines 249-50. The seventh volume, in four parts, is referred to thus: vii, 2, 30.

Christopher Theodor Schwab's edition of 1846 is referred to simply as Schwab, the critical edition of 1913-23 (Hellingrath, Seebaß, and Pigenot) simply as Hellingrath, followed by a volume and page number: e.g. Schwab, ii, 267; Hellingrath, vi, 367.

Hölderlin-Jahrbuch has been abbrebiated to *HJB* in the notes and bibliography.

Whenever possible references have been included in the text, but all other references and all notes, indicated by superior numbers in the text, have been arranged at the end of the volume.

CHAPTER 1

HÖLDERLIN'S POETIC WORLD

There are poets whose works are sited mainly or even entirely in one particular and unchanging context. Their themes, however varied and general, have always the same setting, and ideas are illustrated only in terms appropriate to it. A poet working in this way has a world of his own, one that is characteristically his, in which his poetry is sited, and with which his name is always associated. This world has its own constitution and coherence; it is enclosed and separate, the work of one man, whether he had depicted it carefully from reality, or wholly imagined it, or shaped it out of the hopes and nostalgia of his contemporaries. The world becomes his own, and his work is inconceivable outside the familiar setting.

This is not true of all, or even of very many poets. There is a Homeric world, a world of Thomas Hardy or of Dante, but not, in that sense, a Goethean or Schillerean world. 'The Goethean world' calls to mind ideas, contemporary personalities and events, but in no important or specific setting. Goethe's world is not Weimar. 'The world of Thomas Hardy' sets the ideas, people, and events in a particular and supremely important geographical context, in Wessex. Moreover the place comes to mind first. Hardy limits himself to Wessex, and his themes, as general and significant as Goethe's, are worked out there, in Wessex terms. Goethe's themes have no established, physical world to contain them. There is a Homeric world, the site of a particular past age, in Ionia and the Aegean; and, of a visionary, extra-terrestrial kind, there is a world of Dante, precisely composed. But, in that sense, there is no Kleistian world, no world of Keats or Mallarmé. Their poetry has no consistently preferred physical setting. In fact the setting is often arbitrary or non-existent.

In making his own world a poet may appropriate one region, a real area of the earth accessible to all, and devote himself exclusively to it. Most places have local poets to celebrate them, writers unknown outside the neighbourhood; but only great poetry and the treatment of general themes give the region status beyond its geographical limits and invest things of parochial interest with absolute significance. In Hardy's work, or the German Poetic Realists', general themes are treated effectively in local terms. Such poetry is founded in a strong love for the chosen region and in a vast amount of local lore patiently acquired over many years. Places are in themselves attractive and worthy of attention. The spirit of the place is felt and respected. The poetry deals intimately with real places, and describes them recognizably in a more or less realistic manner. One aim is to celebrate the region, and so fix in art a way of life in a particular environment. The poet's material is factual and detailed. He creates his own world from it by selection, arrangement, and emphasis, and by using the facts and details as terms of his own expression.

Another world is the wholly imagined one, having no discernible resemblance to any area of the real world. It may still be formed in the terms of earthly topography. The author draws his own maps, names his own towns, rivers, and mountain-ranges, and works out his themes in that fictitious setting. This independence of reality may give him scope for symbolism and allegory, so that his hills become Hills of Difficulty and his towns Celestial Cities. Or he may tell a more or less plausible story, siting it in the imagined lands for the glamour they perhaps provide. And the setting may not even be a recognizably earthly one. The poet might invent a whole universe, as Dante did, taking in Heaven and Hell, with landscapes totally unknown on earth. The constitution of such a world is his own doing, although what he imagines may be significantly like what all his contemporaries would imagine. But the creation is in his name, and counts as his world, especially for later generations.

A heroic world, as depicted by a single poet, by Homer, for example, appears complete in itself and is associated with the poet's name. It is his world, in that he becomes the best or only exponent of it. He represents his age in looking back and depicting ideally a better age. He does not invent the heroic world—it is a myth of all his contemporaries—but he re-creates it. His lasting work gives it unity and independence of time. The heroic world is a fit setting for heroes and heroic action. It is sited only vaguely in time and place. Time is simply the ideal past. The geography is often confused, because of the poet's inadequate knowledge of the world beyond his own district. But a general region for action is established, in the Aegean for Homer, in western Scotland for Ossian, and along the Rhine and Danube for the Nibelungen story. Details of the region are not easily fixed. This uncertainty gives a vague glamour to the world. The real and the fabulous are confused, the limits are hazy and distant parts are accessible only through hearsay. But places are distinguished only by association with heroes and great events. In their own right they hardly exist. The tone of the heroic world is solemn and dignified. People and events are exalted beyond what later ages can achieve. Consciousness of this world is shared by the poet and his audience. He is the exponent of their common myth. References and associations are part of a shared heritage and culture, and as such are open to all.

Just as there is a Homeric world and a world of Dante or of Thomas Hardy, so too, although of a different kind, there is a Hölderlin world, one he has created, in which he works out his themes and with which his name may always be associated. It is characteristically his, the creation of one man. Its form and salient features can be understood only through him, because the world was shaped in the likeness of his ideas. Therefore, although the places constituting his world exist independently and are available as material to any artist, the sum total when brought together is the

work and world of Friedrich Hölderlin alone. The whole is greater than the sum of
the parts, a new thing unforeseeable in the disparate pieces.

The purpose of this first chapter is to define, briefly, the nature of Hölderlin's
world, seen at its most coherent in the mature poetry of 1800-02, a world which
has something of the three types mentioned, but which is not entirely any one of
them; and also to begin to consider the imaginative processes by which such a
world is created, to consider what kind of poetic intelligence Hölderlin's was.

Themes broached in this chapter will be treated at length in the chapters that
follow.

Hölderlin's Swabia

Hölderlin was a Swabian, much in love with his homeland, as most Swabian poets
were. He lived nearly all his life there; attempts to live elsewhere failed sooner or
later. In his poetry and in his letters 'Vaterland' is almost always synonymous with
Swabia. In Waltershausen he made a point of looking out his fellow-countrymen:
'Die Schwaben haben sich überall bald aufgespürt' (vi, 106). His relationship with
Schiller was first as one Swabian with another. Schiller called him 'mein liebster
Schwabe' (vii, 2, 30).[1]

Hölderlin knew his homeland intimately: its rhythms of work and the seasons;
the customs, legends, and historical associations of particular places; the achieve-
ments of famous compatriots. And the poetry displays this knowledge; often, in
early poems and the late fragments, in a full, detailed, and realistic manner.[2]

But Hölderlin is not, for all that, a regional poet, not a 'Heimatdichter' of the
poetic-realist type. His world is not Swabia; he is not associated with Swabia in the
way that Storm is associated with the North Sea coast or Annette von Droste-
Hülshoff with Westphalia. Such poets are interested in the place itself; they respect
it and let it be. This is not Hölderlin's way. He celebrates the homeland, or a
particular Swabian site always with a fixed idea in mind. At first this fixed idea is
the conventional one: the ruins of Teck are celebrated in a mood of conventional
nostalgia for the heroic past;[3] later it is Hölderlin's own: Swabia is celebrated as the
ideal homeland, heart of the new Hesperia, to which the archetypal wanderer will
finally return after years of hardship abroad.[4] The places of Hölderlin's world are
almost never described in their own right, but according to whatever overall idea
the poet has imposed on them. For example, in the poetry of 1801 Swabian places
are described in Greek style because to relate west and east, modern and classical, is
Hölderlin's overall poetic purpose.[5]

A visionary world?

The details of Hölderlin's world are real and exact. The places of which it is
composed—Athens, Stuttgart, Patmos—all have a historical reality. And the land-
scapes, for all their glamour, are recognizably earthly. The topography is of this earth;

rivers and mountain-ranges are constituted naturally, and even named and sited in specific regions of the real world. These places and landscape features exist independently and might be visited. Nor does Hölderlin go much beyond the earth when attempting to visualize his Heaven and Hell. He is content with the ether above, in which a Father-God rules, and an abyss below, in which the forces of chaos are uneasily contained. He does not picture precisely the one or the other. Heaven is light, best imagined in the blue Greek sky; Hell is darkness, absence of the sunlight. And so much suffices. The splendour of Heaven brightens the earthly landscapes of Asia Minor, and the unrestraint of Hell is loosed in real forces—armies, frost, or the north wind—over the earth.

Thus although Hölderlin is preoccupied with God and the opponents of God, he imagines no extra-terrestrial setting for their activities but makes them manifest on earth, in the Alps or the Greek islands, and in earthly phenomena, such as day, night, storms, and warfare. Dante describes Hell, Purgatory, and Paradise with the clear precision of the topographer, so creating a visionary world distinct from the real one. Hölderlin keeps within earthly limits, but his act of creation is akin to Dante's. His vision is wide and, for a year or so at least, coherent; its details are manifold.

Nor is the distinction between the real (recognizably earthly) world of Hölderlin and the unreal (unfamiliarly cosmic) world of Dante a sound one. What Hölderlin creates from real places and landscape features is a new world which is arguably as unearthly as Dante's. The coherence given to formerly unrelated places changes their nature and raises their significance immeasurably. Hölderlin is the author of this coherence. His world is an imagined one, although comprising real places. He creates it, and shapes it to his own ends. He never allows the reality of his world's component parts to prevent him from using them for whatever poetic purpose he thinks fit. Bunyan let an imaginary mountain be his Hill of Difficulty, but Hölderlin accords comparable virtues to ranges of the real world.

Hölderlin's world is mapped out to illustrate one fixed idea, and in coherent form Hölderlin has it before his eyes. He *sees* his idea illustrated in mountains and rivers. In two senses, then—first that it is a work of independent imagination, and secondly that it is clearly seen in physical form—Hölderlin's may be called a visionary world.[6]

A heroic world

Hölderlin's world is the setting for great events, in which men and gods are involved. Nothing trivial happens there. Those taking part have stature and prestige Gods have been active on the earth, and will be again, in time. Asia Minor has mountains, rivers, and towns associated with both Christ and Dionysus. Its landscapes, as the poem 'Patmos' describes them, must be supremely beautiful because in those surroundings things of transcendental significance were worked out. When the gods do return it will be to the new Hesperia: fit landscapes must be prepared

for them there. Demi-gods, heroes and great men abound, modern ones, like
Rousseau or Napoleon, and countless ancient ones, Socrates, Heracles, Achilles.
Their names are associated with real places. No second-rate, or even normal people
are admitted to this world. Friends of Hölderlin appear enhanced. Sinclair, Heinse,
Landgraf Friedrich are raised to the status of ideals. The unnamed figures—the
traveller, farmer, pilgrim, trader—become archetypes, and at that level have an
important role in Hölderlin's world. All figures, from gods to traders, are perfected
in their type. Contemporary events, the French Revolution and the subsequent
wars, are idealized to become part of a cosmic scheme. People and events, both
past and present, are mythicized. Hölderlin's world is a heroic one, as Homer's was,
a fit setting for heroes and tremendous events.

The places in this world, towns or features of landscape, hold the glamour of
what happened there. Merely to name a place is to evoke memories of a god, a
great man, or an event. The place distinguished first in its own character by an
appropriate epithet, claims further fame in its associations. This is the Homeric
way, and Hölderlin's too. He can sometimes incorporate the Homeric place, with
its characteristic quality and its associations, into his own mythology. Or, when
other places become important to him, he names them in the Homeric fashion,
but with associations of his own. Or personal and long-established associations may
be mixed.

In Hölderlin's heroic world there are places that have been celebrated since
Homer, whilst others are of Hölderlin's own choosing. But the old and the new
share the same status. The Alps are not inferior to Olympus. Places of Hölderlin's
own homeland whose associations were only local or private to himself are
idealized and stand besides Athens or Parnassus. The heroic tone is maintained;
past and present, far and near, are exalted to the same degree.[7]

Places in the heroic world are famous by repute; often their splendours are
hearsay. They are celebrated in travellers' tales and easily become fabulous. Some
of their glamour is due to this flattering vagueness. Hölderlin's world, like Homer's,
is one for travelling in. It has not been exhaustively explored; Odysseus would be
at home there. Traders and sailors, pilgrims, wanderers, and migrating birds cross
the world from end to end, and their activity has the glamour of an age when travel
and communication were a serious adventure. From personal experience Hölderlin
knew the mystique of travel. He was an excellent walker, and had a passion for
travellers' tales and maps. On his winter journey to Bordeaux he outdid the
archetypal *Wanderer* of his own poems. Images of journeying recur in the works
and the letters. From the Greek world Hölderlin took the image of Hesperia, the
fabulous west, the voyage beyond the Pillars of Hercules into the attractive
unknown; and from his own times the voyages of discovery in the Atlantic and
the South Seas. Most of his mature poems are shaped by nostalgia for Greece and
by the visionary journey there.[8]

Poet and audience share consciousness of the heroic world. The story of Troy, as Homer tells it, is part of his audience's cultural heritage. Places alluded to are widely famous, and their associations are common knowledge. This means, in effect, that much can be left unsaid. The poet can confidently expect his audience to appreciate whatever associations the naming of a place evokes. Homer assumes in his audience an awareness of what Mycenae, Troy, or Dodona should mean to all who are not barbarians. Even if he then briefly characterizes a place, as he does Dodona (*Iliad*, xvi, 233-35), he tells his audience nothing that they do not already know.

Except in his early poetry, when his ideals and enthusiasms were entirely conventional, Hölderlin found no such understanding among his audience. True, they shared the nostalgia and hope out of which his poetic world was created, the nostalgia for Greece and the hope that one day their own country would flourish. But the poetic form in which Hölderlin expressed their common ideas, and the religious intensity of his poetry were incomprehensible to them. Every new development of Hölderlin's thought and poetic technique widened the gap between him and his audience. By 1803 he had withdrawn into a nearly private world.

Nevertheless Hölderlin's attitude towards his audience never significantly altered in all the years of his creative life. He let his poetic world of 1801 seem to be based on the general culture of his age, and assumed, or pretended to assume, in the way that Homer genuinely could, that all his allusions were comprehensible to his entire audience.

Homer did not invent his heroic world. He put it into poetry, but he did not alter or extend it beyond the common, traditional knowledge of his audience. Hölderlin's heroic world, however, was invented by Hölderlin. He shaped it according to his ideas, and as his thinking developed beyond the level of general culture that he shared with his contemporaries, his world, although he still presented it as though it were open to all, in fact became increasingly private.[9]

By what imaginative processes is a poetic world of this kind created? What sort of intelligence sets out its problems in the terms of such a world?

One thing is obvious from the start: Hölderlin's single-mindedness. In creating a world to express his ideas he was helped by the essentially uncomplicated nature of those ideas. He has really only one theme: the hoped-for renaissance of an ideal civilization, and the role and proper behaviour of those awaiting it. Almost every poem he wrote is recognizably relevant to this. The mature work of 1800 to 1803 never leaves the topic, and neither the early poems nor the late fragments ever indicate interests much outside it. Even the most personal experiences, like the love for Susette Gontard, are removed into the context of a general cultural predicament, where they accord perfectly with the other cultural and religious themes. Hölderlin calls her 'die Athenerin' (i, 243).

A coherent interest and philosophy are thus maintained—at considerable cost, it might be thought. Much is forfeited in single-mindedly pursuing the one great theme. No irrelevance is permitted, and even relevant material must be susceptible of enhancement into ideal terms if it is to be used. This exclusiveness is prescribed by the nature of the poetry Hölderlin wrote—and by his own personality, which was quite at one with his poetry. He seems, as a person, to have lacked those qualities which are inimical to the setting up of extensive philosophical systems: humour, for instance, irony, tolerance, common interest in single human beings, and what might be called vulgarity. He was himself aware of this. In a letter to Neuffer he wrote:

Es fehlt mir weniger an Kraft, als an Leichtigkeit, weniger an Ideen, als an Nüancen, weniger an einem Hauptton, als an mannigfaltig geordneten Tönen, weniger an Licht, wie an Schatten, und das alles aus Einem Grunde; ich scheue das Gemeine und Gewöhnliche im wirklichen Leben zu sehr. (vi, 289)

There was nothing in his nature to check his, typically German, tendency to deal in large and ideal terms and his obsession with absolute coherence.[10]

His interests were limited, and the world he created to express them was limited accordingly. There are no gratuituous trips to romantic places in Hölderlin's world; his journeys are serious undertakings. There is no gratuitous poetry of euphonic proper names. Places are included purposefully, or not at all. It is unlikely that any modern poet would limit himself in this way—just as it is unlikely that any modern poet would have a philosophy as limited and coherent as Hölderlin's to expound. If Rilke writes one poem about Venice and another about St Petersburg, then all that links these two places in Rilke's poetry is his having been there and his fortuitous choice of them as subjects of his poems. But if Hölderlin celebrates the Main in one poem, and the Pactolus or the Cephissus in another then a deliberate and meaningful relationship has been created, in the world of Hölderlin's poetry, between these distant rivers. Hölderlin's places are carefully chosen to fulfil his overall poetic purpose. Rilke's places assert themselves, and are in themselves worthy of a poem. Thus for all Hölderlin's preoccupation with locality there are in his works no true poems of place.[11] He could not write a poem like Hardy's 'Lulworth Cove' or D. H. Lawrence's 'Autumn at Taos', in which a place with its own qualities and associations is allowed to assert itself. And yet he travelled, and saw many places and could not have been indifferent to them. But those he wrote about were those that suited the limited themes of his poetry. Thomas Hardy might have written a poem about the low hedge near the poplar trees where Hölderlin passed at 10a.m. on the first Thursday of every month to be seen by Susette Gontard. But it is inconceivable that Hölderlin himself would ever have written such a poem—at least, not before 1803. The hedge and the poplars are too intimate and too particular—they could never be enhanced sufficiently to be admitted into Hölderlin's poetic world.[12]

It should be said that this world, although constituted only of places that externalize ideas and so no wider in range or fuller in detail than are the ideas themselves, is nevertheless by no means bare or uninteresting. More than a hundred and fifty towns, mountains, islands and rivers give it substance. The one theme could be variedly expounded and illustrated.

Selecting certain places to be incorporated into his poetic world Hölderlin simultaneously clears them of all unwanted associations. They appear in his world not as real places in their own right but as illustrations of his thought, bearing the significance he has imposed on them. They are simplified according to the author's fixed idea.

It is significant that Hölderlin's letters are almost totally lacking in precise, detailed descriptions of locality. He was, he said, content with the 'Totaleindruk' (vi, 168) that a place made on him—the overall, general impression of a place, not its peculiarities and incidental details. He apprehended a place in its simplified form. He particularly liked looking down on a landscape from a vantage point, having it spread out beneath him; at his disposal, as it were. There are many such views, in the letters and in the poetry. Particular details are invisible from a height, or appear unimportant; what is lasting and general, the basic, simple structure, is revealed. It is from a 'Totaleindruk' that Hölderlin describes a landscape, and imposes his own sense on it.[13]

Since natural features of landscape, as well as countries, towns and villages, are made to serve a definite poetic purpose within Hölderlin's coherent world it may be worth asking in what sense landscape can be said to be significant, and to what extent it is susceptible of an imaginative interpretation.

There is arguably only one sense in which landscape may be called significant, and that is in its association with human beings. When man acts upon his environment, builds a bridge, makes a path, uses a waterway, then, in his terms, the landscape acquires meaning. The Alpine passes, for example, could fairly be celebrated as the real links between one civilization and another. That has been their historical role—for human beings, their meaning. Similarly, a great river, like the Danube, has been as a matter of historical fact a migration-route, and so a real link between western Europe in the Black Forest and the Greek world on the Black Sea. The significance is inherent in the use human beings have always made of the river or the mountain pass. Or an unremarkable and humanly useless locality may be distinguished and so made meaningful in human terms by an event or encounter there. Perhaps it is the site of an important meeting, or of a battle. Through its association with human life that place thereafter could fairly be called humanly significant. In these ways human beings, living in the world, impose their meaning on it.

But outside their sphere, in areas of the world they have not marked, it could be argued that the landscape has no significance, in human terms, whatsoever. Admittedly such untouched regions are rare, in Europe at least. But unless used by man, or distinguished by a remembered human encounter, a hill is a hill, a plain is a plain, and nothing more. In their natural state they are not open to human inter-pretation. Such landscapes have no human sense; they are unapproachable, indifferent, and can hardly even be discussed in human terms. They are naturally without meaning. It might be considered presumptuous to impose any meaning on them, and sheer arrogance to claim insight into their essential truth, if they have no essential truth. It is reasonable and proper to say of a hill: 'Here King Harold and his bodyguard fought to the last man. This places holds their memory'. Or to say of a river: 'From time immemorial this has been a trade-route down which amber came from the Baltic to the Mediterranean Sea'. And to celebrate the hill or river accordingly. But it is an entirely different matter to say of a range of hills that in their shape and trend God's will and a nation's future are made manifest. Doubtless the hills have had association with human beings and in that sense do have a meaning, but it is a kind of presumption then to accord to them further meaning other than or beyond what is rooted in historical fact. Similarly, to make of a river that could justly be celebrated as a trade or migration route the symbol of a nation's relatedness to and nostalgia for its cultural origins is to impose human meaning on a thing arguably not susceptible of human interpretation. It is not to have insight into the essential truth of the river.

Landscape is significant only in so far as it has been acted upon by human beings. Independently landscape has no meaning. To wish to impose meaning upon it is understandable—human beings must affirm themselves against the disquieting indifference of the natural world—but the exercise is an arbitrary one. For one meaning is as good as the next. There is no essential, final truth to be revealed.

To Hölderlin, as to most of his German contemporaries, such arguments would be unacceptable. For him all landscape is significant, and the poet's responsibility is to interpret it. No poet ever had a surer sense than Hölderlin of the archetypal significance of those landscape features that clearly *are* meaningful in human terms: the high mountain pass, the abyss that intrepid travellers have bridged, the headland that sailors are glad of as a landmark. And he was certainly sensitive to the historical significance of particular places (even though in his poetry he rarely pays particular places their proper due). But beyond this Hölderlin has a highly developed sense of a landscape's *ideal* significance, of what a landscape means other than or more than the meaning that has accrued to it from contact with human beings. He imposes meaning; or, he would say himself, reveals it.

The fragment 'Communismus der Geister', whether or not Hölderlin wrote it, exactly expresses this attitude towards landscape. The two youths, supposedly Hölderlin and Hegel, watching the sunset from a vantage point, are saddened and disquieted as the sunlight leaves the countryside below them:

wenn das Auge des Himmels aus der Natur genommen ist und so die weite Erde da liegt, wie ein Räthsel, dem das Wort der Lösung fehlt. (iv, 307)

It was the poet's responsibility, in Hölderlin's view, to supply the open sesame to the landscape's concealed significance. Landscape was for him inherently meaningful, not arbitrarily arranged this way or that, and his poetic gifts enabled him to make its meaning clear.

Hölderlin thought this function of his poetry a very important one: 'der Trieb des Idealisirens oder Beförderns, Verarbeitens, Entwikelns, Vervollkommnens der Natur' (vi, 328) was, he thought, a basic human urge, in fact the original, moral impulse towards improvement and progress in human affairs. Poetry was to assist this impulse by presenting it with substantial images of the ideals it was striving towards, by prefiguring those ideals in a 'dargestellte höhere Welt' (vi, 329). This is the general function of poetry, and a specific instance of it is the idealization of landscape, the discovery in landscape of correlatives helpful and inspiring to man in his striving towards perfection. Nature is improved upon and given a moral sense (or her inherent moral sense, her part in the moral progress of all creation, is revealed). That is the philosophy behind the interpretation and manipulation of landscape features in Hölderlin's poetic world.[14] It derives from the belief, after Kant, that the mind is unavoidably involved in the creation of what it perceives.

Guardini, in his book *Form und Sinn der Landschaft in den Dichtungen Hölderlins*,[15] writes of Hölderlin's insight into the numinous being of rivers, his ability to experience them first-hand as demi-gods and archetypes, in the way that primitive peoples do. Goethe's 'Mahomets Gesang' is compared unfavourably with Hölderlin's 'Der Rhein' because in the former symbolic meaning is imposed upon the river by the poet, from outside, whereas in the latter the true nature and numinous essence of the river has been revealed. I doubt if any such absolute distinction can be made. When Hölderlin says of the Rhine '. . . und ungeduldig ihn/Nach Asia trieb die königliche Seele' (lines 36-37, ii, 143) is it insight into the essential being of the river, or is it a quite arbitrary imposition of meaning on to something which in itself naturally has no human meaning? Because of the Alpine barrier one branch of the Rhine flows north-east for about fifty miles as far as Chur, where it bears conclusively north. In another poet it might be thought no more than a conceit to make of that an indication of the drive to return to the eastern sources of culture. In the context of Hölderlin's coherent world it should be seen as a deliberate and necessary interpretation of topographical data to suit a precisely limited poetic purpose, rather than as an insight into the primitive, true nature of the river.[16]

A thorough discussion of Hölderlin's poetic method, of the imaginative processes out of which his poetic world was created, would lead too far at this stage. There are some important questions—the relationship of the idealizing and the mythopoeic processes, the degree of intuitive insight and deliberate, intellectual contriving in each—and these will be considered in the chapters that follow.

LOCALITY IN THE POEMS 1784-98

Hölderlin's world, as I described it in my first chapter, evolved at the turn of the century, was stable and, in its idea, coherent throughout 1801 when the great hymns were written, and began to disintegrate early in 1802, after Hölderlin's return from Bordeaux. Before 1799 the places used in his poetry were either quite disparate, or only loosely associated in a conventional manner. After 1802 his world first expanded beyond his control and then shrank back to the scope of his room in Tübingen. This second chapter deals with the use Hölderlin made of locality before 1799.

The technique of using locality to express ideas and the sense of possible coherence, of possible relationships between the places used, developed only gradually. In the Denkendorf, Maulbronn, and Tübingen years (1784-93) less than a third of the poems were at all concerned with place and fewer still made predominant use of it. Nor were places related significantly one with another: Greece and Swabia, for example, were both important from the earliest years, but were not brought together before 1799.

Nevertheless a study even of the very early poems is helpful in several ways. An increasing care in the use of place can be seen, also the changing significance accorded to places at different times, the shifts of emphasis, the loss and revival of interests, and the inclusion of new areas. It can be seen how coherence begins, how it grows from what is most typical in Hölderlin: his schematizing and idealizing habit of mind.

Place *need* not interest a poet; many make little or no use of it. But it was important to Hölderlin, indispensable to him in his mature work. His dependence on places increased, until after 1799 he was obsessively interested in scores of cities, mountains, and rivers throughout the Greek and modern world. He committed himself to them.

The degree of commitment to places is a criterion that can be applied when discussing how and why Hölderlin makes use of them. In the early years there is little or no commitment. Hölderlin frequently makes use of places in what I would call an unserious manner, writing then like the many poets—like many of his contemporaries all over Europe—to whom place never became important. There was no necessity for him ever to develop beyond this. But he did, and it is only because he did that these early, unserious, conventional habits of style are at all interesting. That may serve as an excuse for the rather trivial instances I shall have to use. These examples chosen from Hölderlin's early work could be multiplied by drawing on the *mature* work of many of his lesser contemporaries. Stolberg, Conz, Neuffer, and the others rarely used place in anything but an unserious way.

Certain place-names have become so much a part of poetic jargon that it is difficult to think of them as places at all. They stand for some quality or thing, become 'poetic' synonyms of it, and entirely lose their original identity. They become cyphers, good-tone words acceptable in conventional poetry. Many are Greek—Olympus, Parnassus, Troy—and they, and words derived from them, have developed meanings in which little or no sense of the place itself survives. In the Neo-Hellenist eighteenth century they were sound poetic words that no poet would be shy of using. Hölderlin's early poems are not free of them. For example:

> In Fülle schweben lesbische Gebilde,
> Begeisterung, vom Seegenshorne dir!
>> ('Hymne an die Menschheit', lines 53-54, i,147)

or:

> Folgte mir zu Wies' und Wald
> Die arkadische Gestalt.
>> ('Hymne an die Schönheit', lines 47-48, i,150)

Other places similarly used are: Olympus, Pieria, and the mythological Elysium and Hesperia. No sense of place is intended, 'Lesbisch' is synonymous with 'poetic', Lesbos being the birthplace of Sappho, Arion, and Alcaeus; and 'arkadisch', if it is not meaningless, with 'lovely', 'simple', 'innocent', those qualities being tradition-ally at home in Arcadia.

Place-names as used in these examples are cypher-words. Later Hölderlin almost always paid the place itself more tribute—by celebrating its real qualities and by evoking its associations. This is a second criterion: how much does the place itself matter? In the early poetry it matters scarcely at all. But by 1800, in the poem 'Der Archipelagus', Lesbos is an island among the others, appropriately typified: 'Lesbos glüht . . .' (ii,634). And in the two early Swiss poems 'Kanton Schwyz' (1791) and 'An Hiller' (1793) Arcadia, the place, asserts itself a little. The comparison of Switzerland with Arcadia, although conventional in the extreme, was based originally on a just observation of certain things the two countries had in common. Both were land-locked and surrounded by mountains, and the inhabitants of both lived a hard, simple, pastoral life and were good fighters. Arcadians, like Swiss, made notable mercenaries. So when, remembering the Schwyz valley, Hölderlin writes:

> Wo Fels und Wald ein holdes zauberisches
> Arkadien umschließt, wo himmelhoch Gebirg . . .
>> ('An Hiller', lines 28-29, i,173)

his referring to Arcadia is, although conventional, appropriate, and shows more sense of place than the cypher-phrase 'die arkadische Gestalt'.[1]

A characteristic of the early conventional references is their carelessness. Since they are not intended to carry much weight their accuracy and consistency are often of a low order. The conventions are easily confused.[2] In 'Adramelech', for example, an early poem in the Christian convention, Hölderlin writes: '. . . und meine Gedanken, die den Olympus beherrschen' ('Adramelech', line 5, i,9). The incongruousness of this classical reference in a biblical poem is a mark of how lightly it was made. In 'Keppler' two or three conventions are confused. Kepler was a Swabian and it seemed appropriate to celebrate him in Teutonic idiom:

> Wonne Walhallas! und ihn gebahr
> Mein Vaterland?
>
> (lines 25-26, i,82)

But the homeland itself is given its Latin name: 'Mutter der Redlichen! Suevia! ' (line 33; cf.line 31). Kepler is 'Suevias Sohn' (line 16). Also in the Latin idiom are Albion (lines 9, 32) and Themse (lines 13,26), the home of Kepler's great successor, Newton; although Albion is the Celtic or pre-Celtic rather than the Roman name for Britain. Then another oath, like 'Wonne Walhallas!'—'Heklas Gedonner vergäß' ich so . . .' (line 29). Hekla, an Icelandic volcano, was used by Stolberg and Schiller as a kind of Nordic Etna, and is thus a modern addition to the traditional Teutonic convention.

There is carelessness in the poem 'An die Menschheit':

> So wahr, von Giften unbetastet,
> Elysens Blüthe zur Vollendung eilt,
> Der Heldinnen, der Sonnen keine rastet,
> Und Orellana nicht im Sturze weilt!
>
> (lines 33-36, i,147)

Orellana is the Amazon, so called after Francesco de Orellana who sailed the length of it in 1542. Stolberg lists it among the great rivers of the earth in his 'Hymne an die Erde' (lines 86-89) and Matthisson makes not very apposite use of it in 'Der Genfer See' (lines 131-32). But Hölderlin seems to think of the river as a waterfall: 'Und Orellana nicht *im Sturze* weilt . . .'. He first wrote 'Niagara', for which 'im Sturze' is appropriate. Either he thought the Amazon a waterfall like Niagara, or, having chosen Orellana, he forgot or thought it unnecessary to alter the rest of the line accordingly. In fact neither name matters in the least; anything that could stand for irresistible progress would do.

Accuracy and consistency are hardly called for when the references are so unimportant. Hölderlin need not have gone beyond this. There are poets, even good ones, who never pay more than conventional and superficial attention to place. The interest here is in indicating that Hölderlin *did* develop. The references become more careful and are intended to express more; accuracy and consistency are no longer neglected. Hölderlin takes the trouble to find out about places, and then refers knowledgeably to them. Accuracy in evoking associations and exactness of topographical detail become characteristics of his later poetry. The course of the Rhine, the trend of the hills in south-east Germany, the relationship of Athos to Lemnos are precisely recorded. And on such a precise basis Hölderlin's myths are founded.

This accuracy dates from his reading of the travellers Chandler and Choiseul. They gave him maps, plans, and, especially Chandler, exact descriptions. What he made of this material will be discussed in the chapters to come. There are almost no inaccuracies or confusions in Hölderlin's mature work. In 'Dem Genius der Kühnheit' (lines 5-8, i,176) he incorrectly associates Dionysus with the island Ortygia ('Quail-Island' = Delos). Ortygia was sacred to Apollo; perhaps Hölderlin had Naxos in mind. But this is an early poem (1793). In the rough draft of 'Kolomb' Hölderlin wrote:

> Jason, Chirons
> Schüler, in Megaras Felsenhöhlen . .
>
> (lines 17-18, ii,877)

Chiron's home was in Magnesia, not in Megara. The frequent confusion of the rivers Cephissus and Ilissus, discussed by Beißner, may well be deliberate.[3] Finally, the error in the drafts of 'Mnemosyne'—'Am Olympos aber lag/Elevthera' (ii, 823)—is itself proof of a serious interest in the place. For although Mnemosyne's city was in fact on Cithaeron, as Hölderlin quickly remembered, it was under Olympus, in Pieria, that she bore her nine daughters, the Muses.

These are slight matters in the context of Hölderlin's entire, coherent world. It can be said that once references to place are intended seriously—expressing a great deal in cryptic form—then there is no confusion or inaccuracy.

Place-names may be used rhetorically, for their pleasant sound and for the colour, the exotic flavouring they lend. This is a favourite device of many poets, of Milton, for one. It implies no commitment to the places themselves, and is still what I would call a fundamentally unserious activity. Hölderlin attempts it only in his earliest poems, hardly at all after the Tübingen years. (This is not to say that the naming of places in the mature poems is without rhetorical intention and effect—on the contrary. But the rhetoric is incidental to the main purpose.)

The unremarkable examples will serve to indicate a conventionality Hölderlin grew out of. 'Alexanders Rede an seine Soldaten bei Issus' was written in 1785 whilst Hölderlin was at the 'Klosterschule' in Denkendorf. In all his Swabian schools the Classics were taught; his passion for Greece began there. It is as a school set-piece that this poem, Hölderlin's first celebration of Greek sites, should be seen. It is a speech, put into the mouth of Alexander before the decisive battle of Issus. The challenge for Hölderlin was to write a set-piece of rhetoric on a given subject. Some slight imaginative sympathy with Alexander and his soldiers would be needed, but otherwise only a little erudition and competence in rhetorical versifying. The erudition Hölderlin had from his schooling, and the competence, even at the age of fifteen, from imitation and much practice. And so the place-names are used:

> Kinder, glaubts; kein Thracien,
> Kein steinigtes Illyrien wird's seyn,
> Nein! Bactra, und das schöne Indien,
> Des Ganges Fluren sind der Sieger Siz . . .
>
> (lines 34-37, i,11)

To use place-names in this way is a device of rhetoric, appropriate in a speech urging on any army of mixed nations, Illyrians and Thracians among them. The effect, on the army and on the poet's audience, is hoped for in the reputation places have: 'stony' or 'lovely' (epithets in the classical manner). They are competently used in an appropriate context, and no more. As places they scarcely interest Hölderlin: they are those supplied by his source for the speech, Curtius Rufus (GstA, i,338). The poem is an exercise he might equally well have performed, and doubtless did, on many classical topics: 'Caesar's speech on crossing the Rubicon', or 'Leonidas to his Spartans at Thermopylae'. Any such poem would have its share of knowingly used place-names, just as it would of competent antitheses, apostrophes, and unexceptionable similes.

It is interesting to note the stature and glamour later acquired by places lightly and conventionally referred to in the early years. The biblical lands, for example, in 'Die Meinige', 'Adramelech', or 'Unsterblichkeit der Seele' next occur in the late stages of 'Patmos'. Many of the places mentioned in 'Alexanders Rede' are of central significance in Hölderlin's mythical world: Athens, for example, Boeotia and India. They assert themselves as places, and he commits himself to them. The difference between: 'Des Ganges Fluren sind der Sieger Siz . . .' and:

> Des Ganges Ufer hörten des Freudengotts
> Triumph . . .
>
> ('Dichterberuf', lines 1-2, ii,46)

is one of commitment to the place. The commitment that grows to Dionysus grows also to the places associated with him, just as the later turning to Christ naturally involves the places of his ministry. The Ganges in 1785 was good for an exotic reference; by 1800-01 it had become the eastern boundary of an imagined world. India is similarly enhanced; from its insignificant, merely rhetorical function in 'Alexanders Rede' to its mythical status in 'Andenken'.

Hesperia is another example. There are half a dozen references before this mythological locality takes on any lasting significance at all. Before 1800 and the poem 'Brod und Wein' Hesperia is used loosely in a variety of ways, all purely conventional and slight:

> Hesperiens beglükter Garten bringt
> Die goldnen Früchte nur im heißen Strahle . . .
>> ('An die klugen Rathgeber', lines 10-11, i,223)

or

> . . . in hesperischer Milde glänzt
> Der Winterhimmel . . .
>> ('Der Prinzessin Auguste von Homburg', lines 2-3, i,311)

Hesperia, here, is not much more than a fairyland enjoying a mild climate. The next reference is: 'Siehe! wir sind es, wir; Frucht von Hesperien ists! ' ('Brod und Wein', line 150, ii,95) which establishes the relationship of Greece with modern Europe.

Here are more examples of the slight and merely rhetorical use of place-names, all from the early years:[4]

> Vergiftete das Schnauben ihrer
> Rache, wie Syrias Abendlüfte . . .
>> ('Männerjubel' lines 35-36, i,68)

> . . . und im Sande von Afrika
> Das Gastrecht aufzusuchen . . .
>> (ibid., lines 45-46)

> . . . wann einst
> Des Ozeans Inseln sich küssen,
> Und Kolumbens Welt Lusitanias Küsten umarmt . .
>> ('Gustav Adolf', lines 17-19, i,85)

> Und trauft mir einst von Honigseim
> Das Land Arabia . . .
>> ('Schwabens Mägdelein', lines 33-34, i,78)

These may be compared with the Syria of 'Patmos', the Atlantic of 'Andenken' and 'Kolomb', the Arabia of 'Am Quell der Donau', even with the Africa of 'Der Wanderer' to indicate the different degrees of seriousness and commitment.

In the quotations Arabia and Africa are both cyphers, standing for exotic distance. They have served this poetic function since classical times. The poisonous evening breezes of Syria are also traditional, deriving from a classical source. The two Atlantic seaboards, like Orellana in 'An die Menschheit', are more modern images, but, as they are used here, are still only cyphers, standing for the extremely unlikely: the two coasts will never meet, nor will Gustav Adolf ever be forgotten; the river will never pause, nor will mankind's hopes be disappointed.

There were many such places that served Hölderlin and his contemporaries as concise expressions of distance, exotic beauty and tremendousness. Matthisson, in his poem 'Der Genfer See', uses Greenland, Tahiti, Etna, Stromboli, and, elsewhere, Peru, Golconda, Indus, and Paestum, always as ultimates of the exotic.[5] The popularity with poets of many of these places was due to contemporary voyages of discovery, for example in the South Seas, and to the many accounts of

dilettante travel in Asia Minor and the remoter regions of Europe. The original
enthusiasm for, say, Tahiti or Greenland was genuine and potentially fruitful.
New images were revealed to the imagination as they were during the Renaissance
when the Americas were opened up. Perhaps it was enough merely to refer to these
new places. It is difficult to gauge exactly how much glamour they had, how much
they could enhance a poem, and how much repetition they would bear. A good
deal of their effect has been lost in two hundred years, and the simple, frequent
referring to them seems glib and unsatisfactory. They made up a conventional,
poetic stock in trade, on which Hölderlin and his contemporaries freely drew.

The next, and, really, the last exotic references of this kind occur in the rough
drafts of 'Der Wanderer' (1797). The poem is a useful one here. In its several stages
before the published version of 1797 it indicates the development of a more serious
treatment of place.

The poem was published in the *Horen* in 1797, but the rough drafts go back to
well before that date, possibly to late 1795. They indicate considerable re-
thinking of the poem. The published version has:

> Einsam stand ich und sah in die Afrikanischen dürren
> Ebnen hinaus . . .
>
> (lines 1-2, i,206)

But before choosing Africa Hölderlin tried Egypt: 'Süden kenn ich und Nord. Mich
erhizte der Sommer Aegyptens . . .' (i,513) and Arabia: 'Oftmals ist mir, als
ständ' ich verirrt in Arabiens Wüste' (i,513).

In deciding why Africa was preferred it may help to note certain other changes
that were made. Exotic details of the two extreme regions were either omitted or
toned down. Thus the south loses its apes and tigers; the camel remains, but is less of
a fabulous beast: 'Wasser bewahrte mir treulich das fromme Kameel . . .' (line 14)
in earthenware pitchers, for all we know, and not, as the earlier version had it, in
its remarkable belly (i,516, lines 1-2). The north loses its glaciers. In short, the
regions are simplified. The change is from an easily exotic landscape to a more
carefully composed and mythical one, whose north and south are extremes of
experience rather than of latitude. Obviously it was intended so from the
first—the line quoted, 'Oftmals ist mir . . .' indicates this—but it was some time
before Hölderlin could resist the temptation of the exotic details. When he had
simplified the world of this poem he chose Africa instead of Egypt or Arabia. The
Pole was the obvious choice for the cold north (there was, of course, much
contemporary voyaging in the polar regions, in search of a north-western passage
to India), but neither Egypt nor Arabia would be a good counterpart. They are not
unambiguously south enough, and are too various in their associations, distractingly
rich and exotic, and, since classical times, too well known. Africa suits better as
the southern extreme. It was a continent without much significance for Hölderlin.
He could let it be, as Strabo did for the Greeks, simply the torrid southern zone. He

was probably as vague about its true nature and geography as were the Greeks themselves. In his time the exploration of Africa had scarcely begun. The coast was fairly well known but the interior was still a mystery.

The world of 'Der Wanderer' is composed in a Greek manner. Between the two extremes lies the οἰκουμένη, the inhabited area of the world. In the published version Hölderlin's οἰκουμένη is the Rhineland. But he first wrote: 'Nach Ausonien kehr' ich zurük in die freundliche Heimath' (i,518, lines 29-30). It is curious how false this rings. Obviously the 'ich' of the poem need not be the poet himself. Even in its early versions 'Der Wanderer' has general import. Yet Ausonia is false. 'Aber jezt kehr' ich zurük an den Rhein, in die glükliche Heimath' (line 37, i,207) is a gain in both coherence and truth. (The version of 1800 sites the homeland precisely, beneath the Taunus mountain (line 53, ii,81).) The poet does not increase the general import of his poem by falsifying, for the sake of a convention, the circumstances of his own life. 'Auch den Eispol hab' ich besucht . . .' (line 19, i,206) is an acceptable metaphor to express an extreme of experience. It tells not factual but poetic truth. But his returning to Ausonia, the Italy of conventional verse,[6] tells neither factual nor poetic truth. It is an artificiality, a falsification. When Hölderlin chooses the Rhineland he begins a process that governs all his best work: the making of myths out of the real circumstances of his life. Thus the exclusion of Ausonia is an important step forward in the imaginative use of place. A smaller indication of the same progress in his preferring the Alps to the Atlas mountains in 'An den Aether', a poem written at the same time as 'Der Wanderer' (i,508, ll. 26-28).

Towards the end of 'Der Wanderer' two lines were excluded in the published version:

> Wo ich einst im kühlen Gebüsch, in der Stille des Mittags
> Von Otahitis Gestad', oder von Tinian las.
>
> (lines 28-29, i,520)

These must have been hard to omit. The voyages of Cook, Anson, Bougainville, and La Pérouse were popular reading, and the exploration of the South Seas was inspiring to eighteenth-century writers. It gave them a mythology of travel, an enthusiasm that poet and audience could share, something of a commonly understood culture, almost as Homer and Pindar had. There is a note in the 1792 edition of Matthisson's poems to line 79 of 'Der Genfer See', where the phrase '. . . mit Ansons Heldenkraft' occurs:

Das Andenken dieses großen Seehelden, dessen Reise um die Welt (von 1740 bis 44) zu den merkwürdigsten und gefahrvollsten gehört, die jemals unternommen wurden, bedarf noch keiner Erneuerung.

The great sailors were the age's heroes, and their achievements were fit subjects for celebration in poetry. (The twentieth century has its astronauts, but, quite rightly, can make nothing of them.) In wanting to write about these voyages Hölderlin was only sharing his contemporaries' enthusiasm. Unfortunately Tahiti and Tinian do not belong in the cosmography of 'Der Wanderer'. They would detract from its simplicity. They are too actual, too precise and draw attention away from the Pole and Africa. The associations they carry could not be accommodated in the carefully worked out scheme of the poem. It would be tempting to use them—Matthisson and the others would not have thought twice about it—but Hölderlin saw the need for coherence, the law of his own poem and excluded two places whose appeal would be gratuitously exotic. Again this indicates greater seriousness, more discipline, and more sense of how locality can best be used. Much later Hölderlin understood how these inspiring contemporary voyages might be incorporated into his whole mythology. 'Kolomb' is the unfinished tribute to the great sailors, and interpretation of their achievements.

This is the importance, for my thesis, of 'Der Wanderer'. The changes made from the first drafts to the published version of 1797 show how Hölderlin, in his use of places, was moving away from conventionality and rhetoric towards the deliberate creation, from places of his choosing, of a mythical world.

But the sum of all these early references—conventional, rhetorical, often not seriously intended, and paying scarcely any tribute to the place itself—is in no sense a coherent world. They remain disparate places, casually referred to, nothing drawing them together. Only rarely, for instance in 'Der Wanderer', are they meaningfully associated even within the single poem. Otherwise they are not interrelated nor intended to incorporate important ideas. If they are not mentioned again (Hekla, Bactra, Orellana) then they lapse completely, having contributed very little. If they do recur (Ganges, Syria, Arabia) then it is with a significance immeasurably increased and changed. They are found only in the early work; they are infrequent after 1793 and after 1799 they disappear for good.

There are, however, even in the early poems, places that Hölderlin writes of with great seriousness, celebrating them at length both for their physical reality and for the qualities and ideas they embody. These places are not 'referred to', are not used as flavouring in rhetorical figures, and not as good-tone words or cyphers, but are the subjects, or at least integral parts, of entire poems. The three most important are Swabia, Switzerland, and Greece. Since they are often celebrated it is possible to say exactly what Hölderlin's conception of these places was, what they meant for him. His originality in the treatment of places only emerged when he began bringing them together to form a world of his own. Until then, in his attitude to Greece, Switzerland, or his homeland Swabia, he was entirely conventional and shared the enthusiasms and prejudices of his contemporaries. But once again the conventional attitudes are interesting for the comparisons they offer with the later originality: the Switzerland of 'Kanton Schwyz' and 'Unter den

Alpen gesungen', the Swabia of 'Die Tek' and of 'Die Wanderung', the Greece of 'An den Genius Griechenlands' and of 'Patmos'. And conventionality itself is interesting. When an age is sure of its enthusiasms, when it has certain unquestioned myths, how can a poet avoid devaluing them if his job is their frequent exposition? And how shall he communicate what everybody knows and never doubts if not in conventional—that is, undisturbing, the expected—language? Hölderlin and his contemporaries brought to the celebration of Greece, Switzerland, or the Fatherland such a thoroughgoing unoriginality of thought and expression, so self-effacingly accepted and preached the age's myths, that it must have seemed to them there could be no other proper thing to do. It may simply be that such unquestioned enthusiasms have gone out of fashion, or it may be that contemporary myths can *only* be treated conventionally. Hölderlin was not an original poet until he made his own.

At this early stage Hölderlin undoubtedly shared a common culture with his audience. He thought what they thought of Switzerland, Greece, and the Fatherland, of America, Corsica, or Tahiti. His poetry then—the worst he ever wrote— was based on this mutual understanding, the convention, the agreement not to question the beliefs of the times. Like Homer or Pindar he could assume that his audience would understand. Later, when his idea of those places became more complex and private, he continued to assume that his audience understood. Soon, of course, they did not. The early poems, then, show Hölderlin briefly at one with his contemporary audience, writing for them as they expected him to write.

Germany—sometimes Swabia, sometimes a wider Germanic area—was the first of Hölderlin's themes. His earliest poems celebrate his homeland; between 1786 and 1789 a patriotism of the kind then in vogue was an inspiration to him. Then the interest lapsed for ten years, when a new and more complex patriotism evolved. 'Die Tek' is a product of the early enthusiasm, 'Germanien' of the mature mythopoetry.

Greece, although important from the first (through Denkendorf, Maulbronn, and Tübingen Hölderlin's education in the classics was continuing) began to emerge as a vividly imagined area only after 1793, the poem 'Griechenland' and the early work on *Hyperion*. Until then, despite the many Classical references and the few poems classically inspired, for example 'Hero' and 'Alexanders Rede', there is no poetic evidence of an interest in the places of Greece. The first enthusiasm, more or less conventional, lasted until 1796, typical products of it being 'Griechenland' (1793) and 'Der Gott der Jugend' (1795). It lost its conventionality when Hölderlin met Susette Gontard.

Germany and Greece were brought together in 1799, and the creation of a world outside the contemporary conventions had begun.

The interest in Switzerland, or, at least, poetic proof of it, was due solely to the journey of Easter, 1791. It is more than likely that Hölderlin had a preconception of Switzerland which the journey merely confirmed. There was no development of this until he went to Hauptwyl early in 1801.

These are the places I chiefly want to discuss, but others—America, Corsica, Sweden, for example—will be involved. They are places about which Hölderlin, with his contemporaries, had fixed ideas.

Germany

Hölderlin writes of Swabia sometimes as a patriot celebrating the homeland and sometimes as a private individual remembering places important in his own life. Poems like 'Die Tek' or 'An Thills Grab' combine the two enthusiasms. The patriotism, a public matter, is entirely conventional; the private memories occasionally make more original poems.

To begin with the patriotism. Poems written in the final year at Maulbronn (e.g. 'Die Tek') closely resemble those of the Tübingen years (e.g. 'Burg Tübingen') since throughout the time of Hölderlin's first interest in Swabia the idea of patriotism developed not at all. It was not the kind of idea that could develop. The individual poet could do almost nothing to it, because the idea was not his but a public matter, a convention that poets and audience subscribed to. Hölderlin was bound by it, and wrote poems that were no better or worse than hundreds of others that were written at the time by poets like Thill, Stäudlin or Conz. Patriotism was popular all over Germany, a vague, Germanic patriotism, and specific, regional ones.[7] It refers back to a lost golden age, Swabian poets, whose 'Vaterland' was unambiguously Swabia, let their golden age be the medieval period of their country's supremacy in Europe. Poets born in Hesse, like Sinclair, had to go back further, to the time of Hermann. In Swabia the memory of this golden age was preserved in hill-top ruins, especially in the wilder areas of the Alb. But any medieval castle, Teck or Tübingen, always provoked the same response: a nostalgia for the past, unfavourable comparisons with the present and, mostly, optimism for the future when the old virtues would be fashionable again. There was no alternative: castles in a landscape always had that effect. The castles are indistinguishable from one another, and the landscapes are made up of a few recurrent features, which, like the ideograms of rocks or trees in medieval painting, serve as a kind of shorthand, as reminders to the audience that a certain landscape is intended. Neither the site nor the response it provokes ever varies. All the poems then, thousands of them, having such sites and the ideal of patriotism as their inspiration, are basically the same. The verse form may vary, hexameters or rhyme, but the language hardly does and the sentiments never do. One composite poem would have sufficed for the whole idea and the whole age. Neuffer could provide, ad nauseam, an appropriate landscape:

> Aber den obersten Gipfel, der hoch zu den Wolken emporstrebt,
> Deckt die Trümmer aus voriger Zeit, das graue Gemäuer
> Einer verfallenen Burg.[8]

K. P. Conz does the castle:

Herunter deiner Thürne Höhn:
Wo Tummler kreiseten, da wehn
Durch Nesseln kale Winde nun
Und alle deine Starken—ruhn.

Verwaiset trauren an der Wand
Die Hirschgeweihe, hingebannt
Wie Geister; und der Estrich leer!
Und keines Helden Wiederkehr![9]

Nostalgia for the past and discontent with the present is the theme of all these poems:

Ach! in Staub ist hingesunken
Stauffens grosse Herrlichkeit! [10]

O der Wandlung! Graun und Nacht umdüstern
Nun den Schauplatz jener Herrlichkeit! [11]

But for the future:

Mit deutschem Kuß, mit deutschem Mund
Beschwüren wir den Bruderbund . . .[12]

this ceremony to take place in the ruins.

O dann heb' aus Finsternissen
Noch einmal dein modernd Haar,
Grauer Hügel! laß es wissen
Was Teutonien einst war . . .[13]

Holderlin's poem 'Die Tek' is a typical product of this convention. It is a true celebration of place, very seriously meant, written in the earnest hexameters of Klopstock or Stolberg. The hill is named with all possible solemnity and respect:

Ha! wie jenes so königlich über die Brüder emporragt!
Tek ist sein Nahme.

(lines 21-22, i,55)

Teck is a hill not far from Nürtingen, an outlier of the Schwäbische Alb. The Alb is the heroic background of Hölderlin's Swabia, high, desolate, and littered with Hohenstauffen castles. In Nürtingen and Denkendorf he lived close to these hills; in Tübingen they were always visible, to the south. They are 'heroic', the Neckar valley 'idyllic' (the antithesis is deliberately made in the poem). On the summit of Teck are traces of the castle that was one of the homes of the Dukes of Württemberg and Teck. Their family tombs are in the Tübingen Stiftskirche. The hill is thus a site, like the 'Winkel von Hahrdt' or Thill's grave, in the immediate vicinity of Hölderlin's village, and one that he doubtless often visited. Sooner or later the celebration of these sites would become obligatory. Schwab reports[14] that at this time a poem since lost was written to celebrate the 'Winkel von Hahrdt'. In content and style it will have resembled 'Die Tek', and would have contrasted interestingly with the poem of 1803, showing off the later conciseness to good effect.

A visit to the neighbourhood and a view of the hill are the occasion of the poem 'Die Tek'. The mythical world that Hölderlin later created is composed of places he knew and places he read about. It will be shown that in practice this distinction hardly matters. Places within walking distance of his own village are no more subject to a belittling realism than are the wonders of Asia Minor.

The poet-visitor contemplating the famous local hill gives his version of it. He is between the reader and the place, so that hill and ruins come across only after he has imposed his sense upon them. In Hölderlin's later poems, as in much modern poetry, it often happens that the poet, between the thing and the audience, obscures rather than communicates. In the early poems this never happens. The convention decides what the idea and interpretation of the place shall be, and the poet gives his audience what they expect. He cannot obscure their vision of Teck, since he sees what they would see. Nevertheless, what finally comes into the poem is not a place but the idea of a place. It happens, at this early stage, that poet and audience share the same idea. Later they do not. But in early poems and late the imaginative process is the same. What here interprets Teck later interprets Xanthus, India, or the Alps. The willingness to idealize is thus typical of Hölderlin from the beginning, and it is from this willingness that his ability to create original myths develops.

It is likely that when a place is interpreted and idealized it will lose its identity as a place. For example, in the later poem 'Unter den Alpen gesungen', almost nothing of the place itself (Hauptwyl) remains. Teck is still relatively independent, and does have a physical existence of its own, a certain character, albeit an entirely conventional one:[15]

> ... wo Moder und Disteln die graue
> Trümmer der fürstlichen Maurern, der stolzen Pforten bedeken,
> Wo der Eule Geheul, und des Uhus Todtengewimmer
> Ihnen entgegenruft aus schwarzen, sumpfigten Höhlen.
> ('Die Tek', lines 54-57, i,56)

But Tübingen castle, on which the same interpretation is imposed, disappears almost completely in the welter of patriotism it inspires. The four opening lines of 'Burg Tübingen' are a slight concession to the need for a setting, but the rest of the poem pays no further attention to the place, the sentiments it arouses being more important. This excessive translation into the abstract is, of course, typical of Hölderlin in his Tübingen years. But Teck, too, is interpreted. The facts of the visit are arranged tendentiously. Hölderlin climbs to within sight of the hill on an autumn evening. The valley below him and the distant hill are then brought into a significant relationship. A tendentious landscape painter might have done the same.

The hill is the heroic past, the valley is the idyll of how the present ought to be. This is the kind of manipulation his audience would understand and condone.

Having arranged the landscape so, he articulates what all right-feeling people must feel on seeing it. The sentiments are familiar from the poems of Conz, Thill, Neuffer, Matthisson, and Stäudlin; they are what the audience wants.

This fundamental agreement between the poet and his audience makes the task of communication very much easier than in times when the agreement breaks down. For the audience is eager to help. They are anxious to have the feelings he is attempting to arouse in them, and supplement his verse with their enthusiasm. This applies first in the description of the site. The audience helps out by responding to such words as 'fürstlich', 'stolz', 'königlich', 'herrlich', emotive not descriptive words, which merely remind them of a picture and feelings they already have. Next they respond to the patriotism, and being entirely in agreement with their poet they will not be critical of his rhetoric. I shall discuss this ease of communication more fully later in relation to the poems of the first Swiss journey.

The other patriotic poems of these early years add little to the ideal as 'Die Tek' presents it. There are suitable landscapes in 'Auf einer Haide geschrieben' or 'Emilie vor ihrem Brauttag',[16] ruined castles in 'Burg Tübingen' and 'Am Tage der Freundschaftsfeier'. The virtues of the lost golden age are familiar, exemplified in the Duke of Teck, one of many 'Helden der eisernen Vorzeit' ('Auf einer Haide geschrieben' line 15, i,29) who was restless until he had ridden away and killed three enemies. By comparison the present generation are a poor lot and a poet mindful of the past can scarcely bear to live among them. The hope for the future lies in the brotherhood of a few superior people (the poet and his friends—'Am Tage der Freundschaftsfeier', lines 129-41, i,62). They swear friendship among the castle ruins ('Burg Tübingen' lines 33-36, i,102).

The Fatherland to which this patriotism refers can become wider amd vaguer: the old Teutons and the Hohenstauffen knights are comrades-in-arms ('Burg Tübingen'); the inevitable Hermann is included ('Die Demuth'). It is to Beißner's credit that he left out such early poems from his 'Feldauswahl' of 1943. This nostalgia for the great age of German manliness is unpalatable.

Medieval Swabia could only become an ideal by that rigorously one-sided thinking and that willingness to simplify for the sake of the pleasing type that are characteristic of Hölderlin.

Sweden may be included within the sphere of this early Swabia. A fragment, 'Lied des Schweden', and three poems of 1789 are concerned with Sweden and its foremost hero Gustav Adolf. Swabians shared Protestantism with Swedes, and owed them gratitude for their intervention in the Thirty Years War. (It is said that Hölderlin's ancestors were Swedes who settled in Swabia after the war.)[17] But in the style of Klopstock Hölderlin refers back beyond the seventeenth century, and beyond the Middle Ages, to the pre-Christian Teutonic era, and his poem 'Gustav Adolf' begins:

> Kommt, ihr Kinder von Teut!
> Ihr Kinder von Teut! Zum Thale der Schlacht . . .
>
> (lines 1-2, i,85)

This extends the area beyond medieval Swabia to a wider world in a different age
when Swedes and Swabians were, more or less, of a common race. Gustav then
becomes a Germanic hero, like Hermann, and his age is lost in a vague Germanic
ethos where all Germanic heroes belong. Similarly, in 'Burg Tübingen', the knights
of Medieval Swabia dwell vaguely in the Teutonic sphere of 'Manas Heldenland'
(line 10). Gustav's achievements were his battles, in which he championed the
Protestants against the Catholics:

> Dank dem Sieger bei Lipsia!
> Dank dem Sieger am Lechus!
>
> ('Gustav Adolf' lines 62-63, i,87)

On 17 September 1631 Gustav defeated the Catholic Tilly at Breitenfeld, near
Leipzig, and again at Rain am Lech in April of the following year, when Tilly was
fatally wounded. In November Gustav was himself killed: 'Dank dem Sieger im
Todesthal! ' (line 64). In 1795, five years after Sweden had gone for ever from his
poetry, Hölderlin was still sufficiently interested to visit the battlefield celebrated
in this early poem. He found the site absolutely flat, not a valley at all, and sandy,
and saw how poorly Gustav was commemorated: 'es war mir sonderbar zu Muth,
wie ich an dem erbärmlichen Steine stand, womit man ihn ehren will! ' (vi,166)
Hölderlin was not incapable of observing and admitting, outside his poetry, the
mediocre reality of places that his poetry presented ideally. His journey to
Westphalia in 1796 is another example: idealized in 'Emilie', described realistically
in a letter to his brother (vi,217).

Sweden, at least to poets in Swabia, a Protestant enclave in Catholic South
Germany, meant only one thing: it was the land of the right religion, of solid
Germanic virtues, another site and age of the ideal. But it was an early enthusiasm
that Hölderlin did not re-think at a later date. He might well have done: Gustav's
name would not have been incongrous among those of Fragment 48.

Hölderlin's early patriotism looks back to an ideal past of which only traces
are left in the landscape, inspiring to the present. When he considers the present, the
Swabian places of his own life, he makes them as ideal as the Swabia of the past. In
'Die Tek', having regretted the heroic age, he turns to the present, avowedly so
inferior to the past, but cannot or will not describe it in any but idyllic terms.
Looking from the Alb to the valley, from the past to the present, he moves from
one poetic genre to another, from the heroic to the idyllic.

But Hölderlin saw for himself the details of this idyll in the rural life of Lauffen
and Nürtingen. This then is a more personal Swabia, and although still bound by a
convention (the rules of the idyllic genre) Hölderlin occasionally comes nearer to
original writing than the rules of the public patriotism ever allow. The details are

ably observed and recorded:

Schellend kehren zurük von schattigten Triften die Heerden,
Und fürs dritte Gras der Wiesen, im Herbste noch fruchtbar,
Schneidend geklopfet ertönt des Mähers blinkende Sense.
Traulich summen benachbarte Abendgloken zusammen,.
Und es spielet der fröliche Junge dem lauschenden Mädchen
Zwischen den Lippen mit Birnbaumblättern ein scherzendes Liedchen.
('Die Tek', lines 79-84, i,57)

And doubtless it was so, when looked down on at evening from a vantage point. Idylls are written from hill-tops. It is not that these details have been falsified (they have been enhanced to a, perhaps, unjustifiable archetypal status: '*der* Mäher', '*der* fröliche Junge', '*das* lauschende Mädchen') but that other details, unacceptable ones, have been overlooked. That is the rule of the genre, but also the rule of all Hölderlin's poetry, to choose and exclude according to the dictates of the ideal. It is the rule of his mythical world, and all the constituent places are presented so. He would no more admit poverty or malnutrition into his Swabia than he would goitres and cretins into his Switzerland, or plagues and dried-up river-beds into his Greece.

But it is not enough simply to dismiss such idyllic writing as dishonest and irresponsible. It should be said, first, that Swabia, fertile and pleasant, lends itself to idealization more than most places; and secondly, that the idyll satisfies a profound human need, which the eighteenth century realized better than the twentieth does. The good, simple, rural life is an ineradicable human myth. It is natural that Hölderlin, a great myth-making poet, should in his early work have subscribed to the rules of the conventional idyll. For original myths are made in the same way as were, once, the conventional ones: by choosing, excluding, simplifying, typifying and enhancing. It is not at all surprising that the writer of 'Die Wanderung' and 'Germanien' should also have written 'Kanton Schwyz' and 'Die Tek'.

Other conventions besides the idyllic govern other poems that Hölderlin wrote in praise of Swabian places important to him.

Johann Jakob Thill, although a 'national' figure, one like Wieland, Schubart, or Kepler whom Stäudlin urged Swabian poets to celebrate,[18] seems to have been of considerable *private* importance to Hölderlin. An addition to line 22 of 'Die Wanderung' includes 'Thills Dorf' among the notable places of Swabia, and the late fragment 'Ihr sichergebaueten Alpen . . .', also in praise of Swabia, names 'Tills Thal' with Stuttgart, Tübingen, and the Spitzberg. Hölderlin's friend and fellow-poet Magenau records:

[wir] schwärmten in süßer wehmütiger Stimmung in Thills Tälchen am Uffer des Murmelbächleins [hin], an dem er, der frühverstorbene Jüngling, seine Lieder dichtete . . . (vii, 1,395)

Neuffer, the third member of their 'Dichterbund', is especially praised in the final verse of the poem 'An Thills Grab'. Thill, like Hölderlin and his friends, was educated in the Tübinger Stift, and what they called his valley was close to the town, perhaps the Wankheim valley about a mile to the south. He wrote patriotically, in Klopstock's style, and attempted the usual 'Hermann drama'; his poems were published posthumously by Stäudlin and by Matthisson. To Hölderlin, sharing his enthusiasms, he would be a rather approachable, imitable national poet. He became pastor in Großheppach, east of Stuttgart, and is buried there. Magenau, Neuffer, and Hölderlin were being trained for a similar career.

'An Thills Grab' makes explicit a further association between Hölderlin and Thill: Thill died in 1772, in the same year as Holderlin's father. The two griefs, private (for the loss of his father) and public (for the loss of a national figure) are confused. The subject of his grief changes—unclearly—between the second and third verses of the poem.

The place itself, Thill's grave, visited by the pilgrim, is distinguished by an elder tree:

> du schläfst so sanft
> Im stillen Schatten deines Holunderbaums.
> Dein Monument ist er . . .
>> ('An Thills Grab', lines 21-23, i,83)

Similarly, in 'An die Ruhe', Rousseau's grave at Ermenonville is distinguished by poplars, a detail Hölderlin had from Stäudlin who made a pilgrimage there.[19]

These distinguishing trees were conventional in classical poetry: Ibycus buried at Rhegium beneath an elm, for example. Factual or not the detail stylizes the site, a place, like the 'Winkel von Hahrdt', that Hölderlin knew well.

In 'An meinen B.' another familiar place is stylized, but this time into a different style:

> Freund! wo über das Thal schauerlich Wald und Fels
> Herhängt, wo das Gefild leise die Erms durchschleicht,
> Und das Reh des Gebürges
> Stolz an ihrem Gestade geht--
>> ('An meinen B.' lines 1-4, i,23)

The place is real enough (the Erms is a small tributary of the Neckar, joining not far above Nürtingen) and well known to Hölderlin and Bilfinger, his friend. The associations—the girl (line 9)—are entirely private, yet the setting, as Vietor shows,[20] is entirely conventional. The sombre valley and the deer (especially '*das* Reh des Gebirges') are Ossianic details. A second strophe, left out of the final version, is even more Ossianic:

> Wo vom moosigten Fels stille Erhabenheit
> Auf die friedliche Flur, wo zu der Väter Zeit

Helme klangen, und Schilde,
Ernst und düster herunterblikt.

(Lesarten 4a-d, i,344)

In September 1787 Hölderlin wrote enthusiastically to his friend Nast, urging him to read Ossian:

Den must Du lesen, Freund–da werden Dir Deine Thäler lauter Konathäler–Dein
Engelsberg ein Gebirge Morvens ... (vi,16)

which is what happens in the poem 'An meinen B.'. The girl's name is, of course, also conventional: Amalia from Schiller's *Die Räuber*, Lotte (variant) from Goethe's *Werther*. Thus private sentiments find absolutely no private expression.

It hardly matters that the real landscape may have contained these elements–wooded slopes, a deer, moss-covered rocks. A particular conventional sentiment, apparent in words like 'schauerlich', 'stolz', 'Erhabenheit', 'ernst', 'düster', fuses the bits together. The landscape, which is simply there and open to any interpretation, becomes Ossianic. Another imagination, at another time, would have made something else of it.

At this early stage Hölderlin found it almost impossible to look at even his immediate surroundings without some conventional bias. He made an idyll of the valley below Teck, a classical site of Thill's grave and an Ossianic-heroic landscape of the Erms. Throughout his life he translated landscapes as he saw fit, at first into conventional, later into original mythical terms.

In the early poems it is only the remembered places of Hölderlin's childhood that are expressed in a more personal and independent style. The rural scenes of 'Die Stille' or 'Einst und Jezt' have become familiar by being much quoted. In them Hölderlin comes near to the descriptive poetry he later belittled:

Fernher sah ich schon die Kerzen flimmern,
Schon wars Suppenzeit–ich eilte nicht!
Spähte stillen Lächelns nach des Kirchhofs Wimmern
Nach dem dreigefüßten Roß am Hochgericht.

('Die Stille', lines 21-25, i,42)

Or from 'Einst und Jezt':

Da sucht' ich Maienblümchen im Walde mir,
Da wälzt' ich mich im duftenden Heu' umher,
Da brokt' ich Milch mit Schnittern ein, da
Schleudert' ich Schwärmer am Rebenberge.

(lines 17-20, i,95)

These details are slightly tendentious in that they make unfavourable comparisons with the present, and so repeat privately the national regret of 'Die Tek' or 'Burg Tübingen'; but nevertheless they are remembered with pleasure and something like innocence. They are charming by contrast to the nationally patriotic poems, and the

world they constitute, rural Swabia, is more attractive than the medieval one. This
love of the homeland, the villages Lauffen and Nürtingen, and the longing for
childhood security there, are a theme that the mature poetry raises to a mythical
level.[21]

The almost realistic writing of these few early poems is not met with after the
Tübingen years, until the last stages of Hölderlin's creative life; but by that time
the careful recording of physical data had become a serious, not to say desperate
business.

There is finally one setting of a private experience that is well remembered in a
poem, without any conventionality:

> Guter Carl! —in jenen schönen Tagen
> Saß ich einst mit dir am Nekkarstrand.
> Fröhlich sahen wir die Welle an das Ufer schlagen,
> Leiteten uns Bächlein durch den Sand.
> Endlich sah ich auf. Im Abendschimmer
> Stand der Strom. Ein heiliges Gefühl
> Bebte mir durchs Herz . . .
>
> ('Die Meinige', lines 121-127, i,19)

The ruins of Teck or Burg Tübingen put Hölderlin in mind of his national self.
Place then makes demands on him, being something about which there are proper
feelings to be had. But place as the scene of private experiences should not force
any poses. The memory and the celebration come more naturally, because the
experience and its setting are most often inseparable. As here: the Neckar contributes
to or even inspires the religious emotion. In an easy and intimate manner, appro-
priate in verse addressed directly to his brother, Hölderlin remembers an experience
they shared at a particular time and in a particular place.

In some ways these poems 'Die Stille', 'Einst und Jezt', and 'Die Meinige' are the
most important of Hölderlin's early years. For they testify, in a personal idiom, to
the great love Hölderlin had for his home, and to the intense memory he had of his
childhood there—sources from which a central part of his mythology derived.
Swabia, the mythical Swabia of his lost childhood and his mature poetry, was where
experiences like that described in 'Die Meinige' had happened, where life was lived
in awareness of God's presence.

Clearly the patriotism, the national pride, was also important, but it had to
develop a long way before 1801. By 1801 poems like 'Burg Tübingen' had been
superseded; but the religious apprehension of 'Die Meinige' had been confirmed.

Switzerland

Hölderlin first went to Switzerland during the Easter vacation of 1791, and
wrote two poems commemorating the journey. Before then there is no mention of
Switzerland in his work or letters, but it can be assumed that his idea of the country

was always the conventional one, and that the journey there merely confirmed him in his enthusiasm. For ten years, to judge from the infrequent references he makes, his attitude to Switzerland remained unchanged. Then, early in 1801, he lived for three months in Hauptwyl, and Switzerland took on a new significance in what was by that time a coherent poetic world.

Details of Hölderlin's first Swiss journey are found in a letter to his mother written before he left (vi,67), and in the two poems 'Kanton Schwyz' (1791-92) and 'An Hiller' (1793). That is not much information, but enough: whenever details are lacking—of the route, or of what the travellers felt—they can be surmised. In preparation he got together clothes, knapsack and walking stick, arranged addresses for each stage of the journey and the hiring, from one town to the next, of a man to act as porter and guide. He left on 14 April 1791, accompanied by Memminger, a medical student: Hiller had gone on ahead, as far as Schaffhausen. They were probably no more than three weeks away.

This kind of journey, undertaken almost yearly by those eighteenth-century artists, amateurs, and dilettantes who had money and leisure time, was unique in Hölderlin's life.[22] It was conventional in every detail. Between 1732, when Haller published *Die Alpen*, and 1798, when the Second Coalition War broke out, Switzerland was the goal of thousands of travellers. They were of varied nationality and social standing, all enthusiastic amateurs of something: scenery, geology, mountain-climbing, or the Good Life. They roamed Switzerland in droves along certain traditional routes. Hölderlin and his friends chose one of these. In J. G. Ebel's *Anleitung auf die nützlichste und genußvollste Art in der Schweitz zu reisen*[23] it is Number 16, in the section headed: 'Für diejenigen, die sich nicht lange in der Schweitz aufhalten können, und auf einer kleinen Reise interessante Theile sehen wollen'. This was an easily practicable one: not too far for Swabians, and not involving serious mountaineering.

The first, obligatory, halt was at Schaffhausen, gateway to Switzerland, where they admired the Rheinfall. Via Winterthur they came to Zürich and here, armed with the necessary letters of introduction, they visited Lavater (who was as awe-inspiring to eighteenth-century travellers, and as everlasting as the Rheinfall). They signed his visitors' book; 'NB.', he added in the margin by Hölderlin's name. Then, like Klopstock in his ode, they sailed up Lake Zürich, probably as far as Wädenswil. The walking-tour now began. Catholic pilgrims to Maria-Einsiedeln would be on the road with them. At the great baroque monastery in Einsiedeln the choir, altar, chapel of Mary, library, and treasury were all worth a look; the unscrupulous monks sold relics and souvenirs.

The climb up the valley to the Hagenegg pass took about three hours on foot. At the top there was an inn, good views of the lakes, and travellers wanting to climb the Mythen could hire guides. From here the way was down to Schwyz and the Vierwaldstättersee, the area most travellers chiefly wanted to see.

This first part of the journey was popular, especially in the 70s, 80s and 90s, for

the experience of Swiss scenery it offered. Many notable men had preceded
Hölderlin up that road: Gibbon in 1755, Casanova in 1760, Goethe in 1775,
Lenz in 1777, Matthisson in 1787 and Wordsworth in 1790.[24] Wordsworth's
journey was a student affair, like Hölderlin's. He left Cambridge during the
summer vacation, with his friend Robert Jones, to tour France and Switzerland.
They had £20 each and travelled mostly on foot.[25]

There were half a dozen sites to be visited on and near the Vierwaldstättersee,
all associated with the glorious history of Switzerland: Tell's birthplace at Bürglen;
Altdorf, where he shot the apple from his son's head; Tellskap, where he leapt to
freedom; the Hohle Gasse, where he killed Geßler; Rütli, where the Swiss rebellion
was planned. In June, 1775 Goethe did all these between 2 and 4p.m.[26] Morgarten,
on the Sattelberg, where the Swiss first defeated an Austrian army in 1315, had also
to be seen.

The list of sites had to be gone through; there were really no options. The
programme was carried out as rigorously as any modern travel-agency could wish.

Journeys such as these were pilgrimages to holy places of eighteenth-century
mythology:

> . . . an den Heiligtümern der Freiheit
> Wallten wir dann vorbei in frommer seeliger Stille . . .
>
> ('Kanton Schwyz', lines 65-66, i,145)

The original meaning of 'wallen' was simply 'to go from place to place'. By the
sixteenth century it could also mean 'to go on a pilgrimage' ('wallfahrten') and
under Klopstock's influence this meaning became established, 'Wallen' was more
poetic than 'wandern', and was often preferred when the journey could be
poeticized into a pilgrimage: visits to the graves of famous men, like Rousseau, or
to sites of the nation's great past, like Teck. Amateurs of Swiss scenery were
pilgrims: 'Jäher herunter hieng der Pfad zu den einsamen Wallern' (ibid., line 29,
i,144).

The pilgrimages to Switzerland were very literary in inspiration: Haller, Geßner,
Rousseau were the holy texts. In a sense such literary enthusiasms served when
orthodox Christianity no longer satisfied. The literary pilgrims use the vocabulary
of religion because what they feel seems to merit it; they feel religiously enthus-
iastic about what they see, a mountain, a goatherd, or a monument. And pilgrims,
especially the literary ones, know beforehand what feelings they will have when
they reach the places they set out to see. The meaning of these places is established,
an article of faith. The sites of the Vierwaldstättersee and the sentiments appropriate
to them were known to Hölderlin before he left Tübingen, from his reading, and
simply from living in the late eighteenth century when the philosophers' ideals were
readily attached to certain real places of the world. The literary conventions
obtaining here are akin to religious dogma: to be conventional was to be a believer.
Originality, of thought or expression, is out of place in an established religion.

Thus Hölderlin's sentiments in Switzerland are entirely predictable, just as they are when he contemplates the ruins of Medieval Swabia. Teck and Rütli are alike in that they are both places about which there were certain accepted feelings to be had.

The ability to have these feelings was a prerequisite of the journey. That pilgrim might as well stay at home who would be unmoved by the Rheinfall, by Lavater, the Mythen, or the Rütli. Most of the eighteenth-century travellers seem to have been confident of their sensibility; to feel properly was a point of honour, and a faculty as essential to the eighteenth-century pilgrim as is the camera to the twentieth-century tourist. Those who were sure that they could generally gave thanks and pitied those who couldn't.[27]

It was also essential to be sure of your travelling-companion; useless to go with an insensitive brute or a carping agnostic. But in this matter Hölderlin's companion could be trusted:

> Bruder! dir gab ein Gott der Liebe göttlichen Funken,
> Zarten geläuterten Sinn, zu erspäh'n, was herrlich und schön ist . . .
> ('Kanton Schwyz', lines 6-7, i,143)

And in the first test, the Rheinfall at Schaffhausen, he performed admirably:

> Lieber! wie drüktest du mir die heiße zitternde Rechte,
> Sahst so glühend und ernst mich an im donnernden Rheinsturz!
> (ibid., lines 17-18)

Their friendship is founded largely on confidence in each other's sensibility. Doubtless Wordsworth and Robert Jones behaved similarly.

Thousands of visitors to the Rheinfall behaved like this and recorded their sentiments in verse, not often very well. At least, it seems to have been done badly today, because the original sympathy between the versifier and his audience has faded in the intervening two hundred years. The communication of these sentiments relies on the audience's active sympathy. This was so when Hölderlin tried to communicate his conventional vision of Teck, and in the Swiss poems the appeal for audience participation is made even more strongly. The moment at the Rheinfall is communicated if readers will accept such words as 'zitternd', 'glühend', and 'ernst', words which appeal blatantly for emotional sympathy. Similarly in the description of the Haggen pass:

> Schaurig und kühl empfieng uns die Nacht in ewigen Wäldern,
> Und wir klommen hinauf am furchtbarherrlichen Haken.
> (ibid., lines 26-27, i,144)

'Schaurig' and 'furchtbarherrlich' do not so much describe the mountains as say how Hölderlin is affected by them; but since he can safely assume that his audience would be similarly affected he need not trouble to be more exact. (A modern poet, too, would give his impression—how things affected him—and not simply describe;

but he would not dare assume that his audience was automatically in sympathy with him.) All the descriptive lines of 'Kanton Schwyz' urge the reader in this way: 'wundersam' (line 34), 'staunend' (line 40), 'berauschen' (line 31) all demand a response.

Of course, this is true of most of the Swiss poetry written at the time: Matthisson, Stäudlin, Stolberg[28] were all writing thus, and never developed beyond it. They might easily have written each other's poems; neither the sentiments nor the expression ever vary.

The great events of Swiss history and the peculiar qualities of Swiss life are communicated as enthusiastically and vaguely as is the 'Furchtbarherrlichkeit' of the mountain scenery. The audience helps out. A vast amount of sympathy is there to be tapped at the mere mention of Tell or Walther Fürst, or of Swiss shepherds and hay-makers, their honest wives and contented families. The poet merely reminds his audience of what they already feel; there is no struggle to get across new concepts and emotions. Simply, at the mention of Switzerland all feeling men respond.[29]

The heroes and pastoral folk of Switzerland are reduced to pleasing, simple types, like the knights of medieval Swabia. The whole country is simplified and made to stand for certain qualities, and the awe-inspiring scenery is the setting in which they belong. And, unlike medieval Swabia, the place actually exists and is easily accessible. Germans—the greatest enthusiasts—had only a short journey to be at the very source of the qualities they admired.

In Hölderlin's time the need for places like Switzerland seems to have been imperative. The ideals of freedom and the Good Life needed externalizing somewhere. Switzerland was the nearest. Others were more distant: Corsica, and its chief hero Pasquale Paoli; the new, democratic America; a recently discovered South Sea island. In the real or fabulous past there had been many more: Arcadia, the pastoral biblical lands, the vague homeland of Ossian, medieval Swabia, Tacitus's Germania. In all these places the same ideals, of a free and uncorrupted life, were believed to have been realized, and since the ideals were the same the places themselves became almost interchangeable formulas of them. They were associated and interrelated whenever possible. The last of the old Germans, for example, were said to have taken refuge against the Romans in the inaccessible valleys of the Alps, and so become the ancestors of the Swiss.[30] 'Kanton Schwyz' brings Arcadia (line 45), the biblical patriarchs' lands (line 44), and the country of Ossian (line 34) all into relationship with Switzerland. 'An Hiller' adds Philadelphia (line 58). Hiller was thinking of emigrating: a man so at home among the Swiss would do well among the democratic Americans (lines 15-16). In 'Emilie' Corsica and the Teutoburgerwald are deliberately related (Arminius closely resembles Emilie's brother who was killed fighting for Paoli), and, via Horace, a relationship is also established with Corsica's first settlers, the heroic Phocaeans, who left home and put out to sea rather than submit to the Persians.

Before 1800 Hölderlin, like his contemporaries, sited his ideals in whichever of these countries came to mind. He ceased to need such variety when he committed himself to Greece and let the centre of his poetic world be there. Until then he thought of America, Corsica, or Switzerland what most poets at that time did.

There seems to have been no development in his idea of Switzerland until 1801 when he lived in Hauptwyl. There are only two slight references before then. The first is in a letter of January 1799: 'wie die Schweizerhirten im Soldatenleben nach ihrem Thal und ihrer Heerde sich sehnen' (vi, 311). And in the writing of the poem 'Der Frieden' (late 1799) the word 'Schweiz' (ii,391, line 18) becomes in the final version: 'Und schonst du auch des müßigen Hirten nicht . . .' (line 22, ii,6). Both references indicate an entirely conventional attitude.

Then in the letters from Hauptwyl and the subsequent poems Switzerland and especially the Swiss Alps are given an entirely new significance. Switzerland is perhaps the best example in Hölderlin's work of how the meaning of a locality changes as his ideas develop from the conventional to the private and mythical.

Greece

Not until the 1790s is there any serious treatment of the Greek World in Hölderlin's poetry ('Alexanders Rede', 1785, and 'Hero', 1788, are very slight exercises), but it may be assumed that Greece was always an ideal land for him, as it was for his contemporaries, one more setting of his best ideals.

The poem 'Hymne an den Genius Griechenlands' (1790) is one of the dozen Tübingen hymns written on abstract themes—friendship, boldness, beauty—and like them it lacks body. The spirit of Greece is as abstract as the spirit of harmony or humanity.

The pursuit of Greek ideals later involves an interest in (finally an obsession with) the land itself, those places where the genius of Greece was manifest. Naming places then externalizes the idea. That is not the way of this early poem. The ideas are not given a setting or topographical form (not in the more finished version, at least) but are kept as incorporeal as possible. In the earlier, unfinished, rhyming version there is something of the technique that became characteristic of Hölderlin in his mature poetry. 'Aganippens Flur' (i,424, line 16), that is Mount Helicon, and 'Hämos' (i,424, line 30), the birthplace of Orpheus, specify what aspect of the Greek achievement—the poetry—is to be praised. The later version avoids even this slight precision.

This process, from particular named locality to general abstract quality, can be noted several times in the poetry before 1800. The change from 'Schweiz' to 'pastoral peace' has already been mentioned.[31] There is another example in 'Die Muße': 'von Attikas Schiksaal' becomes 'von menschlichem Leben'.[32]

In the mature poems quite the opposite occurs and places are readily named: it is from real places that the myths are made. For example, reworking the second stanza of 'Du schweigst und duldest . . .' Hölderlin sites the ideal precisely in Olympia. In 'Der Ister' 'Vom heißen Lande' becomes 'Vom heißen Isthmos' (ii, 809, line 4). And in the last year or so of his creative life he was obsessively concerned to be precise. He added place-names to the manuscripts of finished poems: Schweiz, Nekars Ulm, Heidenheim, Thills Dorf, Tenedos, Ida, and Tempe to 'Die Wanderung';[33] Dalberg and Hanau (incomprehensibly) to 'Der Rhein';[34] Ephesus and the adjective 'Tuskisch' to 'Brod und Wein' (lines 6,32, ii,604); Pythos and Alpheus to 'Am Quell der Donau' (lines 4,6, ii,693); 'Wirtemberg ist's' to 'Stutgard' (line 4, ii,587).

Almost three years after 'Hymne an den Genius Griechenlands', with scarcely any Greek-inspired poetry intervening, Hölderlin wrote 'Griechenland'. At that time, the summer of 1793, he was working on *Hyperion*, reading in the Classics and travel literature. He was acquiring factual knowledge of his ideal land, becoming familiar with its topography. In a letter to Neuffer (vi,86) he says how his reading of Plato inspires him in his work on the novel. Plato, and especially the setting of the *Phaedrus*, is clearly an influence on the poem 'Griechenland'. And in the factual details, too, the poem is marked by the reading—of Chandler, Choiseul, the Abbé Barthélemy—for the novel. Similar influences are apparent in other Greek poems of the 1790s, in 'Der Gott der Jugend' or 'Der Main'.

And 'Griechenland' is written in the mood of the novel, elegiac, more backward-looking than the later poems. Stäudlin, as he appears in the poem, has something of Adamas, and there is the conviction that good men like him, unhappy in modern society, would have been at home in Ancient Greece. The ideal land is where good people would be happy to live: Stäudlin is fit for Greece, just as Hiller is fit for Switzerland or Philadelphia; people out of place in the modern world, Sinclair, Heinse and, most of all, Susette Gontard. At the time of this poem Greece was simply one more ideal land, but becoming predominant, the final, best home of the ideal.

Hölderlin affirms his faith in this better world more categorically than ever before, and his regret for its passing more despairingly than ever afterwards:

> Mich verlangt ins ferne Land hinüber
> Nach Alcäus und Anakreon,
> Und ich schlief' im engen Hause lieber,
> Bei den Heiligen in Marathon;
> Ach! es sei die lezte meiner Thränen,
> Die dem lieben Griechenlande rann,
> Laßt, o Parzen, laßt die Scheere tönen,
> Denn mein Herz gehört den Todten an!
>
> ('Griechenland', lines 49-56, i,180)

The ideal land is irretrievably lost. His advice to Stäudlin:

> Stirb! du suchst auf diesem Erdenrunde,
> Edler Geist! umsonst dein Element.
>
> (ibid., lines 39-40)

It is a death-wish, then, to want to journey to Greece. The longing is not like Goethe's for Italy, towards the still existing sites of the lost ideal, but back in time to the age of Ancient Greece. Unhesitatingly Hölderlin abandons the mediocre present in favour of what is irretrievably past. The journey would be pure escapism. In later poems he always resists this temptation and allows himself the journey only on terms of strict loyalty to the present.[35] This whole-hearted nostalgia, unchecked by any sense of responsibility to his own times, is perhaps an indication of how far Hölderlin still was from a mature philosophy of Greece: '. . . mein Herz gehört den Todten an! ' In a sense this was true all his life, but a mark of maturity was the refusal ever again to admit it. It may indicate a certain insincerity, or at least a conventional exaggeration of his feelings, that he could make such a statement in 1793. It is tempting to think that at that time he did not quite realize the seriousness of what he was saying. When the obsession took hold of him later he dared not make such confessions.

Greece, at this stage, was another ideal land about which Hölderlin thought much as his contemporaries did. Many poems like his 'Griechenland', purely elegiac, backward-looking, were being written: Schiller's 'Die Götter Griechenlands', Conz's 'Phantasieflug nach Griechenland'. In line 49 of 'Griechenland' Hölderlin first wrote 'Feenland', which, like Schiller's 'Fabelland', makes a rather unserious fairyland of Greece. Because Hölderlin later outdid all his contemporaries in the degree of his commitment to Greece it is easily assumed that he was wholly dedicated from the start. But in 1793 he was only beginning to commit himself, and still needed several years to develop beyond mere elegy and regret.

The Greece he here regrets is principally Athens at the time of her greatest achievements, in the fifth century. (Alcaeus and Anacreon (line 50) were Ionian poets, and referring to them rather spoils the unity of the poem; another indication, perhaps, of a slight unseriousness: the references are a little gratuitous.) The sites distinguished are the Agora and the Acropolis, the two rivers Ilissus and Cephissus that flow round the town, and the battlefield at Marathon: all stand for aspects of the Greek achievement.

Ilissus and Cephissus are both associated with Plato (cf. the letter to Neuffer, vi,86). He had his Academy on the Cephissus, to the north-west of the city (cf. line 8) and his *Phaedrus* dialogue takes place on the banks of the Ilissus (cf. line 4). In 'Der Gott der Jugend', written the following year, the same area is celebrated:

> Und wie um Platons Hallen,
> Wenn durch der Haine Grün,
> Begrüßt von Nachtigallen,
> Der Stern der Liebe schien,

> Wenn alle Lüfte schliefen,
> Und, sanft bewegt vom Schwan,
> Cephissus durch Oliven
> Und Myrthensträuche rann . . .

(lines 33-40, i,190)

The variants of this poem (of line 39) as of 'Griechenland' (lines 2 and 47) suggest that for Hölderlin Ilissus and Cephissus were almost interchangeable. The Academy on the Cephissus and the plane-trees of the Ilissus under which Socrates sat are confused in one vague area which is cool and pleasant, and rich in associations of the two great teachers. This confusion is probably deliberate. It is likely that from his reading Hölderlin knew the topography of Athens well enough to distinguish between the rivers. Chandler and the Abbé Barthélemy provide detailed maps. Probably Hölderlin allowed the confusion, thinking that the fairyland Greece would not lose by imprecise topography.

Chandler describes both the Athenian rivers. The Cephissus, he noted, was 'a muddy rivulet',[36] most often absorbed into the earth before reaching the sea. The Ilissus he found quite dried up, its waters even when flowing notoriously bad, used by a currier and 'often offensive'.[37] Fully aware that this was the celebrated scene of the *Phaedrus* he comments:

the poets who celebrate the Ilissus as a stream laving the fields, cool, lucid and the like, have both conceived and conveyed a false idea of this renowned water-course.[38]

Despite which it could not be expected that Hölderlin would prefer Chandler to Plato. His vision of the better land was immune against subversion by reality. This remains true all his life.[39] It happens that the 1790s provide several examples of Hölderlin's selectivity in the service of the ideal, because the sources on which he drew in those years for the factual details of his ideal vision are well known. Homer's grotto is another example: Chandler found a grotesque hole, overgrown, and into which a man could barely crawl;[40] but Hölderlin devised something more suitable for Hyperion and Melite (iii, 177).

His sources are either factual accounts and descriptions (e.g. Chandler) or poetic ones that are already as idealized as he could wish. Hölderlin took Plato's passages as he found them, but had to choose carefully in Chandler's work.

There is a second, very pleasant vignette in 'Der Gott der Jugend':

> Wie unter Tiburs Bäumen,
> Wenn da der Dichter saß
> Und unter Götterträumen
> Der Jahre Flucht vergaß
> Wenn ihn die Ulme külte,
> Und wenn sie stolz und froh
> Um Silberblüthen spielte,
> Die Fluth des Anio . . .

(lines 25-32, i,189-190)

Horace is the poet in this landscape. He himself celebrated Tivoli, and especially its trees and waters, in two odes (ii,6 and iv,3) that Hölderlin later translated. Heinse's hero Ardinghello spends some time at Tivoli, and his descriptions of the place are not more prosaic than Horace's.[41] Hölderlin's vision, then, was sanctioned by literary precedents, and he had no need to idealize mere factual information. 'Horace at Tivoli' was, moreover, generally popular with eighteenth-century poets:

> Süß ist's, am Wogensturz in Tiburs Hain,
> Wo Flakkus oft, entflohen den Schattenchören,
> Im Mondlicht wandelt, bei Albanerwein,
> Den Genius der Vorwelt zu beschwören . . .[42]

Hölderlin's version is a better piece of rhyming—the classical bits are put together more mellifluously—but is essentially not very different from Matthisson's; just as his celebration of Athens in 'Griechenland' is not essentially different from Conz's in 'Athen' or 'Phantasieflug nach Griechenland'. In 1793, even 1795, Hölderlin's attitude to Greece was still the conventional one. Greece was the fabulous ideal land—'das Fabelland, Feenland'— to be celebrated in poetry with all possible grace. 'Plato by the Cephissus' and 'Horace by the Tiber' are like certain eighteenth-century classical landscapes, exquisitely done, and more charming than profound; not at all the kind of Greece that later poems present.

In Frankfurt with Susette Gontard Hölderlin became an original and great poet. She was then the centre of his life, and in those years he was able to make Greece the true centre of his ideal world. He could say nothing better in praise of her than: 'Nicht wahr, eine Griechin? '[43] and the greatest tribute he could pay her in his poetry was to call her 'die Athenerin'; 'Athenäa' was his name for her before 'Diotima' (i,526). Years later he wrote that Frankfurt was 'the navel of the earth' (ii, 250, lines 13-16), γας ὀμφαλος, in Greek terms the centre of the world. Nobody would question his right to use Greek terms or to take from Greek mythology whatever would best express his own predicament and his own ideas. He gave ample proof of his integrity. Perhaps even as early as 1796, when the relationship with Susette Gontard was beginning, the Greek terms are permissible and appropriate in his case. He celebrates 'die Unerkannte':

> Die den Dulder, den der Sturm zertrümmert,
> Den sein fernes Ithaka bekümmert,
> In Alcinous Gefilde bringt . . .
> ('An die Unerkannte', lines 22-24, i,197)

The image was commonly used (cf. Conz: 'An die Phantasie') but it was a particularly appropriate one for Hölderlin at that time, when the new relationship was beginning and when in letters, in the novel, and in poems he was attempting to express the uncertainty through imagery of journeying on land and sea, of storms, shipwrecks, and wanderings.[44] His predicament merited comparison with Odysseus's; he was finding himself in Greek terms.

Typically, these personal concerns were before long subsumed in general, political, and religious ones. By calling Susette Gontard 'die Athenerin' Hölderlin places her at the centre of the mythology he was then developing, in which Greece and Germany were to be brought together. Even before 1799, when the two countries were explicitly linked in 'Der Main', there are indications of Hölderlin's readiness to talk in Greek terms of German affairs. Schwab notes that this was typical of him in the Tübingen years: 'er verknüpfte überhaupt das Altertum, das lebendig vor seiner Seele stand, gerne bei jeder Gelegenheit mit der Gegenwart'.[45]

In 1796 the wars came very close, and to escape them Susette Gontard and the children, with Hölderlin, left Frankfurt, which was besieged and surrendered on 14 July. Hölderlin wrote to his brother (all Württemberg was by that time occupied by the French):

Es ist doch was ganz leichters, von den griechischen Donnerkeulen zu hören, welche vor Jahrtausenden die Perser aus Attika schleuderten über den Hellespont hinweg bis hinunter in das barbarische Susa, als so ein unerbittlich Donnerwetter über das eigene Haus hinziehen zu sehen.
Freilich seht ihr auch nicht unentgeldlich dem neuen Drama zu.

(vi, 215-216)

Contemporary events merit comparison with the wars of the Athenians and the Persians. The modern drama is of Aeschylean grandeur, and it gives sense to the wars if they can be seen in such terms. Hölderlin was beginning to affirm the purposefulness of apparent chaos, beginning to make myths of contemporary events, to say what was meant for all time in the happenings of his own age, and to do this he increasingly appropriated the myths of Greece.

In the late 1790s several poems (e.g. 'Die Völker schwiegen, schlummerten . . .', 'Die Muße') deal directly with the wars. 'Die Muße' makes the greatest use of Greece, and already implies its relationship with Germany. At this stage the relating of the two countries is rather clumsily done, and the effect is of confusion, not of careful juxtaposition. Basically the poem is German in character. The landscapes are local: the meadows near the Gontard home, and the uplands surrounding Frankfurt. In the view from the hills there is one Greek element: the town walls stand:

. . . wie eine eherne Rüstung
Gegen die Macht des Gewittergotts und der Menschen geschmiedet . . .
('Die Muße', lines 21-22, i, 236)

But otherwise the scene is entirely Germanic, a poetic description of Frankfurt and the villages lying distinctly around it, reminiscent of contemporary prints.

There are three phases of the poem, and into the third, the same German landscape at night, a purely classical picture is intruded:

Aber ins Mondlicht steigen herauf die zerbrochenen Säulen
Und die Tempelthore, die einst der Furchtbare traf . . .
(ibid., lines 27-28)

This comes as a surprise. Moonlight follows dusk in the poem's sequence and during that natural transition the transference is made. It is reminiscent of many paintings of the 'Ruins in a Landscape' kind, and also of the deliberate confusion of localities in much religious art that has Christ crucified in Dutch or Tuscan surroundings. The temple occurs as though Hölderlin, coming home in the dark, found it across his path. It serves to show how the forces of chaos work; they had once brought down the temple and were then devastating Europe. They become familiar in Hölderlin's poetry, as again and again he tries to accommodate them within a whole mythology. Most often he speaks of them in Greek terms, using the myth of gods and Titans:

> der Unbezwungne, der alte Erobrer
> Der die Städte, wie Lämmer, zerreißt, der einst den Olympus
> Stürmte ... (ibid., lines 30-32, i,237)

He sees in the chaos of his own times a resurgence of those primeval, disruptive forces well known to the Greeks and told of by them in their myths. Hölderlin bases his own mythology on theirs. The Greek ruins in a German landscape show the timeless nature of chaos, just as a Crucifixion in a Dutch or Tuscan landscape shows the universality of Christ.

In the last section of 'Die Muße' the poet is at home reading into the night. The variants are explicit here in again linking the fate of Greece and Germany. Hölderlin first wrote (lines 38-40):

> Hab' ich zu Haußе dann ...
> ... von Attikas Schiksaal
> Ein unsterbliches Blatt zu gutem Ende gelesen ...
> (lines 5-8, i,549)

Perhaps he read of the Persian wars in Herodotus. In the letter to his brother (vi, 215-216) he drew the Greek and German wars together, the liberation of Attica and the advance of the French armies across the Rhine. This variant serves the unity of the poem better than the final version:

> ... von menschlichem Leben
> Ein erzählendes Blatt ...
> (lines 39-40, i,237)

Reference to Attica makes the inclusion of the ruins less incongruous, but perhaps at this early date 'menschlich' seemed better for being more general. The poem suffers from Hölderlin's unwillingness to make explicit the relationship that the inclusion of Greece in an otherwise 'German' poem implies. Its final lines (38-43), far less definite in the MS than they appear in Beißner's text, are in an interesting state of near-coherence. Had Hölderlin worked on the poem to completion he might well, I think, have gone back to 'von Attikas Schiksaal/Ein erzählendes Blatt' (the word 'Attika' was never erased, in fact) and already established here that image of Attica as a holy wood which, in 'Gesang des Deutschen' two years later, serves the idea of palingenesis.

CHAPTER 3

THE COHERENT WORLD, 1800-02

Hölderlin, committed to the Greek ideal, inevitably ran the risk of losing himself in mere nostalgia and escapism. Greece was gone for good, and what the modern world offered in its stead seemed not worth having. The Good Life had become impossible. Hölderlin's indifference, almost his contempt towards the best offerings of life in the present was always remarkable. His hero Hyperion is cruelly careless of personal happiness. Hölderlin remained nostalgic for the Greek past, but, after 1793 ('Griechenland'), refused to regress. He also refused to make do with the present, and instead turned all his hope towards the future. He belonged to the dead—the Greeks—and the unborn: 'das Geschlecht der kommenden Jahrhunderte' (vi,92).

Hölderlin obstinately believed in a revival of the ideal, in another coming of the Greek genius, and because he was a great patriot he believed Germany would be its new home. Germany's backward and fragmented state at the turn of the century gave no promise of this; but many Germans, besides Hölderlin, believed in their country's imminent renaissance.

Schwab noted of Hölderlin's generation: 'Da die Idee eines Freistaates in Frankreich in's Leben getreten war, so glaubte sich eine Jugend, die in den Alten zu Hause war, berechtigt, die Wiederkehr ihrer aus der Vorzeit überkommenen Ideale von der Zukunft zu hoffen' (GStA, vii,1,448). The comment is interesting in two respects. First in that it shows how closely philhellenism and revolutionary politics were connected; secondly in that it characterizes exactly the pattern of Hölderlin's thinking. His nature was elegiac and those are the movements of elegy: nostalgia, unhappiness in the present, and hope. In a quite precise way they structure his poetry.

The chaos of wars as the century ended perhaps seemed to promise something. To people with faith it might have seemed that the chaos was for some purpose. Certainly Hölderlin saw in the present signs of a better future, and his faith was such that the Peace of Lunéville seemed to him the beginning of a new age.

Given a belief, or an *idée fixe*, evidence can always be found to support it. Hölderlin began to expound the one idea, constantly restating it in a variety of ways, never at a loss for indications of its truth. He externalized it by creating an imaginary world, whose constituent places were related as his theory demanded.

It had to be shown that Germany would inherit from Greece. The world had to be arranged to show the genius of civilization recurring, after a long absence, in Germany. The progress of the ideal was mapped out in mythical geography.

For a year or so the idea remained simple and definite, and accordingly, with complete confidence, the poetry gave form to it. The great hymns of 1801 are the clearest expression of the idea, and in them Hölderlin's mythical world is contained; but the beginnings were earlier, in two or three poems written at the turn of the century.

There are two indications in 'Der Main' (July 1799) that the deliberate bringing together of Greece and Germany has begun. Of the poem's ten stanzas hardly three are concerned with the German river, but six are given to Greece. In fact Germany is remembered rather abruptly:

> . . . doch nimmer vergeß ich dich,
> So fern ich wandre, schöner Main!
>
> (lines 30-31, i,304)

which makes a clumsy ending. In 'Der Nekar' (January 1800), the re-written version of 'Der Main', the return to the homeland is less clumsy, in that the German river has already been celebrated before the journey to Greece begins.

To return is to abide by the present; to remain in Greece would be to abdicate from responsibility and be lost in nostalgia for the past. The 'doch' of 'Der Main' and 'Der Nekar' is a profession of fidelity to the present and bears comparison with the more emphatic statements of the later poems: 'Doch nicht zu bleiben gedenk ich' ('Die Wanderung', line 91, ii,141), or:

> . . . treuesten Sinns
> Hinüberzugehn und wiederzukehren.
>
> ('Patmos', lines 14-15, ii,165)

The pattern of journey and return shapes almost all the great hymns.

The second indication is not an explicit one, but in the context of the journey that the poem describes it cannot be overlooked. The Main rises in the Fichtelgebirge (a region Hölderlin travelled through in December 1793) and, with a good deal of meandering, flows west to Frankfurt (where he knew the river well) and to its confluence with the Rhein at Mainz:

> O ruhig mit den Sternen, du Glüklicher!
> Wallst du von deinem Morgen zum Abend fort . . .
>
> ('Der Main', lines 37-38, i,304)

The journey to Greece is eastwards, and the course of the river brings the poet home. The stars, in their progress from east to west, are given a similar significance in later poems. The Main, then, is an inferior forerunner of the Rhine and the

Danube, and the lines are Hölderlin's first essay in mythical geography. His
organizing, interpreting imagination is seen at work in the service of the one great
theme. He is beginning the creation of a world that will variedly and coherently
express his idea.

'Gesang des Deutschen' (written at the turn of the century) explicitly states the
idea and brings Greece and Germany together. The belief on which Hölderlin bases
his poetic world is affirmed:

> Doch, wie der Frühling, wandelt der Genius
> Von Land zu Land.
>
> ('Gesang des Deutschen', lines 37-38, ii,4)

Everything follows from that,[1] all the mythical geography and all the carefully
chosen details binding places together. That is the one theme, to be variedly treated.

The Athenian age was one in which this genius was present, and when it passed
the indestructible spirit was released:

> O heilger Wald! O Attika! traf Er doch
> Mit seinem furchtbarn Strale dich auch, so bald,
> Und eilten sie, die dich belebt, die
> Flammen entbunden zum Aether über?
>
> (ibid., lines 33-36)

The spirit might then recur anywhere:

> Noch lebt, noch waltet der Athener
> Seele, die sinnende, still bei Menschen . . .
>
> (ibid., lines 27-28)

—in Germany, as Hölderlin believed.

'Gesang des Deutschen' differs from 'Der Main' in that it is concerned primarily
with Germany. The poem divides so: 6 + 3 + 6. The three strophes at the heart give
the ideal and example of Greece. The first six deal with the problematic state of
Germany, and the last six, with Greece in mind, are a declaration of faith in
Germany's future. The poem sets the style of those to come: poems concerned
first and foremost with the predicament of Germany (or the wider 'Hesperia'), and
using the example of Greece for inspiration and encouragement. This commitment
to the present combats the nostalgia that 'Griechenland' openly admitted.

Almost all the mature poetry is concerned with the one theme. In most of the
poems the relating of Greece to Germany is explicit, and in the rest the relationship
is implied—poems concerned primarily with Greece (e.g. 'Der Archipelagus')
nevertheless refer to the modern age, and poems concerned primarily with Germany
(e.g. 'Stutgard') derive in many ways from Greece.

New places are added, new relationships made. The theme, although simple, can
be greatly varied and enriched. Before long there is a composite world, which could
be mapped and studied. It is stable and coherent at least until the journey to

Bordeaux, and even after then traces of the former coherence are plentiful, fragments of poems are still written that assume the existence of a coherent poetic world.

This world must now be described; first the places of which it is composed, secondly the many details that bind it together.

The coherence of Hölderlin's world is due largely to his simple conception of the human race's history. Like Herder or Lessing he believed in the meaningful rise and fall of civilizations, in the passing of one age to begin the next, and in a Providence that guided the whole course. Basically, then, the places of his world are linked historically: one inherits from or bequeaths to the next. Germany inherits, though not immediately, from Greece, but Greece, too, had its predecessors. It was an important development in Hölderlin's thought, to give Greece a past. For Winckelmann, whom Hölderlin first followed, Greece was an absolute, outside history, an ideal without past or future, that succeeding generations could do no more than imitate. Herder put Greece into a scheme of history and while acknowledging the Greek achievement warned against treating it as an absolute. Greece, he maintained, was one link in the chain, its achievement was unique, to be admired and learned from, but not to be slavishly imitated. The following civilizations had their own, unique contribution to make. He saw the whole pattern, of which Greece was only a part. These are the ideas that Hölderlin, about the turn of the century, came to accept. His philosophy of history derives to some extent from Herder, from two works: *Auch eine Philosophie der Geschichte zur Bildung der Menschheit* (1774) and *Ideen zur Philosophie der Geschichte der Menschheit* (1784-91).[2]

The sources of civilization—of the Greek, or of the modern European—were further east, in Asia. Hyperion's mentor, Adamas, dissatisfied with the modern Greeks, sets off in search of a mysterious eastern race:

In der Tiefe von Asien soll ein Volk von seltner Treflichkeit verborgen seyn; dahin trieb ihn seine Hoffnung weiter. (iii,17)

They are perhaps the remnants of the original Asian peoples among whom civilization began. Adamas's journey is back to the source. In a sense a journey to Switzerland, where there were remnants of the old Germanic tribes, or to Corsica, where there were remnants of the virtuous Phocaeans, would have done almost as well. Travellers to such places always felt they were returning to the unspoilt sources. Adamas, setting off eastwards, after a lifetime spent in search of the ideal, is making an ultimate effort: the East is his last and best chance.

In Hölderlin's mature philosophy Asia always has this significance. It is the source, where human history began, and from there all the following generations with their own unique achievements ultimately derive. He calls Asia 'the mother'.[3] When the Rhine turns east instead of north ('Der Rhein', lines 36-37, ii,143) that is the blind wish to return immediately to the source. Asia is a vague land, further east than Asia Minor, at least as far as India (including Tibet and China in Herder's scheme).[4] Often Hölderlin says simply 'the East':

> so kam
> Das Wort aus Osten zu uns . . .
>
> ('Am Quell der Donau', lines 35-36, ii,126)

or 'the Orient':

> Daß schauen mag bis in den Orient
> Der Mann und ihn von dort der Wandlungen viele bewegen.
>
> ('Germanien', lines 37-38, ii,150)

The East is the vague time and place behind Greece. Certain areas of it are occasionally emphasized. India, and especially the two rivers Indus and Ganges, is important. Herder thought Eden might be the modern Kashmir and that the Indus and the Ganges might be two of Eden's rivers.[5] For Hölderlin they are associated chiefly with Dionysus who was from the East and who returned there to spread the vine.[6] But God's messenger, the eagle, began his flight from the Indus—'der Adler, der vom Indus kömmt' ('Germanien', line 42, ii,150)—or his origins are there:

> Anfänglich aber sind
> Aus Wäldern des Indus
> Starkduftenden
> Die Eltern gekommen.
>
> ('Der Adler', lines 9-12, ii,229)[7]

It was Herder's idea that human life began in the East because in the beginning (after the Flood?) the Asian mountains were the only land-mass in a world of water.[8] Probably this is the sense of Hölderlin's lines:

> Der Urahn aber
> Ist geflogen über der See
> Scharfsinnend, und es wunderte sich
> Des Königes goldnes Haupt
> Ob dem Geheimniß der Wasser . . .
>
> (ibid., lines 13-17)

When Hölderlin saw the Atlantic, early in 1802, India was in his thoughts again. There were two ways to India, as the first discoverers believed, the known way, travelling east overland, or the unknown way that they thought possible, sailing west across the Atlantic:

> Mancher
> Trägt Scheue, an die Quelle zu gehn;
> Es beginnet nemlich der Reichtum
> Im Meere.
>
> ('Andenken', lines 38-41, ii,189)

Either way, inland or over the sea, the journey is back to the source, which is India. By 1803, when 'Andenken' was written, the coherent world of the hymns had largely disintegrated, but the significance of India remained unchanged; it was still the source, in the new terms of the Hesperian mythology, the source to the mariner of the fifteenth century.

The cities of the Euphrates, Palmyra the most notable, are briefly mourned after their destruction ('Lebensalter', ii,115). They were cities of old Asia, of the historical stage before the Greeks.

The Caucasus mountains, reputedly where the Ark landed after the Flood, are another area of this earliest world. 'Ich aber will dem Kaukasos zu! ' ('Die Wanderung', line 25, ii,138) is a wish to return to the source, a nostalgia that the rest of the poem modifies.

> Auch eurer denken wir, ihr Thale des Kaukasos,
> So alt ihr seid, ihr Paradiese dort . . .
> ('Am Quell der Donau', lines 77-78. ii,128)

Paradise was the first environment of the human race. Men lived first, according to Herder, a patriarchal life, nomadic and pastoral, in paradisial surroundings: 'ewig wird Patriarchengegend und Patriarchenzelt das goldne Zeitalter der Kindlichen Menschheit bleiben' (v,481). This was in the East, somewhere in Asia: 'M o r g e n l a n d, du hiezu recht auserwählter Boden Gottes! ' (v,483). Hölderlin duly remembers the patriarchs, as ancestors of the Greeks:

> Und deiner Patriarchen und deiner Propheten,
> O Asia, deiner Starken, o Mutter!
> ('Am Quell der Donau', lines 79-80, ii,128)

It is the primitive biblical age, one of the many ideal ages—once used conventionally in a comparison with Switzerland ('Kanton Schwyz', lines 43-44, i,144), now included carefully in a coherent world and history.

In Herder's philosophy civilization spread westwards:

Die Vorsehung leitete den Faden der Entwicklung weiter—von E u p h r a t, O x u s und G a n g e s herab, z u m N i l und an die P h ö n i c i s c h e K ü s t e n . . .
(v,487)

The Egyptians were thought to be an Asiatic people in the eighteenth century. Theirs was the next civilization. Egypt fits similarly into Hölderlin's historical scheme as an older culture than the Greek. In the greatest years of the Greek civilization, when the Greeks extended their influence throughout the Mediterranean, traders sailed to Egypt for corn, flax, and papyrus: 'hinab zum alten Aegyptos' ('Der Archipelagus', line 77, ii,105). In the Tübingen essay *Geschichte der schönen Künste unter den Griechen* Hölderlin acknowledges the earlier achievement of the Egyptians (iv,189)—at the same time emphasizing, as he does again in *Hyperion* (iii, 80-82), how inferior, for reasons of climate and national character, their achievement was to that of the Greeks. But in *Empedokles*, he confronts his hero with the older wisdom of Egypt in the person of Manes, to make him understand all the implications of his intended suicide.

It should be stressed, however, that while Herder is interested in the whole chain of civilization's development, paying tribute to every important link of it, Hölderlin is more selective, and concentrates his attention on only three of the stages—Asia, Greece, and Hesperia—making only nominal references to those stages which interest him less, like Egypt and Rome. He ignores the Phoenicians, an outstanding people in Herder's view (v,492 f.). He is glad to put Greece into a historical context, and is glad of the historical philosophy that links Greece with Germany, but he is selective, as a poet, and does not pretend to the thoroughness and impartiality of the philosopher Herder. He is not interested in the particular achievement of the Egyptians—their mathematics, agriculture, public order—but includes Egypt simply as an older civilization than the Greek. The same is true of Arabia. He speaks of the gifts from the East:

> die aus Ionien uns,
> Auch aus Arabia kamen . . .
> ('Am Quell der Donau', lines 64-65, ii,127)

Ionia, clearly—an area that obsessed him. But Arabia is of no importance in his world. It may be that he had Herder's writings in mind:

Selbst, da Griechenland zum z w e i t e n m a l auf Europa würken sollte, konnts nicht u n m i t t e l b a r würken: A r a b i e n ward der verschlämmte Kanal—Arabien der 'under-plot' zur Geschichte der Bildung Europa's. (v,563)

The Arabs passed on Aristotle to the scholastic theologians of medieval Europe (unfortunately, in Herder's opinion). It may be that Hölderlin included Arabia for those associations, although they are not relevant to his main concerns. But more probably Hölderlin's Arabia simply belongs, rather vaguely, in the classical area and times to which modern Europe owes a debt of gratitude. It happens more than once that areas of no particular interest to Hölderlin are simplified to fit conveniently into an overall scheme. The Persian civilization is so treated in 'Der Archipelagus' Persians are simply 'des Genius Feind' (line 86, ii,105). Likewise in the letter to his brother of 6 April 1796 (vi, 216) he speaks of 'das barbarische Susa'. But then in Fragment 67 Persia occurs exotically in a list of flowers. Places get their freedom as the coherent world disintegrates.

Greece

Greece is the central area of Hölderlin's poetic world. Everything leads to or derives from Greece. This ideal land is passionately but also precisely and carefully imagined. To give it topographical form Hölderlin chooses those places that can best stand for the aspects of the Greek achievement he most admired.

Within Greece the development of civilization continued from east to west,
from Ionia to Sparta and Athens;[9] but from first to last the Greek world was a
unity, an achievement complete in itself throughout its successive stages:

> doch von
> Parnassos Quell bis zu des Tmolos
> Goldglänzenden Bächen erklang
> Ein ewiges Lied . . .
>> ('Die Wanderung', lines 72-75, ii,140)[10]

It was this unity that the German Hellenists coveted for their own fragmented
country.[11] In his poems Hölderlin has clear visions of the whole geographical area of
Greece: most extensive in 'Der Archipelagus', where the wholeness of the Greek
achievement is perfectly figured in the harmonious integration of geographical
features—rivers, mountains, islands—features so large and celebrated, the Nile, the
Tmolus range, Delos, or Salamis, that only a total vision, as from an impossible
height, can comprehend them. But it is all *seen*, and at once; as though the symbols
on the map were quite plain realities, not in the least reduced.

The Greeks had a common language and, for all its local variations, a common
religious culture; and it is this that made a unity of the country, despite the
multiplicity of small city-states, and gave to the Greeks a quite clear sense of what
it meant to be Greeks and not barbarians. Unity was most apparent in the religious
festivals that brought Greeks together from all quarters of their world. They met at
Olympia, Delphi, Corinth for the games, on Delos for the festival of Apollo, and
these are the places Hölderlin uses most frequently to epitomize an aspect of the
Greek ideal. Delos, centrally situated among the Aegean islands, themselves
stepping-stones, peaks of human achievement, between the east and west of Greece,
was perhaps the best instance of the unity that Hölderlin admired and wanted for
his own country. Delos, like Delphi, was called by the Greeks 'the navel of the
earth'.

Having a common religion the Greeks revered all the holy places throughout their
land, the oracles at Delphi, Dodona, and Thebes, the mountains associated with the
gods—Olympus, Parnassus, Tmolus, Cithaeron—and the many places where their
myths, involving gods and men, were sited—Colonus, Cos, or Troy. These places
had the same associations for Greeks everywhere. It gives expression to the ideal of
unity when Hölderlin names them. The Muses' mountains—Pindus, Helicon,
Olympus, Cithaeron, Haemus—were of particular importance.[12] It was the poets,
especially Homer and Pindar, who made the Greeks aware of their unity, by
giving poetic form to their myths. Greeks everywhere could understand what Homer
and Pindar said or implied. An ideal situation, as Hölderlin recognized, an ideal
relationship between the poet and his audience, and one that Hölderlin, when
writing his best poems, never enjoyed. His own land was fragmented and godless,
and he could not base his poems on the traditions and myths of a common culture.

His mature poetry assumed a sense of community in his audience that was lacking. Only his early poems, treating the commonplaces and prejudices of his age, found anything like the understanding that Homer and Pindar had among the Greeks. Germany, then, needed not only a Delos and an Olympia to make a community of the people, but also a Pindus, Helicon, and Parnassus to give poets, the spokesmen of the people, the hearing due to them.

The greatest age of Greece, and so the age of her greatest unity, was the fifth century in Athens. Warfare against the Persians initiated this ideal time. In the battles of Salamis, Marathon, and Thermopylae the Greeks united against a common, barbarian enemy.[13] Typically, the Greeks turned everything to good. They derived positive benefit from the wars, re-building their destroyed cities more beautifully than before, and growing more conscious than before of community among themselves and with their gods. Athens flourished and extended her culture throughout the known world. The traders were the heroes of this expansion:

> Siehe! da Löste sein Schiff der fernhinsinnende Kaufmann,
> Froh, denn es wehet' auch ihm die beflügelnde Luft und die Götter
> Liebten so, wie den Dichter, auch ihn, dieweil er die guten
> Gaaben der Erd' ausglich und Fernes Nahem vereinte.
>
> ('Der Archipelagus', lines 72-75, ii,105)

Traders, like poets, bring about or express the unity of a people. Their status is high in Hölderlin's mythology.[14]

The Greeks owed their geographical unity largely to the sea. Communication over land was difficult, and land-locked peoples, like the Arcadians, were severely handicapped. But, in the sailing season, March to October, conditions in the Aegean were ideal for navigation. It was rare to get out of sight of land; the sailors, having no instruments, navigated from one island peak and headland to the next, between mainland Greece and the coast of Asia Minor and Egypt. Hölderlin recognized the primitive importance of these salient landscape features, of Poseidon's temple on the Sunium promontory, for example, visible to sailors;[15] and in his own visions of Greece, in 'Die Wanderung' or in 'Patmos', he moves from one landmark to the next.

Physical conditions—above all the Archipelago—favoured the unifying of the Greeks. The eighteenth-century Hellenists saw this; Herder makes much of it. The Greeks were nature's favourites: the geography, and the climate of their land helped them achieve their peak of civilization.[16]

Hölderlin always imagined Greece as the supremely beautiful land. Beauty was the prime achievement of the Greeks, and the country they lived in had to be beautiful also. The ideal race lived in ideal conditions. The beauty of Greece is that of perpetual spring—the Greeks were the youth of the human race, their age the spring-time of history. All the landscapes are in flower. The islands:

Deiner Inseln ist noch, der blühenden, keine verloren.
Kreta steht und Salamis grünt . . .

('Der Archipelagus', lines 12-13, ii,103)

Attica:

Schon auch sprossen und blühn die Blumen mälig, die goldnen,
Auf zertretenem Feld, von frommen Händen gewartet,
Grünet der Ölbaum auf . . .

(ibid., lines 175-77, ii,108)

The Cephissus and Ilissus flow abundantly at all times. The people themselves
are said to blossom:

. . . noch andere wohnten
Am Tayget, am vielgepriesnen Himettos,
Die blühten zulezt . . .

('Die Wanderung', lines 70-72, ii,140)

Of all the landscapes those of Ionia are the loveliest. Hölderlin pays a constant
tribute to Athens, but seems to be attracted most of all to the coastline of Asia
Minor. This is the oldest part of his Greek world, having Asia, the source, as its
hinterland.[17] It is not so clear as Athens; its age is a vague one in which the ages of
Troy, Homer, and the colonists from the mainland are confused. It is more exotic,
more mysterious, probably because of its vaguer history and its closeness to the
obscure but glamorous beginnings inside Asia. In Ionia Greece is constantly
reminded of her origins—by the moon:

Wenn von Asiens Bergen herein das heilige Mondlicht
Kömmt . . .   ('Der Archipelagus', lines 30-31, ii,104)

and the sun:

Wenn die allverklärende dann, die Sonne des Tages,
Sie, des Orients Kind, die Wunderthätige, da ist . . .

(ibid., lines 35-36)

These signs testify, even in the absence of the gods, that the course begun in the
east continues.

Ephesus, Smyrna, and the nearest islands, Tenedos and Chios,[18] have the snow-
covered mountains at the back of them:

aber im Lichte
Blüht hoch der silberne Schnee . . .

('Patmos', lines 38-39, ii,166)

an indication of the gods' presence at the source—the high land of Asia. In this vision
of Asia ('Patmos') Jung found archetypal images of the source, the mother-land,[19]
and although almost every detail can be explained in terms of Hölderlin's reading

and work,[20] it is true that, subconsciously or not, he was seeing in 'Patmos' a landscape of the beginnings of his world. His poetry celebrates the mountains Tmolus, Taurus, Messogis, and the rivers flowing down from them, the Maeander, Cayster, Pactolus, and the estuary towns, Smyrna, Ephesus.[21] In this Asian landscape, as in the Hesperian landscape of 'Heimkunft', the gods, living above the snow of the mountains, communicate with human beings through rivers, the intermediaries (demi-gods) between heaven and earth. The rivers of Ionia bring culture westwards down from the Asian mountains where it began.

Hölderlin's personal preference for this most distant area of Greece will have grown from the writing of *Hyperion* and the reading of the travellers that involved. Certain regions of his world are richer in associations because they were celebrated years before in the novel. The Troad peninsula and the hinterland of Smyrna are the old haunts of Adamas, Alabanda, and Hyperion—they have an even stronger attraction for Hölderlin because of the significance his own writings have already given them. The islands Calauria and Delos are similarly enriched.

The landscapes of the novel lose none of their beauty when they appear—with enhanced significance—in the poems. Ionia is as colourful, fresh, and spacious as before. It blossoms like the rest of Greece:

> Aber blühet indeß, bis unsre Früchte beginnen,
> Blüht, ihr Gärten Ioniens!
> > ('Der Archipelagus', lines 278-79, ii,111)

> Und voll von Blumen der Garten,
> Ein stilles Feuer . . .
> > ('Patmos', lines 37-38, ii,166)

The golden Pactolus, the silver snow, the peach and cherry—typical details of Hölderlin's Ionia.

All the places and the details he selects in the poems were used earlier in the novel and were probably read about in Chandler, Choiseul, or the Abbé Barthélemy. But in the novel they made up local colour, in the poems they contribute to the making of myths.[22]

The natural beauty of Greece is not marred in any way. There are no plagues or droughts—such details, that Hölderlin knew of from Chandler, are rigorously excluded. For the fate of Greece there is great sorrow and regret, but almost no mention of the degenerate modern Greeks and no diatribes against their barbarian Turkish overlords. Hölderlin accepts that the ideal age is over, what remains is the landscape—the people still living in it are more or less irrelevant.[23] The renaissance will be elsewhere, among a different people.

Hölderlin omitted or made very little of many places greatly important to the Greeks. There were some, like Crete and Mycenae, whose importance he could not know, living when he did. Others, like Eleusis or Cythera, had a significance that did not interest him. Nor was he ever concerned to draw up complete lists: he names Olympia, the Isthmus, and Pythius (= Delphi, ii,693) but not Nemea, although the games held there were also important; Dodona, Delphi, and Thebes, but not the fourth great oracle at Ammonium in the Libyan desert. He chose what suited the purpose of each poem. A coherent world was formed because his interests were constant, not because in each poem he worked at shaping it. He favoured certain mountains and rivers, when he might equally well have chosen others to express the same ideas. And if he paid less tribute to certain places than the historian would do, to others he paid far more. The mountains and rivers of Asia Minor have greater prominence in his Greece than in the historical Greece. He gives his own sense to places—to Xanthus (in 'Stimme des Volks') or Eleutherae (in 'Mnemosyne')—and where, for the Greeks, there was no sense at all—the island of Patmos—he makes one for his own mythology.

Hölderlin's prime concern was to relate Greece to Germany, and what came after Greece and before Germany in the course of civilization interested him very little. He makes almost nothing of the western Mediterranean, the Greeks' own Hesperia. True, in 'Der Archipelagus' the sailors get beyond the Straits of Gibraltar 'zu neuen seeligen Inseln' (line 80), but this is one more example of Athens's manifold activity and not really an indication of the western civilization to come. Empedocles, in Sicily, is on the borders of a new age, but the play makes nothing of his country's *geographical* position in relation to the civilizations of Egypt and Athens.

The Etruscans, whom Herder greatly admired, are indicated in 'Der Adler' (line 3) as a stage in the progress of culture, along with the Gotthard and the notable mountains of Greece. And in 'Brod und Wein' a late variant of line 96 reads: 'Richten in Tuskischen Ordnungen Völker sich auf' (ii,604, line 6) where the earlier version had simply 'herrlichen'. It is typical of Hölderlin, at this late stage, to particularize with a proper noun or adjective, but why 'Tuskisch'? [24] Herder paid special tribute to the Etruscans' gifts of organization in social matters, and in art, especially architecture where they created the Tuscan column.[25] It may be that, from Herder or elsewhere, Hölderlin had these national qualities in mind. Probably the building of temples, the raising of the columns, is the image behind line 96 of 'Brod und Wein'.[26] The Greeks, who then create works of art, temples, and cities, are themselves, naturally, a perfect work.

Rome is the next stage. Hölderlin's eagle, en route for Germany, passes over the hills of Italy ('Germanien', lines 44-45, ii,150), and thus the great age of Rome is acknowledged. Hölderlin doubtless shared his contemporaries' idea of Rome, and conventionally admired the 'Roman' virtues of 'die alten Eroberer' ('Der Frieden', line 21, ii,6). But he pays no more attention to their particular achievements than to those of the Egyptians. If we are all either Greeks or Romans then Hölderlin was clearly a Greek, and what sympathy he had for empire-builders he gave to

Napoleon. Italy mattered more to him as Napoleon's battle-ground than as the centre of the Roman world.[27]

The passing of Rome ends the classical era in the old world south and east of the Alps:

> Drüben sind der Trümmer genug im Griechenland und die hohe
> Roma liegt . . .
>> ('Der Archipelagus', variants, ii,645, lines 11-12)

After Rome, in Herder's phrase: 'N o r d e n wars' (v,514).

The whole course of civilization is thus resumed:

> . . . so kam
> Das Wort aus Osten zu uns,
> Und an Parnassos Felsen und am Kithäron hör' ich
> O Asia, das Echo von dir und es bricht sich
> Am Kapitol und jählings herab von den Alpen
>
> Kommt eine Fremdlingin sie
> Zu uns, die Erwekerin,
> Die menschenbildende Stimme.
>> ('Am Quell der Donau', lines 35-42, ii,126)[28]

These are 'die Gipfel der Zeit' ('Patmos', line 10, ii,165), the high-points of human history. Herder often uses similar imagery: '. . . sie waren R ö m e r. Auf einer W e l t h ö h e, und alles rings um sie T h a l! ' (v,507). 'Gipfel gränzt an Thal' (v,508). And Hölderlin writes elsewhere:

> . . . die Zeiten des Schaffenden sind,
> Wie Gebirg,
> Das hochaufwoogend von Meer zu Meer
> Hinziehet über die Erde . . .
>> ('Der Mutter Erde', lines 67-70, ii,125)

He abides by this imagery. In his survey of history mountains stand for the achievements of each age. He resumes the history of Greece so: from Tmolus to Parnassus.[29] Often he refers to a city by the mountain above it—Taygetus for Sparta, Hymettus for Athens[30]—as though the peak were the visible indication of the city's greatness. Like Herder, he thought mountains important in the shaping of human history, and, also like Herder, he often seems to be reading that history from a relief map of the globe.[31]

So it is that after the high plateau of central Asia, the mountains of Asia Minor, the peaks of the Aegean islands, Cithaeron, Parnassus, Taygetus, and Hymettus, the Roman Capitol, finally come the Alps. And lying below the Alps, like Ionia below Taurus and Tmolus, is Hesperia:

Hesperia

Herder continues paying tribute to each new effect of the 'Gang Gottes über die Nationen' (v,565), to the Middle Ages, the Renaissance, and the Reformation. None of these stages interested Hölderlin in the years when his poetic world was most coherent. He simplified the historical scheme, and his Hesperia, in an ideal but imminent future, inherits directly from the classical age.

It is typical that Hesperia should be in the future, however imminent. An age of darkness is interposed between the Greek and the new Hesperian daylight. Even Herder, having fairly meted out praise to successive past ages, was unable to be anything but ironic and sceptical towards his own (v,545 f.). The spirit of civilization, these eighteenth-century philosophers found, was temporarily absent, but about to re-appear. Thus most thinkers, whether Christian or not, looked forward to another coming of their ideal. They were all hopeful.

Pietists, like Bengel and Oetinger, confidently prophesied, for the early nineteenth century, the coming of the millenium to Swabia. It seems likely that Hölderlin was influenced by them. He had a Pietist upbringing and traces of Pietism are evident, particularly in the vocabulary, even in his mature work. But chiliastic philosophies were so current in the eighteenth century that Hölderlin's debt to the Pietists is hard to estimate. He was on common ground, thinking as he did. However, there are some remarkable parallels.[32]

The Pietists were waiting for the millenium, and preparing for its coming in the meantime. 'Die güldene Zeit'[33] was imminent, and it was the duty of all believers to announce it. They understood passages in the Book of Revelation, notably Chapter 12, to mean that Germany was to be the site of Christ's kingdom. They saw the Church progressing from the East, to a recent peak in Bohemia (Hus) and to the promised climax in Germany:

Die Kirche mußte in zerstreuter Kraft von Morgen gegen Abend ziehen, sie mußte in die Wüste. Die Wüste war anfangs Böhmen, hernach Deutschland.[34]

God was preparing Germany to receive the Church.

Oetinger uses one of Hölderlin's favourite images, the eagle's flight, to illustrate the Church's coming from the East. One of the chapters of his book *Die güldene Zeit* is headed: 'Flug der Kirche mit Adlersflügeln nach Teutschland'.

In a typically Swabian manner Oetinger included the Greeks in this renaissance of the Christian Church: 'Die Philosophie der Alten, wiederkommend in der güldenen Zeit'.[35]

From January until early April 1801, Hölderlin lived in Hauptwyl, in sight of the Alps. On 9 February France and Austria signed the Treaty of Lunéville, and temporarily brought the European wars to an end. The Peace of Lunéville encouraged Hölderlin in his belief that a new and better age was imminent, and the poem 'Friedensfeier' is a measure of his confidence. Living in sight of the Alps, the high, snow-covered Säntis peaks, clarified his vision of the ideal world into which this new age would come. He wrote to his sister on the day when the news of the Peace reached Hauptwyl:

Ich konnte auch diesen Morgen, da der würdige Hausvater mich damit begrüßte, wenig dabei sagen. Aber das helle Himmelblau und die reine Sonne über den nahen Alpen waren meinen Augen in diesem Augenblicke um so lieber, weil ich sonst nicht hätte gewußt, wohin ich sie richten sollte in meiner Freude.[36]

The Alps are a kind of visible correlative of the good news. From this time onwards Hölderlin could give his Hesperian ideals a precise geographical setting.

The ideal homeland of his poetry, Swabia, lies directly below the Alps:

> Und Alpengebirg der Schweiz auch überschattet
> Benachbartes dich . . .[37]

This was not in fact true of the Swabia Hölderlin lived in; but it was true of Hohenstauffen Swabia, which extended south of Lake Constance to include St Gallen (and so Hauptwyl) and the Alpine regions of Chiavenna and Chur. And since it was important for Hölderlin's mythology that his Swabia should lie close under the Alps he kept the medieval, and not the modern boundaries in mind. The real world was arranged to suit an ideal pattern, political and geographical facts ordered to serve the idea.

In the poems that resume the course of civilization by naming successive mountain peaks the Alps follow naturally, and the series is concluded without anti-climax. This is important; the new Germanic age must hold its own against the Greek.

The Alps, on the southern border of Swabia, make visible the civilization flourishing at their feet. But more, since the ideal life is only possible in the presence of the gods, they are a guarantee of the closeness of divinity. Simply, they are the new throne of the gods. This was the vision Hölderlin had in Hauptwyl. He wrote to his sister:

Du würdest auch so betroffen, wie ich, vor diesen glänzenden, ewigen Gebirgen stehn, und wenn der Gott der Macht einen Thron hat auf der Erde, so ist es über diesen herrlichen Gipfeln.   (vi,414)

Then in the poetry after Hauptwyl the Alps have this significance. In 'Der Rhein' they are: 'die Burg der Himmlischen' (line 6, ii,142). In 'Unter den Alpen gesungen', 'Heimkunft' and 'Die Wanderung', all written in 1801 and influenced strongly by the months in Hauptwyl, the Alps are the source of divinity or simply the gods' throne. Even in some of the fragments, written when Hölderlin's poetic world was no longer coherent, much of this significance remains: in 'Wenn aber die Himmlischen . . .' and 'Ihr sichergebaueten Alpen . . .', certainly, and possibly also in 'Tinian'.

The Alps are that place in Hesperia where communication is easiest between gods and men:

> wo aber
> Geheim noch manches entschieden
> Zu Menschen gelanget . . .
>
> ('Der Rhein', lines 7-9, ii,142)

Hölderlin found imagery for this communication in the view from the Gonzenbach house in Hauptwyl:

> wie vom Aether herab die Höhen alle näher und näher niedersteigen bis in dieses freundliche Thal . . . (vi,414)

He had noted a similar feature of landscape much earlier, in the vineyard terraces around Tübingen and in the level-topped, one-behind-the-other hills of the Schwäbische Alb, and intruded it, incongruously, into the landscapes of Greece:

> wie Stuffen gehn die Berge bis zur Sonne unaufhörlich hinter einander hinauf. (iii,48)

Swabia is a typical 'Trias Stufenlandschaft', as Swabian critics point out; but Greek mountains tend to be steep and sharp, rarely flat-topped.[38] At the time of the writing of *Hyperion* that topographical observation was without mythical significance. But in 1801, seeing the Alpine peaks descending through their foothills into the Hauptwyl valley, Hölderlin had the imagery he needed to express his new myths. God cannot communicate directly with men, because men could not bear the contact. Intermediaries make communication possible:

> Immer stehet irgend
> Eins zwischen Menschen und ihm.
> Und treppenweise steiget
> Der Himmlische nieder.
>
> ('Der Einzige', lines 71a-d, ii,745)

Demi-gods, like Castor and Pollux:

> . . . und othembringend steigen
> Die Dioskuren ab und auf,
> An unzugänglichen Treppen, wenn von himmlischer Burg
> Die Berge fernhinziehen
> Bei Nacht . . .
>
> ('Wenn aber die Himmlischen . . .', lines 78-82, ii,224)

And demi-gods like the great rivers. The Rhine, rising in the Alps and flowing through Germany relates the gods and the men of the new age. The river makes its way gradually down from its source, from a divine into a human sphere, like the sunlight ('Der Rhein', lines 2-4, ii,142). The Gotthard massif, where the Rhine, with four other rivers, has its source, was a place of the greatest importance and holiness in Hölderlin's mythology: as a source of divinity; as a turning-point between the ages (north, with the Rhine, into Hesperia, south with the Ticino or the Rhone into the old Mediterranean world); and as a pass between these ages, a bond relating them.[39]

The gods' messenger, the eagle, finds Germania immediately below the Alps. This is the privileged situation of Hölderlin's Swabia, close to the source, in communication with the gods through the streams that flow down from the melting snow.[40]

Hölderlin's vision of Hesperia clarified in 1801 after the months in Hauptwyl. Before then, in 'Der Archipelagus' or 'Brod und Wein', his Hesperia was only a vague counterpart to his clearly imagined Greece. He did not name any equivalents of Parnassus, Cithaeron, or the Ismenus, not until the hymns of 1801. Then he was confident enough to be quite precise. Landscapes he had known from his childhood were thought fit to be the components of a world comparable in its achievements and physical beauty with that of Greece. Most of the landscapes are Swabian. Only one other area of Germany is included in the poetic world, the Rhein-Main plain and Frankfurt, an area of the greatest personal importance to Hölderlin. The ideal world of the past was composed entirely of places that Hölderlin knew only from his reading, but Hesperia of places he had personally experienced. It is relatively easy to idealize inaccessible lands (to the Germans Greece seemed inaccessible), but Hölderlin had the ability to idealize and make convincing myths of places that were present and commonly visited. As the one great idea of his poetry possessed him he applied it and looked for indications of its truth wherever and as often as he could. The idea was always with him.

> Oft stand ich überschauend das holde Grün,
> Den weiten Garten hoch in deinen
> Lüften auf hellem Gebirg' und sah dich.
> ('Gesang des Deutschen', lines 14-16, ii,3)

When he walked, alone, over the Alb or the Taunus he looked for evidence in the landscape of the one great idea. The enjoyment he had from wide views was largely due to the freedom they gave him to interpret and schematize the landscape below. Similarly, the pleasure he had from Germany's rivers lay in the sense he could impose on them: 'An deinen Strömen gieng ich und dachte dich . . .' (ibid., line 17). Crossing the Alb to visit his sister in Blaubeuren—climbing from the Neckar into the Danube valley—he will have thought of the course eastwards to the Black Sea, just as, seeing the mountains near Regensburg in 1802, he thought of the course north-westwards into Germany.

Hölderlin possessed in a high degree that ability to see a pattern (his fixed idea) developing over vast expanses of space and time that Herder thought indispensable in the historian-philosopher.[41] It is this 'Überblick' that encourages him to idealize, and from such a vantage point, with the one idea in mind, he looked out over his homeland and interpreted its mountains and rivers.

Swabia, like the Alps, was celebrated in Hölderlin's early poetry, then largely ignored for several years when Greece was the main concern. When, in 1801, Swabia again preoccupied Hölderlin it was not for its great medieval past—there are no equivalents of 'Die Tek' or 'Burg Tübingen', not until 1803—but as the mythical ideal homeland.[42] Lying close under the Alps it allows the ideal life in innocence, such as the poem 'Unter den Alpen gesungen' celebrates. Real places, Lauffen, Heidelberg, Tübingen, Stuttgart, the Neckar and its tributaries, and the particular Swabian roads and hills are the component parts of this ideal land. It is for his own well-loved, well-known country, actually for the villages and landscapes of his childhood, that Hölderlin conjures up the renaissance of the Greek ideal.

Herder always maintained that any attempt simply to revive the Greek achievement was doomed to failure:

... der Geist war Staub; der Sprößling blieb Asche: Griechenland kam nicht wieder. (v, 562)

And Hölderlin's frequent affirmations of loyalty to the present indicate that he thought as Herder did. The new age that his poetry announced was to be Germanic and not Greek. It was sited unequivocally in Swabia.

Despite which it is obvious that Hölderlin could not imagine this new ideal Germanic world—either its qualities or its physical setting—in any other than Greek terms. His Hesperian civilization is not simply one more peak in the long development from Asia, Germanic and unlike any before it—it is a revival, admittedly on German soil, of all that was best in Greece. The paradox is that Hölderlin must maintain himself and his times against the temptation that the Greeks represent, but for inspiration and for examples of his ideals he goes again and again only to the Greeks (whereas Herder might have gone to the Greeks for one thing, to the Romans for another and to the Egyptians for a third). Greece is his sole ideal and obsession; he seems permanently on the brink of giving way once and for all to its attraction. He lays far less emphasis than Herder does on the *uniqueness* of each age's achievements and needs.

What he wanted for Germany was a Greek harmony, unity, and community, he wanted equivalents of Olympus, Delos, and Helicon even though Germany, at the turn of the century, had problems that were peculiarly her own. 'Herz der Völker', the phrase used in 'Gesang des Deutschen', and commonly by other writers, aptly describes Germany's situation in Europe (hence the obsessive fear of *Einkreisung*. This central situation, Hölderlin hoped, would favour her role in the new age:

Germania, wo du Priesterin bist
Und wehrlos Rath giebst rings
Den Königen und den Völkern.

('Germanien', lines 110-12, ii,152)

But this is wishful thinking, for the ideal future. In fact, as Hölderlin well knew, Germany's central position, lying between France, Prussia, Russia, and Austria,

made her the battlefield of Europe. Significantly, Germania is 'wehrlos'.
Hölderlin's mature patriotism was not militaristic. In an age of war the virtues he
urged on his countrymen were patience, love, and conscientiousness. Possibly this
was the most he could ask. Passive virtues—virtues of necessity—were all his country
could hope to show. The heroics and the flamboyant chauvinism were for nations
with more say in the direction of the wars. Germany needed the patience to bear
what could not be avoided. The German virtues are those of the earth: 'Allduldend,
gleich der schweigenden Mutter Erd' . . .' ('Gesang des Deutschen', line 2, ii,3).
Germany is 'Tochter . . . der heiligen Erd' ' ('Germanien', line 97) and, like the
earth, 'unzerbrechlich' (ibid., line 59). Germany survives wars and all catastrophes,
just as the earth survives.

It is the Greeks who provide examples of those virtues that Hölderlin saw or
wished for in his countrymen:

> Kennst du Minervas Kinder? sie wählten sich
> Den Oelbaum früh zum Lieblinge . . .
>
> ('Gesang des Deutschen', lines 25-26, ii,4)

Athene was the patroness of conscientious craftsmen. Her image in Athens was of
olive wood. The olive takes thirty years to reach maturity, and frequent warfare
makes its cultivation impossible. For that reason it has become a symbol of peace,
but other symbolic aspects should not be overlooked: the tree's toughness, its
survival and growth despite hardships, the patience needed to cultivate it to
maturity—eminently the virtues Germany was in need of.

The greatest virtue is love. Germany is 'Du Land der Liebe' (ibid., line 10). But
love, too, in Hölderlin's mythology at least, was the prime Greek virtue, the
inspiration of their civilization.[43] Later, when more concerned than ever with
Hesperia, Hölderlin celebrated the Madonna as the Hesperian goddess of ἀγάπη
love:

> und gewaltet über
> Den Menschen hat, statt anderer Gottheit sie
> Die allvergessende Liebe.
>
> ('An die Madonna', lines 24-26, ii,211)

Obviously these qualities, love, patience, conscientiousness, are absolutes, more
or less present in any age and not at all peculiar to the Greeks. But, in Hölderlin's
view, no people was ever more full of them, and when examples are needed they are
drawn from Greece.

Hölderlin's Hesperia is orientated back to Greece, and related to it, deliberately,
as often and in as many different ways as possible. Paradoxically, the more Greek
this Hesperia can be shown to be the more established it becomes as a new ideal
civilization. The more Greek, the more ideal, since there has never been a higher
achievement than Greece. Hölderlin's Hesperia would be no more than a classicistic
abstraction were it not rooted so firmly and with greater and greater particularness

in the Swabian landscape. And as Hölderlin turns more and more certainly to the
Swabian landscape, in the months after Hauptwyl, and professes ever greater
fidelity to his own times, so, in order to enhance and make clear the nature of his
Hesperia, he draws more and more frequently on Greece.

To describe the Alps, having established them in his mythology as the throne of
the Hesperian gods, he uses the word 'göttlichgebaut ('Der Rhein', line 5, ii,142),
which is Homer's epithet Θεοδματος for the towers of Troy, built by Poseidon.[44]
(Hölderlin himself uses it in line 45 of 'Patmos' for the Greek buildings of Asia
Minor: 'die göttlichgebauten Palläste'.) The landscape with which 'Der Rhein'
opens has other typically Greek elements:

> Von Treppen des Alpengebirgs,
> Das mir die göttlichgebaute,
> Die Burg der Himmlischen heißt
> Nach alter Meinung . . .

(lines 4-7, ii,142)

'Burg' suggests Olympus, and also the Acropolis of Athens: 'die seelige Burg der
Mutter Athene' ('Der Archipelagus', line 149, ii,107). 'Nach alter Meinung' is most
interesting. The phrase attributes a long tradition of holiness to the Alps. But they
had no such tradition; they were never a holy place of Christian Europe. When they
became popular in the eighteenth century it was for their Gothic beauty, or for the
thoughts of Rousseauesque simple living they inspired. At most they aroused a
pseudo-religious awe in sentimental pilgrim-tourists. Nor had they always been
holy in Hölderlin's own poetry. They were not the throne of the gods when he first
saw them in 1791. In fact their holiness is only a few weeks old: it dates from the
time in Hauptwyl. 'Nach alter Meinung' is what a Greek might justifiably have said
of the holiness of Olympus, Parnassus, or Tmolus. Hölderlin sanctifies with the
weight of a long tradition a myth he has just invented.

He uses Greek terms, deliberately, to imply that the renaissance in Swabia will
be a renaissance of those qualities that were best realized among the Greeks. But
also because he saw that there were no Germanic terms of comparable force. He
uses Greek traditions and beliefs because those available to him in his own land
and times were not adequate. He did attempt to make use of the myths of his own
age—the voyages of discovery, for example—and he created new myths out of
contemporary events—the Revolutionary Wars, for example—but always by drawing
on the traditions, beliefs, the style and vocabulary of Greece, so forming a strangely
private mythology.

The places of his Hesperia are unquestionably German, but to give proof of the
ideal, mythical status to which they have been enhanced Hölderlin can do no other
than characterize them in a Greek manner, often with loan-translations of traditional
Greek epithets. The ideal cannot be conceived of in any but Greek terms. Thus
Swabia is 'von hundert Bächen durchflossen': Homer's Mount Ida was πολύπιδαξ

'of the many streams'.[45] The Main is styled 'du Glüklicher':[46] the Greek word εὐδαίμων was commonly used of places. Lindau is 'wellenumrauscht' and 'glükseelig':[47] Sophocles gives very similar epithets (ἀλίπλακτος and εὐδαίμων) to Salamis in verses that Hölderlin translated:

Berühmte Salamis, irgend wohnst
Du meerumwoogt, glükseelig . . .

(v,278)

Hölderlin's Rhine is 'das göttliche Wild': Pindar calls the centaur Chiron φήρ θεῖος;[48] Stuttgart is 'die gepriesene': Hymettus 'viel gepriesen' (Greek: κλειτός, πολυύμνητος).[49] And there are many more such epithets, some exact equivalents of the Greek—'wohlgeschmiedet' (εὐεργής), applied to the hills near Regensburg[50] — and some Greek in style—'schiksaalskundig' (Heidelberg castle),[51] 'weißblühend'[52] (Swabian fruit-trees). The effect of both types is the same: to give a classical glamour to homely German places, proving the renaissance of the ideal by indicating how Greek these German places are. (I refer to these epithets here as being one means of relating the two main spheres of Hölderlin's poetic world. But the use of epithets is an important aspect of Hölderlin's descriptive style, and as such they will be discussed again in the chapter 'Hölderlin's poetic-descriptive art'.)

The epithets are a small indication of the coherence Hölderlin established in his poetic world early in 1801. With the one unifying idea in mind—that the Greek ideal would flourish again on German soil—he looked constantly for indications of its truth, and for details that might help in its expression. In his Hesperia he found many hints, some small, some obvious, of the relationship with Greece. The largest and best known are the rivers. The Main, flowing east to west, was the first to be interpreted.[53]

The Danube was more difficult. Rising in the Black Forest and emptying into the Black Sea it undeniably links Hesperia and Greece. It was a river that Hölderlin knew well, from visits to his sister in Blaubeuren, from the journey to Hauptwyl through Sigmaringen, and from his stay in Regensburg with Sinclair. It was a valuable reminder to him, at home, of Hesperia's direct relatedness to the eastern source. The west-east course of the river is appropriately used in 'Am Quell der Donau'. At the Danube's source Hölderlin is naturally mindful of Asia, and the river offers an obvious means of acknowledging Hesperia's debt to the east. Further, it is a reminder that now the west must reply to the original inspiration from Asia with comparable achievements of her own.[54] Here the symbolic interpretation of the river is entirely unforced; it accords well with geographical and historical fact. The Danube always has served as a trade and migratory route, perhaps even as Hölderlin suggests in 'Die Wanderung', between western Europe and the Black Sea regions. But Hölderlin cannot leave it at that. In its west-east course the river is not finally satisfying to him (even though trade and influence can just as well come upstream as down), and he sets about improving on nature to suit his own poetic ends:

> Der scheinet aber fast
> Rükwärts zu gehen und
> Ich mein, er müsse kommen
> Von Osten.
> Vieles wäre
> Zu sagen davon.
>
> ('Der Ister', lines 41-46, ii,191)

This is, I think, an appropriate point at which to continue the discussion, begun in Chapter 1, of the imaginative processes through which Hölderlin's poetic world was formed. 'Der Ister' is a particularly illuminating poem.

What Hölderlin is asking of the Danube is to provide him with a clear image of civilization's progress from Greece to Germany. Or, more than that: not simply to be an image, but to be an indication, to be a proof of what he himself believes. But the river puzzles him; in a sense, its sluggish west-east course fails him. It is clear from the rough drafts and the variants (ii, 808-10) that the lines quoted above—the 'insight' into the physical nature and symbolic significance of the river—are the nucleus of the poem, the part Hölderlin began with and repeatedly worked over. In fact there is an almost obsessive insistence upon them. In one form or another they recur six or seven times during the poem's composition. They are then further emphasized by a long bracket in the margin drawing them together and setting them prominently at the head of a new strophe.

The river is a problem:

> Aber allzugedultig
> Scheint der mir, nicht
> Freier, und fast zu spotten.
>
> ('Der Ister', lines 58-60)

The Rhine, on the other hand, is an easy river to understand; Hölderlin had already done so, and interpreted it—its eastern and abruptly northern course—in accordance with the one great idea that shaped all his poetic world. But the Danube leaves him puzzled:

> Was aber jener thuet der Strom,
> Weis niemand.
>
> (ibid., lines 71-72)

He is puzzled by the geographical fact of the river's notorious sluggishness, almost motionlessness, in its upper reaches—a fact he had noted for himself on several occasions, most recently in the autumn of 1802. The river ought, by rights, to have been rushing headlong east, as the young Rhine does, back to the source. Instead it almost stagnates.

That is a difficult fact to accommodate into the coherent world: Hölderlin cannot make of the river a symbol of the blind instinct back to Mother Asia. Instead, he imposes on the river's course a significance which he would far rather it had. He would far rather the Danube flowed east-west, from the Black Sea to the Black Forest. But that cannot be, so instead, as a *pis-aller*, he takes advantage of a particularly indeterminate part of the river's course and, rather hesitantly, with 'seemings' and subjunctives, imposes his own sense on it.

Is this mythopoeic insight into the true nature and meaning of the river? Or is it simply manipulation on behalf of the one fixed idea? The latter seems the more likely. 'Der Ister' is a late poem (summer 1803) and it can fairly be discussed in this chapter only because its theme is still quite clearly that of the coherent poetic world that the great hymns of 1801 express. The theme is the same, but the poet's myth-making imagination (or, at the very least, his just sense of symbolism) is failing him. In their crudeness those central lines of 'Der Ister' indicate how close the myth-making poet may often be to conscious, forced contriving—or perhaps how much intellectual contriving there is always in the making of myths. And there may be no objective criteria for deciding which is which. It may simply be a matter of how well the contriving is concealed, and how convincing the poet's myths turn out to be.

The poem 'Das Nächste Beste', in its third version, provides a further and more striking illustration of this problem. Like 'Der Ister' it was written after Hölderlin's coherent world had largely disintegrated, but its theme is recognizably the old one (indeed, it is only because the old theme is recognizable that sense can be made of the poem), and in its use of geographical features as poetic images or indications of relatedness and coherence it continues the technique successfully used in the best poems of 1801.

Probably Hölderlin shared Herder's view that mountains are important in the development of any country's culture.[55] 'Das Nächste Beste' is an attempt to put such theories into poetic form.

The poem looks forward to the end of that familiar transitional period of chaos which its opening lines (1-6) describe. And it finds an encouraging image of the new dawn—the gods' return and the coming of the ideal civilization to Germany—in the starlings' homecoming from their winter habitat in south-western France. This begins as an image—'Drum wie die Staaren . . .' (line 9) —sustained in Homeric style, one that Hölderlin was particularly fond of.[56] It is a phenomenon that human beings observe and interpret:

> Menschlich ist
> Das Erkenntniß.

(lines 38-39)

But, Hölderlin believes, the gods, too, will be influenced by it:

> Aber die Himmlischen
> Auch haben solches mit sich, und des Morgens beobachten
> Die Stunden und des Abends die Vögel. Himmlischen auch
> Gehöret also solches.

(lines 39-42)

They too are watching the starlings' flight and deciding from it, so Hölderlin believes, as though like human beings they too were taking the auspices, that the times are now propitious for their return. The iamge of the starlings' return is becoming more than an image; like much of Hölderlin's imagery, it is becoming an *effective* indication of the facts—facts about men and gods that ordinary people are blind to. It has become more than a simile: 'Just as the starlings . . . so, too, I believe, the gods . . .'—more than a human approximation at a religious truth. In the normal simile a familiar phenomenon is used to illustrate, probably inadequately, an unfamiliar or unimaginable one. But here the starlings do more than that: they are an omen, they are themselves effective.

The poem then goes on to discover a further indication of the gods' imminent coming in landscape, in the course of mountain ranges. Because of the times and the loss of religion between men and gods, the poet cannot say it directly: 'The gods are returning'—but only obliquely by revealing the significance of landscape (lines 42-47). What Hölderlin then offers is not a simile, but an interpretation of what the landscape means. The key-words are 'Umsonst nicht' (line 51). Therein lies the justification of the passage, and indeed of Hölderlin's treatment of all the landscape features in his poetic world. It is not for nothing that the mountains are as they are, they are not fortuitously shaped this way or that. Their course is meaningful and its meaning can be revealed. The same applies to the course of the Danube, and in 'Am Quell der Donau' Hölderlin's revelation is convincing and satisfying; less so in 'Der Ister', and here, in 'Das Nächste Beste', his revelation seems contrived and extremely unconvincing. But in all three poems the imaginative or intellectual process is essentially the same; and only that kind of mind, at its best, could shape a poetic world like Hölderlin's of 1801.

Only a very careful reading of the poem, and a close study of the rough drafts and variants make the passage in 'Das Nächste Beste' (lines 47-56) comprehensible. Maps must be consulted, and drawn. The starting-point is Vienna (cf. ii,869, line 4). From there the Alps tend westwards across Austria, north-eastern Italy and Switzerland, so by-passing Germany to the south. For this reason they are unsuitable as an indication of the gods' coming to Germania. Following the trend of the Alps,[57] and the trend of the main Alpine valleys the gods would be led astray to such regions as north-western Italy or south-eastern France (lines 54-56). Fortunately, near Vienna, the Alps put out a minor range that leads north-west over the Böhmerwald and the Bayrischer Wald to the very heart of Germany, through the Fränkische Jura and on to the Fichtelgebirge:

Abendlich wohlgeschmiedet
Vom Oberlande biegt sich das Gebirg, wo auf hoher Wiese die Wälder sind wohl an
Der bairischen Ebne. Nemlich Gebirg
Geht weit und streket, hinter Amberg sich und
Fränkischen Hügeln.

(lines 47-51)

Their course is not fortuitous; it is the deliberate work of a god, who turned them aside from the Alpine trend and directed them 'home', to Germany (lines 51-54). Landscape is not used as an image but as a sure indication of what the gods intend.

The poem has all the appearance of having been painstakingly contrived from a study of the map. It represents the failing of Hölderlin's mythopoeic gift. The element of intellectual contriving always present even in the most satisfying mythopoetry is now all that remains.

Perhaps one last example might be given, a small one that occurs in the late, unfinished poem 'An die Madonna'. Again, this is a poem written after 1802 in which the coherent world of the hymns is still, to a large extent, assumed or maintained. By a quite false etymology Hölderlin associates the Germanic mountain Knochenberg with the Greek mountain Ossa,[58] so binding together, in a poem primarily concerned with the Hesperian goddess Mary, the antique and the modern worlds. It is not the whole mythopoeic imagination which is at work here, but a rather tired intellect still obsessed by the one idea.

In the finished poems of Hölderlin's maturity the indications of coherence, of Hesperia's relatedness to Greece, although not essentially different from those occurring in later poems—in 'Der Ister', 'Das Nächste Beste', or 'An die Madonna'— are nevertheless more satisfying. They work quite subtly, as true details and as apt, effective images.

Indications in 'Die Wanderung' are the cherry and peach trees, and the swallows.[59] Both trees originated in the east (the peach in Persia, the cherry in China) and spread westwards. Swallows spend the winter in Africa and migrate to western Europe for the summer. The thought of their route across the Mediterranean encourages the poet to make his visionary journey to Greece ('Die Wanderung', lines 25-28, ii,138-139). The stars, too, are an indication of coherence:

> auch unter den Sternen
> Gedenk' ich, o Ionia, dein!
>
> (ibid., lines 85-86)

Their course is similarly interpreted in 'Der Main' (line 37) and 'Deutscher Gesang' (lines 26-29).

The Swabian vineyards are a constant reminder of the classical world and of the earlier Asian sources from which the vine was brought. In the poem 'Stutgard' the Swabian hills, at the time of the vintage, move in an unequivocally Bacchic dance. The whole poem, celebrating the German landscape, is Greek in its inspiration and style.

Swabia is associated with Italy, the nearest to home of the antique lands, by its southern breezes: 'Ihr milden Lüfte! Boten Italiens! ' ('Rükkehr in die Heimath', line 1, ii,29), its many streams and by the Alps ('Die Wanderung', lines 1-8, ii,138). These are the kind of indications—the north-east wind in 'Andenken' is another—that occur to a poet who clearly sees his imagined world mapped out before his eyes.

In Hölderlin's mythology the Aegean island of Patmos is a place of Hesperian significance. To celebrate it fittingly, to make it the equal of the fabulous Ionian mainland that the poet-traveller has turned from, Hölderlin naturally adopts a Greek style, and offers many indications of Patmos's relatedness to Ancient Greece. As an Aegean island it can be named with Cyprus ('Patmos', line 58, ii,166) —'die quellenreiche' (πολυπῖδαξ), although its nature is quite different. 'Wohnen' (line 60) is a deliberate Graecism— ναίω —used by Hölderlin in 'Der Ister' (line 22). Sophocles uses the word of Salamis in the lines already quoted (p. 61). Similarly 'gast-freundlich' (line 61)—Greek: εὔξεινος . The lines:

> Und wenn vom Schiffbruch oder klagend
> Um die Heimath oder
> Den abgeschiedenen Freund
> Ihr nahet einer
> Der Fremden . . .

(lines 64-68)

hold many classical associations. The shipwrecked sailors Odysseus and Peleus (in a later version of 'Patmos' Peleus and the island that received him, Cos, are named)— the exile Philoctetes, Achilles mourning his friend Patroclus. Obviously John, too, is literally or metaphorically shipwrecked, exiled and bereaved, but as 'der gott-geliebte (διΐφίλος) Seher' (line 74) he shares the status of the Greek heroes who suffered similarly. He was the intimate of a god—a very Greek god, for all his Hesperian role: Christ is 'der Gewittertragende' (line 78)—one of Zeus's titles—and he has the physical beauty of a Greek god (lines 137-40).

John's Patmos is reminiscent of the island on which Philoctetes was marooned, Lemnos. This was a place and Philoctetes was a character of some importance to Hölderlin.[60] In certain details the Patmos that Hölderlin describes in his poem closely resembles the Lemnos of Sophocles's *Philoctetes*. The dry barrenness of Patmos, the dark cave, in which John lives, are details typical also of Lemnos (e.g. *Philoctetes* 1-2, 159-60, 1081 ff.) One detail is repeated several times in Sophocles's play: the echoing among the rocks of Philoctetes's cries of pain.

> Nur die geschwätzige Nymphe
> Echo, fernher schallend,
> Gibt ihm zurück sein bitter Gestöhn.

(lines 188-90)

and:

> Wie oft warf mir des Hermes Gebirg
> Wenn ich in Stürmen der Qual aufschrie,
> Den Widerhall meiner Stimme zurück.

(lines 1458-60)[61]

Typically, Hölderlin makes the echo more comforting to the sufferer:

> Sie hören ihn und liebend tönt
> Es wieder von den Klagen des Manns.

('Patmos', lines 72-73)

These associations are probably as deliberately intended as are the poem's Greek vocabulary and style. Hölderlin was anxious to associate both the heroes and the places of his Hesperia as closely as possible with the source and inspiration of classical Greece. Patmos had no significance for the Greeks; they left Hölderlin nothing to work from, not even a descriptive epithet. He turned instead to Lemnos, and thus associated his Hesperian hero John with the Greek Philoctetes. That is not to say that he *equates* John with Philoctetes—the associative range is much wider: Peleus, Odysseus, Achilles. He draws on the glamour that classical heroes and places have, and so raises Patmos, John, and Christ to equality and association with the Greeks.

In his Hesperia Hölderlin discovers associations with Greece: he deliberately relates his homeland to the antique past. Does the process work the other way? Does he deliberately infuse Hesperian elements into his vision of Greece? It has often been pointed out[62] how Swabian, under their exotic local colour, are the Greek landscapes of the novel *Hyperion*. The flat-topped, terraced hills have already been mentioned earlier in this chapter and they are Swabian, not Greek. There is one very striking passage, a description of Salamis, omitted from the final version of the novel:

Reifer grünt die verbrannte Wiese noch Einmal auf im kühlen Reegen des Spätjahrs, and die Zeitlosen blühen und schimmern im dunkeln Grase und auf den Stoppeläkern waiden die Schaafe und die Zugvögel versammeln sich lärmend in den abgeerndteten Zweigen und schiken zur Reise sich an. Lieblich mild sind izt die Spiele der Wolken . . .

(iii,256-57)

The third reaping (the emphatic 'Einmal' indicates that it is the third, the variants iii,389 say so specifically) and the autumn crocuses ('die Zeitlosen') are characteristically South German details. The whole landscape is too fertile and gentle to be Greek. But although this is certainly a vision of Greece into which German tones have been infused it is not significant in the way that the later Greek-inspired Hesperian landscapes are. At this early date (1796-97) it is partly ignorance that causes Hölderlin to imagine Greece thus; but partly also it is the passionate love of the landscape around him, in the light of his love for Susette Gontard, which makes that transference appropriate. In the MS, the *Homburger Quartheft*, the passage occurs in the company of poems to Diotima, together with 'An den Aether', 'Die Eichbäume', and 'Die Muße.'

In 'Brod und Wein' Hölderlin has this vision of Greece: 'Festlicher Saal! der Boden ist Meer! und Tische die Berge . . .' (line 57, ii,92). The landscape thus evoked is more Swabian than Greek: the hills of the Schwäbische Alb would make far better tables than the abrupt mountains of Greece. And it is more than likely that Hölderlin had the Swabian hills in mind, or even before his eyes; since the poem moves from a description of a town, as it might be Tübingen or Stuttgart, surrounded by its hills, to a vision of Greece, a vision in which real elements of the present, well-known landscape are still preserved.

Hölderlin remembered the image three years later when working over the finished version of 'Patmos': 'Von tausend Tischen duftend', he wrote then, 'Tischen' replacing 'Gipfeln' (line 30, ii,174). Certainly in 'Brod und Wein' and possibly even in 'Patmos' this is a 'Swabian' detail that has been intruded into a Greek landscape; but, probably, not consciously and not with any intention to bind the two spheres together. It indicates simply how naturally Hölderlin's visionary journeys happened. He looks from the familiar town below him south to the level Swabian hills, and the transition is made, from one ideal vision to another.

In the mature poetry I can find only one instance of the purposive introduction of Hesperian elements into the Greek world, and that is the legend, used in 'Die Wanderung', of a Germanic migration down the Danube to the Black Sea. Michel calls this 'eine wissenschaftliche Vermutung':[63] I should call it a useful poetic notion, a good and convincing one that serves Hölderlin's purpose as well as the course of the river in 'Am Quell der Donau'. It is another indication, like the flight of the swallows, of the truth of the One Idea, another binding component of the coherent world.

It will be seen that the process really only works one way. Greek elements are found in Hesperia, not Hesperian elements in Greece. This is reasonable, of course. Greece is the example in the past, finished and unalterable—but Swabia is the coming land, the land about which something has to be proved. If the renaissance in it is to be Greek-inspired, then, obviously, as many Greek elements as possible must be discovered there. The Hesperian sphere of Hölderlin's coherent world hardly resists the pull of the old Greek sphere. It is unequivocally orientated back to Greece, and were it not fixed in the present reality of Swabian places and landscapes it would not have an independent identity. Hölderlin was fully aware of this danger. What he attempted after the return from Bordeaux was the further definition of his own Hesperian sphere. This will be the subject of the chapter 'The Disintegrating World'.

CHAPTER 4

THE JOURNEY

Hölderlin was not a great traveller; chiefly, because his active life was so short and so full of material complications and misfortunes. Successful writers, like Goethe, could afford almost yearly trips, to refresh their minds, get inspiration, collect artistic or scientific material; but Hölderlin, after leaving Tübingen in September 1793, had neither the free time nor the money to travel for pleasure.

His years of education, unpleasant in most other respects, did allow him to do a little amateur travelling, at his mother's expense. His schooling was free, and he was not costing her much besides. She paid for two short journeys, one in 1788 to Speyer and one in 1791 to Switzerland, probably considering them a part of his education.

The first, for five days in early June, was primarily a practical trip to visit relatives. Hölderlin, then a slightly conceited young seminarist, made rather more of it in the long account he wrote for his mother (vi,32-39). His letter is a *Reisebeschreibung* in the manner of the times, when the most ordinary travellers visiting the most ordinary places, thought their impressions worth recording. So although his own journey was a slight and largely practical affair, Hölderlin will have had in mind the more interesting journeys of more famous men, and in his account he did his best to enhance the sights he saw and the feelings he had. The journey, the first outside his immediate homeland, gave him a chance to prove his sensibility. He was pleased and grateful whenever he responded warmly to a scene:

ich gieng gerührt nach Haus, and dankte Gott, daß ich empfinden konnte, wo tausende gleichgültig vorübereilen . . . (vi, 39)

The gift stood him in good stead on his second journey, to Switzerland during the Easter vacation of 1791, a journey stereotyped in all its details, a three-week pilgrimage, in the company of two suitable college friends, to the most accessible of Switzerland's holy places, a 'Geniereise' of sorts, like Goethe's in 1775.

This kind of journey, that his more successful contemporaries undertook frequently, for profit and amusement, throughout their lives, was impossible for Hölderlin as soon as he left Tübingen and had to find his own money and manage his own affairs.

A short, solitary walking-tour in the Rhöngebirge and Fulderland at Whitsuntide 1794, a week's walking in the Leipzig area, visiting Gustav Adolf's battlefields, in

March-April 1795, or short excursions in the immediate vicinity of wherever he happened to be living—around Frankfurt, for example, in 1797, when his brother visited him—this was all the travelling he did for his own pleasure, on his own initiative, after leaving the Tübinger Stift.

He went to Bad Dribourg, July-October 1796, with Susette Gontard and her children, but that was a duty, however pleasant, for which he was paid. Sinclair invited him to the Congress at Rastatt, in November 1798, to help him through his unhappiness in Homburg, and paid for the trip. And in the autumn of 1802 there was another therapeutic journey, again at Sinclair's invitation, this time to Regensburg. These journeys, especially to Westphalia and Regensburg, were important—they affected Hölderlin's poetry—[1] but they were not journeys he chose independently to make. Fortunate circumstances brought them about.

And that is typical of Hölderlin's life: he went wherever circumstances, fortunate or unfortunate, sent him, having neither the time nor the money to go anywhere else. Thus the journeys to Waltershausen, Frankfurt, Hauptwyl, and Bordeaux. He went wherever a job was offered him. He might have gone almost anywhere; at particularly unsettled times of his life, between jobs, there were offers or rumours of employment in many parts of Europe—in Switzerland (not Hauptwyl), Frankfurt (not the Gontards'), Heilbronn, Copenhagen, or Swedish Pomerania. To be the travelling-companion of a young gentleman was another possibility.[2]

He travelled to his place of employment, and when he had given up or been dismissed from the job he travelled home again. These journeys home, and visits to friends and relatives, were almost all the independent travelling he did in adult life. He covered much of Swabia: Nürtingen, where his mother lived, over the Alb to his sister's family in Blaubeuren, to relatives in Löchgau and Markgröningen, to friends in Stuttgart, Vaihingen, Kloster Murrhardt, and Leonberg. But in a sense even these were essential journeys; for maintaining contact, especially with his family, was essential to Hölderlin. And they were mostly short and over familiar ground.

Circumstances were against his becoming a great traveller, but if travelling had been his passion they would not have discouraged him. Without a job, and without much money he might have gone on the road as many of the Romantics did. Why did he never try to reach his ideal land? The Romantics set out enthusiastically for the south—their poetry needed the inspiration of the real journey. Even Goethe got as far as Sicily. But Hölderlin never made the least attempt to see Greece, nor even the surrogate Italy, although a journey no more strenuous than the one to Bordeaux would have got him on to classical ground. This shyness of seeing the ideal land was, of course, a characteristic of German Hellenists; French and English travellers and poets went there without qualms, but no important Germans followed until late in the nineteenth century. Winckelmann and Goethe both refused excellent offers to travel through Greece. It seems never to have occurred to Hölderlin that he might make the effort. Other Hellenists sometimes publicly wished that they might one day somehow be transported there, a curious hypocrisy that Hölderlin never indulged in. True, introducing *Hyperion* he declares:

Von früher Jugend an lebt' ich lieber, als sonstwo, auf den Küsten von Ionien und Attika und den schönen Inseln des Archipelagus, und es gehörte unter meine liebsten Träume, einmal wirklich dahin zu wandern, zum heiligen Grabe der jugendlichen Menschheit. (iii,235)

But this belongs firmly in the world of Hölderlin's poetry; in reality he never entertained the idea. Greece, all important in his poetry, never suggested itself as the possible goal of a real journey; and journeying itself, a main theme of the poetry, was not so attractive an activity in Hölderlin's life that he would whole-heartedly set about pursuing it. He wrote to Neuffer of his 'ewiges Sehnen von einer Stelle der Welt zur andern' (vi,124) and to his friend Hiller, who was thinking of emigrating, he wrote:

> Oft flammt der Wunsch, unendlich fortzuwandern,
> Unwiderstehlich herrlich in uns auf . . .
> ('An Hiller', lines 63-64, i, 174-75)

but in his day-to-day life it was not so much wanderlust as material necessity that kept him on the move. On the whole it may be said that he travelled when he had to. Often, in his letters, he complains: about the discomforts of travelling, and about having to travel at all. What he most wanted was peace and quiet, and enough money to live independently, for his poetry (vi,404). His art would have benefited, he claimed, had he been allowed to live peacefully and quietly with Susette Gontard (vi,370).

Hölderlin had the kind of genius that needs only a small amount of real experience to inspire it. Whatever happened to him affected him basically. Similarly in his reading: he read comparatively few books, but he knew them well and was profoundly influenced by them. And so it was with his travelling: he travelled comparatively little, and not often from choice, but the few journeys were of the greatest importance for his work, not so much in the memories and descriptions of places he saw (although these *are* important, especially in the later poems) as in the experience he gained of the basic human activity—travelling. And so, as an archetypal activity, travelling matters most in Hölderlin's work.

An activity cannot be considered archetypal if it is not an essential one. It is because most of Hölderlin's journeys were essential that they became basically important in his poetry.

Walking as a sport, especially Alpine walking, was already popular in the second half of the eighteenth century. Hölderlin's friend Ebel in his Swiss handbook[3] urged the tourists to travel on foot. This enthusiasm for walking is an indication that it was becoming more common for more people to travel on horseback, or by private or public coach. As today, when everybody can travel by bus or train, most by car and many by plane, the enthusiasm is an attempt to get back to travelling in the simplest manner. Walking from Land's End to John o'Groats, a wholly artificial activity, sport (first the journey *need* not be made, secondly it could be done by car) is an attempt to regain the lost experience of simple travelling, and today it is only through this artificiality that a faint sense of the archetypal activity can be had. The nostalgia was beginning to be felt in the eighteenth century.

Probably in this spirit, Hölderlin and his two companions walked a stretch of Switzerland in 1791, hiring a man to carry their things (vi,67). The journey was a pilgrimage and pilgrimages are done on foot. But after that time Hölderlin rarely walked unless he had to. His tours around Leipzig and in the Rhöngebirge were on foot, but otherwise, like most people, he travelled by coach whenever he could afford it.

However, he could not often afford it. His employers generally paid his travelling expenses, but only after his arrival. He rarely saved enough from his salary to travel by coach at his own expense. Frequently, then, Hölderlin was obliged to walk.

He was a good walker, by modern standards. He walked from Tübingen to Maulbronn (18 hours) to visit Louise Nast,[4] frequently between Stuttgart and Nürtingen (4 hours),[5] over the Alb to Blaubeuren, between Homburg and Frankfurt (3 hours). In Jena, when offered a job in Frankfurt, he talked of walking there via Nürtingen: 'Sehr beträchtlich wäre ja der Umweg nicht. Ich gienge des Tages 8 Stunden; menagirte mich . . .' (vi, 174). He proposed another visit home, from Homburg: 'Daß ich dann ein paar Meilen weiter zu wandern habe, thut nichts, besonders in den schönen Maitagen' (vi,294). Neither of these proposals came to anything, but the reasons were the weather, the unsafeness of the roads, or Hölderlin's unwillingness to come home, not the distance he would have had to cover. As he said, Nature had provided him 'mit ein paar rüstigen Beinen' (vi, 135). On his walking tour in the Leipzig area, 1795, he averaged twenty miles a day for seven days.[6] He walked most of the way to Hauptwyl and, probably, all the way to Bordeaux. Both these were winter journeys, the latter a serious and dangerous undertaking.

Bordeaux was the farthest Hölderlin went from home; his other posts were only two or three days' journey out of Swabia. He saw very few exotic places (probably only Bordeaux and the Atlantic and the wilder parts of France were truly foreign), and hardly made contact outside his own race (even in Bordeaux he lived among Germans).

It is remarkable, then, how 'abroad' he felt himself to be as soon as he had crossed the frontiers of Württemberg. Waltershausen and Jena, Frankfurt and Homburg were all emphatically abroad, and the people he lived among there were foreigners. In part this was a characteristic of the times when people travelled far less than they do now and when their loyalties were not to 'Germany' but to the region of Germany in which they were born; officially, anywhere outside Swabia was 'im Ausland' (vii,I,310). But the feeling was particularly strong in Hölderlin. It meant that his journeys, even when not often very enterprising nor to very distant places, were sufficient to affect him deeply. Going abroad—if only as far as Frankfurt—aroused in him an archetypal longing for home.

Hölderlin had a very strong sense of what and where home was, and so of what it meant to live away from home, abroad. Home was Nürtingen, the village where his mother lived, and the homeland—'das Vaterland'—was the wider area of Swabia where he had spent his childhood and where his relatives and many of his friends were still living (whilst he, perhaps less wisely, was attempting to make his own way abroad). Living abroad he compared the landscapes, the food and wines with those of home, made a point of looking out fellow-Swabians, searched for traces of emigrant relatives. He missed the country itself, the Neckar and the characteristically Swabian orchards and hills. But above all he missed his family, his half-brother Carl, his sister Heinrike and his mother.

The affection he had for his family, and especially for his mother, is well attested in the letters he wrote. The letters were his way of celebrating what he knew to be exceptionally strong emotional ties. The family was close-knit and held loyally together through considerable hardship. Hölderlin's visits to Nürtingen and Blaubeuren were for his own sake as much as for his family's.

It may be that this affection was excessive and, in the end, harmful, a symptom of his chronic inability to manage his own life. He was never quite independent of his mother and her household.[7] But excessive or not, it was this affection that gave the intensity to his thoughts of home. Swabia was the homeland because of the strong emotional ties that bound him to his family there.

Hölderlin must have realized his probable fate, one aspect of which was homelessness, quite early in life. He readily idealized other people's lives and compared his own unfavourably with them. He liked to think Neuffer and Rosine Stäudlin perfectly happy together (vi,124); in his sister's married life he saw the ideal (vi,94). The fact that Neuffer's fiancée soon died of consumption, and that after not many years' domestic happiness Heinrike's husband died of a heart attack could not affect Hölderlin's vision of the ideal. He needed opposites of himself, people to represent what he most admired and wanted. Almost always when congratulating his sister on her happiness he explicitly contrasted it with his own fate:

. . . ich ehre das, was Du bist und hast, um so eher, weil ich es entbehre. (vi, 315)

Und Du erlaubst mir, in Deiner glüklichen Haushaltung zu leben, als gehört' ich auch dazu.—Wenn und wo werd' ich denn Dich einmal zu mir zu Gaste bitten, Liebe? (vi,352)

This ideal life was being lived in the homeland Swabia. Living abroad, Hölderlin came to think of Swabia as a lost paradise to which he could never permanently return. Like John Clare, he made an Eden of his birthplace and the villages of his childhood.

He always maintained that true happiness could be found in quiet domesticity in a Swabian village, and was forever reassuring his mother that one day such a life would be his. In fact it was repeatedly offered him. A country parson could have lived in the way Hölderlin professed to find admirable, and both his mother and the Württemberg Consistorium were urging him to take on the parson's job. He would marry (his predecessor's daughter, they suggested [vi,234]) and live quietly ever after. For his poetry's sake he could not agree. His poetry was not of a kind to be pursued as a sideline to anything else; nor could the religion it professed possibly be squared with the dogma of orthodox Christianity. Hölderlin spent his life avoiding the fate that Thill before him, Neuffer, Magenau and even Renz, his contemporaries, and Mörike after him all accepted. (Others who resisted, like Waiblinger, came to unhappy ends. The best way to resist was to become famous, like Schelling and Hegel.) It was this fear of being pressed into the Church, among other things, that kept Hölderlin abroad (vii,2,579). To settle in Swabia, his homeland, he would have had to accept a country vicar's job. In this way the ideal homeland and the quiet life there he called ideal became unattainable. Being loyal to his poetry he had to live abroad. His home-sickness could never be cured.

This predicament—a practical one of adverse circumstances and conflicting loyalites—became, through an imaginative process that is typical of Hölderlin, a general, impersonal, mythical fate. And not merely in his poetry (that will be discussed later) but in the life he led. His journeys, his homelessness, his living away from the ideal homeland are the ingredients of a generally significant myth (his own life) in which he played the leading role. His life lent itself increasingly to the kind of mythical interpretation he was fond of. Thus he saw himself as the archetypal wanderer. When discussing his own predicament he discussed the archetypal one, and for this reason many of his complaints have a general tone and significance:

Glaube mir, wer ohne eignen Heerd, und häufig unter Fremden lebt, der weiß es erst zu schäzen, und vergißt es nicht, wenn ihn ein Freund oder Mutter oder Schwester im Hauße freundlich aufgenommen hat. (vi,276)

His sense of the mythical significance of his own life increased as the pattern of journeying, living abroad, and failure repeated itself. By 1801 his letters were more and more confidently asserting his role, almost celebrating his own downfall. They have a high, tragic tone:

Einige ruhige Tage, bei Euch, Ihr Theuersten! werden mir noch zum Seegen auf meine dritte Wanderschaft werden. (vi,406)

nimm zum Abschiede die stille, aber unaussprechliche Freude meines Herzens in Dein Herz . . . (vi,407)

The climax is the journey to Bordeaux:

Und nun leb wohl, mein Theuerer! bis auf weiteres. Ich bin jezt voll Abschieds. (vi, 427)

It is as though all merely circumstantial factors fall away, and his real journey becomes the clearest imaginable symbol of the tragic course of a man's life. It is obvious from the letters that he knew himself to what symbolic status he had been raised. He was acting the tragic role of his own mythology. That is why the journeys to and from Bordeaux are so disturbing. They are myths, and research into their real details, however interesting, cannot get at the truth of them. Clearly whatever did happen—his arrest in Strasbourg, the flooded roads, the snow and ice, the fear of robbery, and the dangers and suffering only hinted at—whatever happened in reality had, more importantly, symbolic significance, and was the kind of revelation or infliction that happens to the heroes of myths:

... da hab' ich auch ein Gebet gebetet, das bis jezt das beste war in meinem Leben und das ich nie vergessen werde.
Ich bin erhalten—danken Sie mit mir!
Ihr Lieben! ich grüßt' Euch wie ein Neugeborner, da ich aus den Lebensgefahren heraus war ...
Ich bin nun durch und durch gehärtet und geweiht ... (vi,430)

At this stage the simplest facts of his experience, simply expressed, are more than themselves, like the details of myths:

Wie wird mir der sichere erquikende Schlaf wohl thun! Ich wäre froh an sicherer Einfalt. (vi,430)

In the letter to Böhlendorff of 2 December 1802, Hölderlin resumed the stages of his journey home. Again, beyond the personal, is the mythical. The language is clear and simple, but the sense is baffling; the details are particular to his journey— his probable route can be deduced—and yet general, symbolic, and hard to interpret:

die traurige einsame Erde ... das gewaltige Element, das Feuer des Himmels ... das wilde kriegerische ... das rein männliche ... das Athletische der südlichen Menschen ... (vi,432)

Particular observations are at the source of these generalities, but the particular has been obscured and the general, in its simple expression, is hardly explicable. The account is irreducible, as myths are. It is clear that Hölderlin knew the mythical implications of his experience:

und wie man Helden nachspricht, kann ich wohl sagen, daß mich Apollo geschlagen. (vi,432)

In an earlier letter to Böhlendorff he compared his own likely fate to that of Tantalus (vi,427). At this late stage of his life he was living in a way that merited such comparisons. For his experience only the myths were adequate expression.

He was the equal of Tantalus, or of Marsyas whom Apollo flayed alive, and could draw on their myths to illustrate the myth he was living out himself; Phaeton, Icarus and Oedipus were other kindred figures. His journey home from Bordeaux, ending in madness, was the myth's last act.

This living out a mythical role may be the peculiar privilege of the mad and those going mad. John Clare's experience was similar on his 'journey out of Essex'. He escaped from the lunatic asylum at Epping and walked home to his Northampton-shire village, confident of finding the woman he loved there, who had died years before. Like Hölderlin's it was a mythical journey, in that its real details were enhanced symbolically within a scheme, of general significance, peculiar to the traveller's mind. Clare thought he was going home to Eden, where Mary lived.

Certainly it was in the months before the onset of madness that Hölderlin saw and lived his life in the clearest mythical terms. But long before then the inclination to generalize from private experience, which is essential in the making of myths, was Hölderlin's characteristic.

His poetry derived largely from his own experience; he knew this and thought it right:

jedes Gedicht . . . [muß] aus poetischem Leben und Wirklichkeit, aus des Dichters eigener Welt und Seele hervorgegangen seyn . . . weil sonst überall die rechte Wahrheit fehlt, und überhaupt nichts verstanden und belebt werden kan . . . ('Grund zum Empedokles', iv,150)

It is not always obvious in the poetry, because the private experience is rarely directly expressed, rarely in its particular details:

Die Empfindung drükt sich nicht mehr unmittelbar aus, es ist nicht mehr der Dichter und seine eigene Erfahrung, was erscheint . . . (ibid.)

In the creative process private experience is removed into an objective equivalent of it: 'das eigene Gemüth und die eigene Erfahrung in einen fremden analogischen Stoff übertragen' (ibid.). But private experience is the original source, even of the most universal themes. The years of preoccupation with *Empedokles* will have had Hölderlin's own thoughts of suicide as their beginning. The long struggle to bring Greece and Germany together was first a personal predicament, a private intellectual quandary, a division of Hölderlin's own loyalties. His love for Susette Gontard—'die Athenerin'—clarified his vision of the Greek ideal. But these general themes have been far removed from and expanded beyond the private interests out of which they originated. Personal experience had to be translated, which Hölderlin was always very ready to do.

In certain aspects of his life, however, less translation was necessary. His own predicament already obviously had the general import that he demanded for his poetry.

He knew the mythical sense of his own journeying, his homelessness, his living abroad. In this aspect his life lent itself to the making of myths, which was a function of his poetry. He worked the material of his own life, at first deliberately, generalizing and idealizing as his poetic doctrine demanded, but later almost involuntarily, as the particular facts of his life and their mythical counterparts merged.

It is because this apprehension of the mythical and this inclination to mythicize were in him already that his own comparatively small experience of travelling sufficed.

For certain themes, then, the material was there in personal experience and needed very little interpreting or translating. For this reason what he wrote in the poems reminds again and again of what he wrote in the letters. This could be expected in a forthrightly lyrical poet chiefly concerned with private and particular truths, but it is more interesting in the case of Hölderlin, whose concerns were general. From his own experience he could write about homelessness:

> Ein heimathloser Sänger; denn wandern muß
> Von Fremden er zu Fremden, und die
> Erde, die freie, sie muß ja leider!
>
> Statt Vaterlands ihm dienen . . .
> ('Der Main', lines 26-29, i,304)

And the peculiar dangers of permanent homelessness, the risk of dissolution:

> Und daß mir auch zu retten mein sterblich Herz,
> Wie andern eine bleibende Stätte sei,
> Und heimathlos die Seele mir nicht
> Uber das Leben hinweg sich sehne . . .
> ('Mein Eigentum', lines 37-40, i,307)

By contrast, out of his own longing, he could celebrate the homeland, in his day-to-day life an area of such primal significance that it could go unenhanced into the poetry:

> . . . der Heimath
>
> Verehrte sichre Grenzen, der Mutter Haus
> Und liebender Geschwister Umarmungen . . .
> ('Die Heimath', lines 12-14, ii,19)

And he could celebrate the kind of domestic happiness he ascribed to his sister, and that was offered him with the country parson's job:

> Beglükt, wer, ruhig liebend ein frommes Weib,
> Am eignen Heerd in rühmlicher Heimath lebt . . .
> ('Mein Eigentum', lines 21-22, i,306)

Several poems have the homecoming as their theme. 'Heimkunft', specifically addressed 'An die Verwandten', celebrates a particular return, from Hauptwyl in April 1801. The poem could not be more directly related to Hölderlin's life, but of all the poems treating the theme of homecoming it is the one whose import is most general, in which the largest, most coherent myth is given form. The Alps, Lake Constance, Lindau, and Swabia are places of Hölderlin's coherently imagined poetic world, and his journey home is the archetypal journey, an episode in his poet-hero's myth. At that stage of his life there was probably little difference between what Hölderlin actually thought and felt, how he really lived, and the myth that the resultant poems gave form to.

The homelessness and wandering abroad might have been exchanged at any time, so Hölderlin's mother argued, for the quiet domesticity of a country living. Hölderlin steadfastly refused the alternative, and it is unlikely that he was ever seriously tempted to accept. He can hardly be said to have chosen the life he led (he could not choose not to be a poet, and the consequences were, precisely, the homeless, wandering existence abroad) but in that he saw its unalterability and made no unwise attempts to escape it, he at least chose to accept an unavoidable fate. By doing so he gave some sense to his life abroad: it was a necessary time of trial for the sake of his art.

Clearly, he always wanted to come home and be back with his family and friends in familiar country. The letters are proof of his frequent homesickness. And he always *intended* to come home—'Ich werd' auch wol nicht ewig ausbleiben' (vi, 161)—just as soon as circumstances would allow it. But in the meantime there were a few years abroad to be got through. Before returning home he had to prove himself abroad.

It is significant how often during his longest period away from home (December 1795-April 1800) his promises and plans to visit his family came to nothing. There were practical objections to the journey: the roads were unsafe because of the war, the weather was bad for travelling, he had very little money, his job kept him fully occupied. He was furthermore in love with Susette Gontard. All these considerations might have been settled, however, but not the overriding one, which was his sense of duty, his responsibility to his art. Especially in Homburg he was holding out as long as he could for his art's sake: working on *Empedokles* and the aesthetic essays, trying to publish a journal. All this in difficult circumstances, working against time as his money, his means of independence, dwindled. From Homburg he wrote home, hearing that Elise Lebret had married:

So wie ich jezt mich und unsere Zeit kenne, halte ich es für Nothwendigkeit, auf solches Glük, wer weiß, wie lange Verzicht zu thun . . . (vi, 362)

The years in Jena were his 'Wanderschaft' (vi,145), the time abroad obligatory for all apprentice craftsmen, which he refused to cut short by accepting a pastor's job at home. He looked forward to the time in Hauptwyl as his 'dritte Wanderschaft' (vi,406). Leaving for Bordeaux he wrote: 'Aber ich fühl' es, mir ists besser, draußen zu seyn . . .' (vi,424).

Inevitably, since Hölderlin gave this moral sense to his enforced living abroad, the untimely homecomings counted as so many defeats. He only came home when for one reason or another he could no longer manage to live abroad. The home-comings, from Jena, Homburg, Hauptwyl, and Bordeaux were all admissions of failure; and after the initial pleasure of reunion with his family he was soon ill at ease among them and discontented with himself. He felt he should not be there, without a job, without money, an embarrassment to his mother, not having proved himself. Not enough had been gone through or achieved. His vocation could only be followed abroad. Before long he was planning to leave home again.

This theme—the necessary period of trial and journeying abroad—a theme of his own life, appears, enlarged beyond the personal, in his poetry:

> nemlich zu Hauß ist der Geist
> Nicht im Anfang, nicht an der Quell. Ihn zehret die Heimath
> Kolonie liebt, und tapfer Vergessen der Geist.
> ('Brod und Wein', variants, ii,608)

Like the other main themes it derived from his private experience:

> Verbotene Frucht, wie der Lorbeer, aber ist
> Am meisten das Vaterland. Die aber kost'
> Ein jeder zulezt . . .
> ('Einst hab ich die Muse gefragt . . .' lines 6-8, ii,220)[8]

As he knew for his own easy conscience the journey abroad had to be undertaken first, and only after that could the homeland be settled in:

> dann
> Giebt der Geläuterte dir sich lieber.
> ('Rükkehr in die Heimath', lines 19-20, ii,29)

The theme of journeying and return, widened beyond personal experience, is integrated into the main preoccupation of the poetry, which is to relate Greece and Germany and bring about the ideal Hesperia. The interim age, before this is achieved (that is before there is a homeland to return to and settle in), is character-ized by wanderings in darkness and through wildernesses. The paths are obscured and untrustworthy:

> und gehalten nicht mehr
> Von Menschen, schattenlos, die Pfade zweifeln . . .
> ('Patmos', lines 62-63, ii,180)[9]

Travellers of all kinds are the typical figures of this age of night. Christ's apostles suffer the typical fate, dispersal over the earth:

> Doch furchtbar ist, wie da und dort
> Unendlich hin zerstreut das Lebende Gott.
> Denn schon das Angesicht
> Der theuern Freunde zu lassen
> Und fernhin über die Berge zu gehn
> Allein . . .
>
> ('Patmos', lines 121-126, ɪɪ,168-169)

They initiate the age, and their wanderings prefigure all the journeys and homelessness to come. Crusaders and pilgrims engage in similar journeys, as the times demand.[10] The Christian era, not one of fulfilment but one of chaos and, at best, expectancy, allows no other life. Its heroes are the explorers and sea-voyagers.

One figure epitomizes the age: 'der Wanderer'. He occurs repeatedly in Hölderlin's poems, in most of the landscapes, on most of the paths, crossing mountain cols, turning into villages at night (where he enjoys, at most, a reflection of other people's contentment), and finally coming home, after years away, to find himself a stranger there.[11] He is not a man out walking for pleasure—not an amateur of travel—nor, in the mature poetry at least, has he much in common with the typical Romantic hero of the open road: he is a man engaged on an unavoidable journey, more often than not a homeless man. As such he is a sign of the times, a reminder that journeying is what the times demand. (He occurs also in the Greek landscapes of 'Der Archipelagus' (line 148), but this is an oversight or unseriousness on Hölderlin's part. 'Der Wanderer' is a Hesperian figure, out of place in Greece. The Greeks, in their ideal age, had none of his unsettledness.)

In poems directly celebrating his own journeys, Hölderlin is himself 'der Wanderer', in 'Heidelberg' for example ('Ein vertriebener Wandrer/Der vor Menschen und Büchern floh . . .') or in 'Heimkunft'.[12] His own fate was the typically Hesperian one.

All this has to be. The times between the Greek and the new Hesperian age are unavoidably so and have to be endured: Hölderlin was similarly helpless to do more than suffer the adverse circumstances of his own life. But the chaos is interpreted for the best: in the overall scheme it is purposeful, it prepares the harmony and community of the ideal age to follow. Similarly, for his poetry's sake Hölderlin accepted the homelessness and suffering, interpreted it as positively as he could, and always trusted there would be an end to it. He did not believe that either the personal suffering or the political chaos could be futile. His poetry constantly announces the end of journeying, and the establishment of community and order in an ideal Graeco-Germanic time:

> Seines jedem und ein Ende der Wanderschaft
> Einen Orden oder
> Feierlichkeit geben oder Geseze
> Die Geister des Gemeingeists
> Die Geister Jesu
> Christi
>
> (Fragment 62, ii,334)

He never understated the difficulties of the interim age—to get through it is like crossing a high and dangerous mountain pass, and inevitably some travellers lose their lives en route[13] —but he kept his belief in the better future.

The journeying, then, is both unavoidable and, with faith, worthwhile and purposeful.

In early poems, it is true, the journey is inspired by not much more than a romantic wanderlust:

> Wohl manches Land der lebenden Erde möcht'
> Ich sehn, und öfters über die Berg' enteilt
> Das Herz mir, and die Wünsche wandern
> Über das Meer . . .
>
> ('Der Main', lines 1-4, i,303)

The hero of 'Der Wanderer' leaves home after reading the accounts of the great voyages in the South Seas. Sometimes it is the sight of ships on the river, or the sound of streams that wakens the desire to travel.[14]

But even this wanderlust is an existential necessity, and the journey, however gratuitous its goal, cannot be avoided. It is still a period of restlessness that must be gone through before a quiet life in the homeland can be had.[15] And it may be said that the private restlessness of every traveller derives from the general restlessness of the times.[16]

In later poems Hölderlin attempts to direct the wanderlust and to ensure that the journey is purposeful. His journeys are to Greece and their purpose is to bring about the ideal time and homeland Germania. The journey has a definite goal, and must not be escapist, nostalgic, or gratuitous. It is undertaken only on terms of strict loyalty to the present. This discipline is necessary, for 'immer/Ins Ungebundene gehet eine Sehnsucht' ('Mnemosyne', lines 12-13, ii,197). Hölderlin's singleness of purpose is ceaselessly threatened.

The streams that often initiate the journey are a particularly suggestive image. By streams, small tributaries of the Neckar, the imagination is led naturally to the river, along its whole course, to its confluence with the Rhine, and so into the infinite distance:

> Der Berge Quellen eilten hinab zu dir,
> Mit ihnen auch mein Herz und du nahmst uns mit,
> Zum stillerhabnen Rhein, zu seinen
> Städten hinunter und lustgen Inseln.
>
> Noch dünkt die Welt mir schön, und das Aug entflieht
> Verlangend nach den Reizen der Erde mir . . .
>
> ('Der Nekar', lines 9-14, ii,17)

The streams, easily and frequently come upon in familiar surroundings, thus have the power to dispatch the imagination into the distance, in themselves they point infinitely far. They are reminders, in the homeland, of abroad, 'die sehnsüchtigen

Bäche der Heimath' ('Patmos', lines 23-24, ii,165), always restless. They suggest pure travelling, endless, directionless journeys.

In this respect their sense, as Hölderlin implies it, is ambivalent. They initiate the journey—the sound of them so disturbs the poet that he leaves his homeland—but give no direction. The journey, unless it can be controlled, becomes aimless wandering and ends in dissolution. The streams, subversive elements at home, suggest the boundlessness, the aimlessness, and the dissolution of abroad. Their only course is into self-annihilation in the sea. They are a temptation to unrestraint:

> Um unsre Weisheit unbekümmert
> Rauschen die Ströme doch auch, und dennoch,
>
> Wer liebt sie nicht? und immer bewegen sie
> Das Herz mir, hör' ich ferne die Schwindenden,
> Die Ahnungsvollen meine Bahn nicht,
> Aber gewisser ins Meer hin eilen.
>
> ('Stimme des Volks', lines 3-8, ii,51)

They typify 'das wunderbare Sehnen dem Abgrund zu' (ibid., line 17) and the danger is always that the traveller will abandon his own direction for theirs. The temptation is acknowledged: 'das Ungebundene reizet' (line 18).

Thus, initiating the journey, they indicate its dangers too: that the inevitably ensuing homelessness, which should be temporary, only for the time of the journey, will become a chronic, inescapable condition. This happened to Hölderlin himself. He always knew the danger—of having no home or centre, being engaged for ever in increasingly aimless journeying—and he struggled hard to escape it. But what he hoped was a limited period of trial consumed his whole life. He never got out of the chaos.

In Hölderlin's poetry the temptation to unrestraint that the streams suggest is always resisted, although sometimes not easily, and the journeys undertaken have direction and purpose.

The purposeful journey to Greece

There are no poetic journeys to Greece in Hölderlin's work until 'Der Main' (July 1799) and 'Der Nekar' (May-June 1800). 'Griechenland' and, to a lesser extent, 'An den Genius Griechenlands', list the memorable sites of Greece, and 'Der Gott der Jugend' has two classical settings, by the Anio and by the Cephissus, but these places are simply put into the poems: the poems are not journeys to them.

The journeys of 'Der Main' and 'Der Nekar' are, untypically for Hölderlin, almost gratuitous ones, excursions to exotic places, inspired, as has already been said, by nothing much more than a desire to travel. The Greece that the poet travels to is the beautiful, exotic land of his novel *Hyperion*. There is more detail, more local colour, than in any other poem, and all the details are of the *Hyperion* kind, remembered from reading Choiseul and Chandler.[17] The places too—Sunium, Smyrna, etc.—are picked out rather at random, probably because Hölderlin was fond of them after writing his novel: the vision of Asia in 'Patmos' shows how deliberately and carefully places and descriptive details *can* be used.

The longing for Greece in 'Der Main' and 'Der Nekar' is comparable to Goethe's longing for Italy; the two poems share the mood of 'Kennst du das Land . . .? ' It is a longing to be at the scene, as it still exists, of the great happenings of an ideal age, to visit a land that is still supremely beautiful. Merely, in fact, to visit Greece, as Byron and others did, but as the German Hellenists were unwilling to do. Had Hölderlin gone himself he might have seen all the sights his poems celebrate. A feasible journey, then, not back in time but to contemporary Turkish-occupied Greece,'zum heiligen Grabe der jugendlichen Menschheit' (iii, 235).

In 'Der Nekar' the journey is almost entirely gratuitous; less so in 'Der Main' where the river's east-west course is interpreted.

The journey is both a device and an image. As a device it shapes the poem, rather crudely in these first attempts, but subtly later. Its structural purpose is either to introduce the argument, or to be the form of the argument throughout. But simultaneously it is the expression, an image, of the poem's main concern. For the purposeful journey is a way of communication, of synthesizing things far apart, which is Hölderlin's intention with Greece and Germany. The journey binds together the places of his world.

'Patmos' shows how the journey can best be used.

'Patmos'
The purely nostalgic longing for Greece, for the ideal it represented and for the physical beauty of the land, remained with Hölderlin to the end of his creative life. In poems as late as 'Thränen' and 'Der Einzige' he confesses the longing quite simply:

> Ihr lieben Inseln, Augen der Wunderwelt!
> Ihr nemlich geht nun einzig allein mich an,
> Ihr Ufer . . .
>
> ('Thränen', lines 5-7, ii,58)

and is at a loss to explain it:

> Was ist es, das
> An die alten seeligen Küsten
> Mich fesselt, daß ich mehr noch
> Sie liebe, als mein Vaterland?
>
> ('Der Einzige', lines 1-4, ii,153)

In 'Der Rhein', primarily concerned with the cultural predicament of modern Europe, the temptation to escape to Greece twice breaks through:[18]

> denn noch kaum
> War mir im warmen Schatten
> Sich manches beredend, die Seele
> Italia zu geschweift
> Und fernhin an die Küsten Moreas.   (lines 11-15, ii,142)

('Jetzt aber . . .' (line 16) brings him abruptly back to the present.) And the first instinct of the river itself is eastwards to Greece (lines 36-37).

In all the poems where the journey does take place (e.g. in 'Die Wanderung', lines 64-78) Hölderlin's pleasure in describing the beauties of Greece is obvious. His imagination is as passionate as in *Hyperion* or 'Der Main' and 'Der Nekar'; only the vision is more controlled.

He disciplines himself, and gives a purpose to his enthusiasm, only allowing himself the visionary journey on certain strict conditions.

The times, Hölderlin decides, make the journey necessary. Separateness and disunity are characteristics of the interim age. The journey—to the ideal age of the past—is, then, an act of communication and the contact will help in dealing with the present. So the journey is justified in 'Patmos', the poem beginning with statements and images of the modern predicament: God hard to apprehend, although near, and humanity disintegrated. This is the modern condition and to better it the journey is undertaken, not only in 'Patmos' but in most of the great hymns. The Greeks had the unity that the modern world lacks.

The journey is not an escapist or nostalgic flight; Hölderlin always affirms his intention to return:

> treuesten Sinns
> Hinüberzugehn und wiederzukehren.
> ('Patmos', lines 14-15, ii,165)[19]

Fidelity to the present is a means of countering the temptation of dissolution; a definite goal and a strict purpose help avoid the way 'ins Ungebundene'.

Each journey to Greece should be of positive value to Hesperia. This is clearest in 'Die Wanderung' where the Charites of Greece are invited back to the western homeland Swabia. In 'Germanien' the longing for Greece, only just resisted, brings about the eagle's flight and the annunciation of Germany's new role. In 'Brod und Wein' and, to a lesser extent, 'Der Archipelagus' it is through the journey to Greece that the Hesperian problems are examined. Similarly in 'Am Quell der Donau'.

So the journey can be justified. Moreover, certain conditions in his homeland encourage the poet in his longing to go:

> Es dämmerten
> Im Zweilicht, da ich gieng
> Der schattige Wald
> Und die sehnsüchtigen Bäche
> Der Heimath . . .   ('Patmos', lines 20-24)

The conditions that justify the journey impinge on the landscape: the spiritual darkness and the restlessness of the age are expressed in woods and streams. Similarly, in 'Germanien' the streams and the heavy sky are expressions of the longing and oppression that characterize the times. In 'Patmos' as in 'Brod und Wein' the journey begun in darkness ends in Greek daylight.

These details—the twilight or total darkness, the streams, the oppressive sky—are at once images of a spiritual state, and, within the structure of the poem, a means of transition to the journey itself.

But how shall the journey be done? How shall communication be established when isolation is the characteristic of the times? The eagles and the Alpine dwellers are encouraging examples. Eagles communicate between God and men. The men in the Alps span the abysses and cross over. Communication is possible despite the difficulties and the danger. Encouraged, he wishes the requisite conditions for the journey:

> So gieb unschuldig Wasser,
> O Fittige gieb uns . . .
>
> ('Patmos', lines 13-14)

By air and water, pure elements, he makes his journey: first in a visionary flight, like the eagles', then by sea from the coast to the islands. In other poems similar means of communication are found. In 'Am Quell der Donau' the river itself offers a feasible means. In 'Die Wanderung', too; alternatively, the way of the swallows:

> Denn sagen hört' ich
> Noch heut in den Lüften:
> Frei sei'n, wie Schwalben, die Dichter.
>
> (lines 26-28, ii,138-39)

It is sufficient, for the imagination, to picture the swallows' migratory route, or the course of the Danube, or, in 'Andenken', the way of the wind blowing from the north-east towards Bordeaux, and in the poem the visionary journey can be made. Such means of communication, indications of an over-all unity, are typical of Hölderlin's coherently imagined mytho-poetic world.

The journey is begun in the Pindaric (or biblical) manner that Hölderlin favoured:[20]

> da entführte
> . . . ein Genius mich
> Vom eigenen Hauß'.
>
> ('Patmos', lines 16-20)

He has his vision of Asia Minor, at once the most beautiful, intense and the most controlled in all his poetry. Coming from an age of darkness he is blinded by it, and even this blindness is an indication of the purposefulness of his journey. He has not come merely to be delighted by Asia Minor (the area of Greece he loved best); but soon turns his back on it and faces west, already looking home. He has come to Greece on behalf of Hesperia, and is not distracted from his purpose by the supreme beauty of the Ionian coast. He turns from an entirely Greek landscape, all colour and light, to the dark cave on Patmos, an island with only Christian associations, to something more like the darkness of home.

The journey continues by sea. It was the sea that made the Greek unity possible. The sailor is the great communicator, going freely from island to island, the separate peaks of time.

Fidelity to the present, abruptly and even crudely affirmed in other poems, is guaranteed in 'Patmos' by the course of the journey itself. The journey is at once the structuring of the poem and an image of the poem's argument. The main concern of 'Patmos' is Christ. Christ is the god of the interim age: turning to him (turning from Asia Minor to the island Patmos) affirms Hölderlin's loyalty to the present, in that the attempt to understand Christ is an attempt to make sense of the whole modern predicament. The journey, over the first one and a half triads, leads into the poem's main concern, and thereafter the places themselves are forgotten; just as in 'Der Rhein' the river, having been used to initiate the argument, is forgotten.

The promise 'wiederzukehren' has been kept—the journey ends at a place of Hesperian importance. It is not necessary, as it is in 'Die Wanderung', to bring the poet home to Swabia. His fidelity is obvious in the direction the argument takes. Similarly in 'Brod und Wein' the poet's concern is so obviously the present that it need not be explicitly stated that he resisted the temptation of Greece. In 'Die Wanderung' the temptation seems so strong that he must emphatically reaffirm his loyalty to Swabia: 'Doch nicht zu bleiben gedenk ich' (line 91), and in 'Germanien' he dare not even make the journey, but has the eagle come to him, so doubtful is he of his ability to return. 'Germanien', in its first strophes, swings to and fro between past and present, between the ideal Greece and the real problems of Germany. Protestations of loyalty to the present counter the temptation of the past.

There is not this uncertainty in 'Patmos'. The journey is the perfect expression of Hölderlin's greater confidence: his loyalty is obvious in the course his journey takes.

CHAPTER 5

HÖLDERLIN'S POETIC-DESCRIPTIVE ART

Even in his letters Hölderlin rarely described the places he lived in or visited when travelling. There is one exception—the account of the journey to Speyer that he wrote for his mother. He had promised her a long description, and, for once, he kept his word. It was a considerable effort—'Sie müssen eben vorlieb nehmen mit dem Gesudel, ich schriebs oft halb im Schlaf, eh ich zu Bette gieng'—that he would gladly have been spared: 'Wenn ich nur auch mündlich erzählen könte' (vi,32). He wrote very briefly and, if often seems, impatiently of wherever he happened to be.

This paucity of description is remarkable in one so concerned to maintain contact with his family and friends. His letters will scarcely have helped them imagine his situation in places they had never seen. The letters to his mother least of all. Only occasionally, writing to his sister, he gives helpful details. In two letters from Homburg, for example, he describes the furnishing of his rooms, and the view from the house (vi, 352 and vi,316). (In general, the letters to his sister differ from those to his mother and half-brother in their greater simplicity, directness, and detail.)

But quite often journeys and new places are not described at all:

Über meine Reise von Stutg. bis Nürnberg kann ich euch nichts sagen. Ich schloß meist die Augen . . . (vi,100)

The journey to Rastatt is not described, nor is Dankenfeld, the von Kalbs' residence, nor Frankfurt, nor the city and port of Bordeaux. Hölderlin made his biographers' task all the more difficult by saying so little about the real circumstances he lived in.

Occasionally, feeling that *something* ought to be said, he offers brief, general, and obvious comments: 'Die Gegend von Jena ist treflich . . .', 'Gotha ist ein hübscher Ort . . .', 'Erfurt ist enorm groß . . .' (vi,142). And sometimes, knowing his description to be inadequate, he promises a fuller one at another time: 'Die Gärten von Luisium u. Wörrliz . . . beschreib' ich Dir ein andermal . . .' (vi,167). But he fails to keep his promise. He promised Carl a description of his walking tour in the Rhöngebirge, but never wrote it.[1] When Carl visited him in Frankfurt Hölderlin was pleased to be excused much of the necessary account: 'Über die Mainzer Gegend soll Dir Karl selbst etwas sagen' (vi,239).

And of the few longer descriptions that his letters contain most tend to be
sketchy and uninteresting. Or is it simply the things he chooses to describe? A
graveyard and school-house in Dessau, the orphanage in Halle (vi,167). Beck notes
how slight an impression Nürnberg apparently made on him (vi,654).

Clearly, Hölderlin disliked describing and felt he had no talent for it. He makes
general, unexceptionable remarks because he will not trust himself to be more
particular or original. He warned against setting too much store by his
observations: '. . . will ich . . . gerne gestehen, daß mein Urtheil nur flüchtig und
äußerst unzuverlässig ist' (vi,142). Writing to Neuffer he excused himself from an
account of his Leipzig journey:

Ich kan Dich nicht mit Reisebeobachtungen plagen, ich mochte das Wesen nie
recht leiden, wahrscheinlich, weil ich keine Gaabe dazu habe . . . (vi, 168)

If full topographical descriptions are rare in the letters they are almost entirely
absent from the poetry. This should not be surprising since Hölderlin accepted the
view of poetry advanced by Lessing in *Laokoon*. Description was for the visual
arts: a painter could communicate the coexistent details of a landscape, group, or
setting far better than a poet. The poet's strength lay in the relating of the
consecutive details of an action. Moreover, even when, in the early poetry,
attempting to communicate a scene that an artist might have painted—a ruined
castle, Swiss mountains, a wide view—Hölderlin always obeyed his instinct to
idealize and interpret—his poem never simply described. There are almost no
factual descriptions in his poems; he was opposed to that kind of writing.[2] But the
absence of descriptive passages from his letters, where, as many writers do—Flaubert,
for example—he might have relaxed the principles that governed his art, suggests
that in prose or poetry factual description was something he was incapable of.

And this is interesting in a writer to whom so many places, near and exotic alike,
were so attractive and important; who travelled and was an avid reader of other
travellers' accounts, and who had a vision of his homeland and of Greece that he
must communicate. How then is the vision communicated, if not through factual
description? That is the question to be considered in this chapter.

All Hölderlin's knowledge of the topography and physical appearance of Greece
was got from reading. First the classics: the historians, geographers, and travellers—
Herodotus, Strabo, and Pausanias—whom Hölderlin probably knew well, at least
from the references and quotations in contemporary books on classical subjects,
in the *Laokoon, Geschichte der Kunst des Alterthums*, and the *Voyage du jeune
Anacharsis en Grèce*, and, of course, in Chandler and Choiseul who both refer
constantly to Strabo and Pausanias; and the poets, whom he certainly knew well,
who characterize places briefly with an epithet or typical detail, or celebrate them
at greater length in lyrical passages. Works that particularly served Hölderlin were
the *Bacchae* (Cithaeron and Asia Minor), *Phaedrus* (the setting by the Ilissus), *Ajax*
and *Philoctetes* (Salamis and Lemnos), and he took many details from other works

by Sophocles (details of Colonus, for example), and from Pindar, and, most notably, from Homer. When he named and celebrated places in his poems he almost always had traditional details in mind.

Hölderlin's second source of information on Greece was the travel literature of his own time, above all the works of Chandler and Choiseul, where the classical world is described in the greatest detail with the aid of maps, diagrams, and engravings.

He saw Greece through these two quite different perspectives and evolved his own vision out of them, one closer to the poets' than to the travellers', but quite his own, and of his own age, nostalgic (*sentimentalisch*) and hopeful in a modern way.

Since his sources, at least in the earlier writings, are well known (Beißner gives many parallels in the Stuttgart edition of *Hyperion*) it is possible to see Hölderlin at work transmuting chosen material for his own poetic ends. Obviously, when he draws on classical poets—borrowing an epithet, accepting a characterizing detail—no such transmutation is necessary, for their vision was as ideal as his. But when he makes use of Chandler and Choiseul much revision is necessary before their prose material—their factual accounts—suits his novel or poem.

Chandler's account of his travels in Asia Minor and Greece[3] is soberly and objectively written. His was a scientific expedition, financed by the Society of Dilettanti, and he had his instructions to carry out. His observations are as exact as he can make them (an architect and a painter were with him to substantiate his measurements and descriptions); his prose is clear. He rarely allows himself to be enthusiastic: he carefully notes the ingredients of a curious or beautiful scene—identifying the exotic trees and flowers, for example—and does not intrude his own sentiments. His writing is not tendentious: he makes very little pathos out of the modern Greeks' predicament. The German edition, that Hölderlin probably used, is a faithful translation, with maps and plans.

Choiseul[4] is less objective, more enthusiastic and more tendentious. He is always pleased to indicate how low the Greeks have sunk. His translator, Reichard, deliberately exaggerates this pathos and even falsifies the original whenever an opportunity of maligning the modern Greeks presents itself (cf. especially his perverse translation of Choiseul's account of the Siege of Coron—fully examined by Beißner in G StA, iii). Hölderlin almost certainly read Reichard's translation, a shoddily produced and incomplete version of the sumptuous French edition.

In fact, though, Choiseul's sentiments, even when exaggerated by Reichard, were very much Hölderlin's own at the time of writing *Hyperion* and the poems 'Der Main' and 'Der Nekar'. He accepted the tendentiousness of Choiseul's account and where tendentiousness was lacking, in Chandler's account, he readily supplied it himself. Chandler's descriptions are lucid and neutral; he gives Hölderlin objective facts, which Hölderlin then transforms. This process can be studied by comparing descriptive passages in *Hyperion* with their probable sources in Chandler's travel books. The point is not to prove that Hölderlin re-wrote poetically whole paragraphs of Chandler's prose (he certainly did not), but to attempt to show what the poet's vision owes to the traveller's careful observations, and so to discover differences between prose and poetic description.

I have chosen two passages from *Hyperion* whose details clearly derive from Chandler. The first describes Hyperion's wanderings through Greece with his mentor Adamas:[5]

an den Athos hinauf und von da hinüberschifften in den Hellespont und dann hinab an die Ufer von Rhodus und die Bergschlünde von Tänarum, durch die stillen Inseln alle, wenn da die Sehnsucht über die Küsten hinein uns trieb, in's düstre Herz des alten Pelopones, an die einsamen Gestade des Eurotas, ach! die ausgestorbnen Thale von Elis und Nemea und Olympia, wenn wir da, an eine Tempelsäule des vergeßnen Jupiters gelehnt, umfangen von Lorbeerrosen und Immergrün, in's wilde Flußbett sahn . . . (iii,14)

Athos, the Hellespont, Rhodes, Taenarum, Eurotas, Elis, Nemea, and Olympia are a list of almost arbitrarily chosen evocative names, rather than the stages of a feasible journey. Naming places in this way is a technique often employed by Hölderlin, in the poems too, as a means of compressing a broad vision of the whole of Greece into the small space of a single paragraph or stanza. Chandler visits or mentions all these places and describes them more or less fully. Perhaps Hölderlin read the names from the maps the volumes provide. Here, in an obvious way, one important aspect of the process of poetic description is made clear; disparate details are brought together, raw material is reduced and compressed.

Nemea and Olympia, for example, are on opposite sides of the Peloponnese, but it is not clear which site is intended in the phrase 'wenn wir da'. The three chosen details—the pillar of the Temple of Zeus, the abundance of laurel and evergreen, the river-bed—could be taken as equally typical of both. It seems probable, however, that, originally, they were details of Nemea. Chandler describes the way there thus: 'Der Weg läuft an einem tiefgehöhlten, mit dichten Gebüschen von Lorbeerrosen, Myrten und Immergrün verwachsenen Flußbette hin . . .'[6] He found two pillars of the temple of Nemean Zeus still standing.[7] But nothing in his very brief description of Olympia (he found little to see there)[8] is traceable in the *Hyperion* passage. Hölderlin's poetic purpose is served by compressing the two sites into one scene that could be either, and arranging the details he had from Chandler to suit his own ends—so Hyperion leans on the pillar and, overhung by laurels and evergreen, gazes down into the river-bed. Out of the disparate, neutral details a tendentious picture has been made.

And this is the second element in the poetic process. Chandler writes objectively, Hölderlin has an axe to grind. Details that are neutral in Chandler are tendentious in Hölderlin. Hyperion leaning against the pillar broods sorrowfully on his country's past. Most of the adjectives are similarly tendentious: 'still', 'düster', 'alt', 'einsam', 'ausgestorben', 'vergeßen'.

The description continues:

da saß ich traurig spielend neben ihm [Adamas], und pflükte das Moos von eines Halbgotts Piedestal, grub eine marmorne Heldenschulter aus dem Schutt, und schnitt den Dornbusch und das Haidekraut von den halbbegrabnen Architraven, indeß mein Adamas die Landschaft zeichnete, wie sie freundlich tröstend den Ruin umgab, den Waizenhügel, die Oliven, die Ziegenheerde, die am Felsen des Gebirgs hieng, den Ulmenwald, der von den Gipfeln in das Thal sich stürzte; und die Lacerte spielte zu unsern Füßen, und die Fliegen umsummten uns in der Stille des Mittags . . .(iii,15)

Far from being Chandler's Nemea ('Die Trümmer ist kahl, und der Boden umher war neulich gepflügt worden'[9]) or his Olympia, this is simply a typical ruined site, composed of details picked up anywhere. Chandler writes in his first volume, *Travels in Asia Minor*:

Unter dem Schutt, der sich weit erstreckt, findet man wenige Marmorstücke und Reste von Bildhauerarbeit . . . Der Bauer zeigte mir ein marmornes Fußgestell . . . Nahe dabey fanden wir noch ein Paar andre Fußgestelle, von welchen eins über halb in Schutt vergraben war.[10]

This was a site in Troas.

The neutral details are used tendentiously by Hölderlin: he crowds them together to form almost a caricature of a classical ruins scene of the kind commonly produced by eighteenth-century painters. The landscape that Adamas sketches is similarly composed. Typical details (none of them, however, noted by Chandler at Nemea or Olympia)—olives, goats, a lizard—all the proper ingredients, are mixed to give a Greek landscape which, like the ruins, is tendentiously intended. It is 'freundlich tröstend' (that is why Adamas sketches it), being what remains of the Greek world.

The whole scene, then, is a poetic composition, independent of the factual accounts it uses, having its own mood and intention. Poetic composition implies free choice, compression, and tendentious arrangement.

Another example is the description of Hyperion's walk in the hinterland of Smyrna (iii,20-21). There is the same compression into unreal distance and time: the real journey, Smyrna-Sardes-Tmolus-Cayster-Smyrna would be 130 miles or more, including a climb of 6,000 feet. Tmolus seems within easy reach of Smyrna in Hölderlin's account. Before beginning his climb Hyperion spends a night at the foot of the mountain:

Ich hatt' am Fuße des Bergs übernachtet in einer freundlichen Hütte, unter Myrthen, unter den Düften des Ladanstrauchs, wo in der goldnen Fluth des Pactolus die Schwäne mir zur Seite spielten, wo ein alter Tempel der Cybele aus den Ulmen hervor, wie ein schüchterner Geist, in's helle Mondlicht blikte. Fünf liebliche Säulen trauerten über dem Schutt, und ein königlich Portal lag niedergestürzt zu ihren Füßen.

(iii,20)

The exotic and evocative details, the myrtle, laudanum, and swans, have been gathered here and there in Chandler.[11] and brought together, almost to excess. The main features—the hut, the river, and the temple—are related more closely and more clearly than would be likely in reality. They *feel* close together; the imprecise 'wo' encourages the reader to picture them as closely related.

Details are enhanced in Hölderlin's compositions beyond what Chandler found them to be: 'die freundliche Hütte' among the myrtle and laudanum bushes will have had as its original the *khans* in which Chandler's party often slept. They were rarely so idyllic. The phrase 'die goldne Fluth des Pactolus' deliberately implies that the water of the electrum-bearing river was golden in appearance. Chandler found the river at best shallow, sandy, and reddish-yellow, at worst 'foul and dull'.[12] Chandler describes the temple of Cybele in detail.[13] Hölderlin selects two precise instances—the five pillars still standing and the fallen gateway—and with the words 'lieblich', 'trauern', and 'königlich', charges them with his own nostalgia. They are a tendentious summary of the scene.

Even in the novel the descriptive passages are almost never an end in themselves but are subordinate to an overall purpose. They are coloured by the author's nostalgia for the lost Greek ideal; describing the Greek landscape he is acutely aware of the ideal civilization that has gone from it. But there is, nevertheless, room in a novel for a certain amount of not strictly relevant 'picturesqueness' and local-colouring. Or, rather, the author has room to indulge his passion for the physical beauty of Greece in long and frequent descriptive passages that serve his novel's *Tendenz* only in so far as more and more description may be said to increase the reader's sense of the beauty of Greece and so his sense of loss. But in the poems, where places, although important, are never themselves the main concern, there is no room whatsoever for gratuitous description. Least of all in the odes, and hardly more so in the Pindaric hymns. There is most room in hexameters and iambic pentameters, and early poems in those metres do contain descriptive passages of an untypical length.[14] But in the mature poetry there is no room to spare.

This means that the process of selection and compression, already noted in the writing of the novel, must be greatly intensified in the lyrical poetry. The intensification can be shown by comparing earlier and later poems in which descriptions of Greece occur.

'Der Main' and 'Der Nekar'

Both poems, especially 'Der Nekar', still have *Hyperion* and ultimately Chandler and Choiseul as the source of their descriptive details. The verses are crowded with evocative instances—the *embarras de choix* is obvious. Hölderlin has two simple intentions: first, to indicate the degenerate state of the modern Greeks; secondly, to indicate the surviving beauty of the landscape. A plethora of possibilities must have come to mind. For his first purpose he chose the songs and the labyrinthine dances that, according to Choiseul,[15] are a comfort to the Greeks in their enslaved condition; also the pillars of the Olympieum that are still standing, a reminder of the great past ('Der Nekar', lines 28, 32, 18, ii,17-18). Other details would have served the same purpose more or less well. Remembering his reading he might have chosen the antique sarcophagi now used as cisterns (typically, Chandler merely notes this detail, Choiseul points the moral of it), or the sections of antique pillars or altars now used as grind-stones. Jackals among the ruins or cranes migrating at the approach of winter are details objectively noted by Chandler already used tendentiously by Hölderlin in his *Hyperion*.[16]

For his second purpose—to conjure up the surviving beauty of the landscape— Hölderlin had an inexhaustible supply of suitable details at his disposal. He chose the cooling sea-breeze, the laurel, pomegranate, orange, and mastic trees ('Der Nekar', lines 24-30). He might equally well have chosen oleander, laudanum bushes, jasmine, myrtle, tamarisk, or lemon trees.

'Der Main' and 'Der Nekar' are unlike the later poems in the amount of exotic detail they contain, and in that the details themselves are not absolutely necessary and unalterable, as details of later poems are. There might have been more or fewer of them, and others would have done as well. Nevertheless, there has been greater selection than in the writing of the novel, and the selected details have been enhanced beyond the significance they had in, at least, Chandler's account.

An important aspect of the poetic descriptive process is this choosing of details that, in a poetic context, will be able to sustain a symbolic significance, details that will be, unforcedly, more suggestive and significant than they would seem to be in reality. Perhaps a distinction can be made between details whose innate, true significance the poet, in his poem, *brings out* and details that are of themselves neutral and to which the poet attributes his own significance. Jackals among ruins and migrating cranes would be of this latter kind—the poet gives them a, fairly obvious, significance of his own choosing. Most satisfying are details of the former kind, where the poet justly evaluates the detail's significance—his poem *reveals* and does not impose significance. The 'Hadrianstor' in *Hyperion* would be an example of this.[17] In itself it *does* illustrate the passing of a civilization—the new city has spread round it and has no more use for it. It is a gate that nobody goes in or out of. It has become symbolic, of its essential nature, and Hölderlin, in selecting it, lets its essential symbolic nature be revealed.

But perhaps the distinction is not just. It may simply be that all details are of themselves neutral and the poet always imposes significance, sometimes convincingly and sometimes not. Either way it can be said that Hölderlin had an eye for the detail that would bear symbolic significance. For poetic description he selected such details—things he had observed himself and things other people had observed—and immeasurably enhanced them.

Details evaluated or enhanced in this way produce Hölderlin's most satisfying imagery. In the opening lines of 'Patmos', for example:

> furchtlos gehn
> Die Söhne der Alpen über den Abgrund weg
> Auf leichtgebaueten Brüken.

(lines 6-8, ii,165)

The detail is a component part first of a real landscape, and secondly of a complex of images indicating a metaphysical predicament. It is first a fact observed by Hölderlin himself or remembered by him from his reading. He may have seen such bridges on his way home from Hauptwyl, if he went through the mountains to the Rhine gorge. Or perhaps he transferred them from Chandler's Asia Minor. Chandler notes of a cave at Hylae that it was sacred to Apollo, whose image gave his devotees extraordinary skill in all their undertakings:

His servants leaped down the steep rocks and precipices; or, felling tall trees, walked on them, with burthens, over the narrow passes of the mountain.[18]

This will be the meaning of 'leichtgebauet', whether Hölderlin had Chandler's observation in mind or not. Alpine bridges might be similarly built. In being used thus as an image the detail loses nothing of its essential nature: the poet attempts a bold act of communication, exactly as the bridge-builders did.

The same kind of imagery occurs in 'Mnemosyne':

> da, vom Kreuze redend, das
> Gesezt ist unterwegs einmal
> Gestorbenen, auf hoher Straß
> Ein Wandersmann geht zornig,
> Fern ahnend mit
> Dem andern . . .

(lines 29-34, ii,198)

This is the perfect expression of Hölderlin's theme—the difficult transition into the new age. It is an image, like the bridges of 'Patmos', of a religious situation and it is the more satisfying for being firmly of this earth. Hölderlin knew about passes; in the Alps, the Black Forest, the Auvergne he had learned the significance of the image with his own feet. The metaphysical idea finds its exact correlative in the revealed significance of the mountain pass.

The cross, commemorating travellers who have died, is an interesting detail. Such crosses are erected by the roadside in Alpine regions. Wordsworth observed them in 1790, when travelling through the Reuss valley: 'And crosses rear'd to Death on every side'. He notes: 'Crosses commemorative of the deaths of travellers by the fall of snow, and other accidents very common along this dreadful road'.[19] Hölderlin will have seen them for himself. Later the remembered detail became a perfect image.

I should like now to examine Hölderlin's final and most intense vision of Asia Minor, the area of Greece that his novel and earlier poems had already often described.

The vision of Asia Minor: 'Patmos' (lines 25-45)

It may be worth examining the lines phrase by phrase.

Asia appears 'in frischem Glanze' (line 25)—in obvious contrast to the twilit world of Hesperia. The Greeks enjoyed an age of light. In Greek poetry a common circumlocution for 'dying' is 'leaving the light'.[20] There are factual and commonly understood reasons for thinking of colour and light as being prime qualities of the Greek civilisation, but the phrase 'in frischem Glanze' has its full meaning only within the context of Hölderlin's whole mythology of cosmic day and night.

> Geheimnißvoll
> Im goldenen Rauche . . .   (lines 26-27)

This is how Hesperian eyes must see the Greek past—through the veils of legend, myth and nostalgia, through 'ein goldner Rauch, die Sage' ('Germanien', line 25, ii,149).

'Blüthe' (line 27) is the verb most often used to describe the Greek achievement.[21] But first, in the vision, it is the supreme beauty of Ionia, of which Hölderlin had precise factual details—the flowering shrubs and trees, the snow, the rivers, etc.—from reading the travellers. 'Blühen' is a descriptive word whose potential has been raised.

> Schnellaufgewachsen,
> Mit Schritten der Sonne . . .   (lines 28-29)

This is, first, the speed, the light, and the enormous scope of the vision. It dawns on the poet. Then, in the whole mythology, the course of the sun from east to west is a metaphor of civilization's development from its Asian source.[22]

> Mit tausend Gipfeln duftend . . .   (line 30)

These are the mountains of the Ionian hinterland, precisely named later, that Hyperion climbed. They were, literally, 'duftend' as Hölderlin knew from Chandler, scented with laudanum, tamarisk, and oleander. This one line has its more expansive equivalents in many *Hyperion* passages and in the descriptive strophes of 'Der Main' and 'Der Nekar'. In 'Patmos' there is maximum compression—and not only that, but also an enhancement and an enrichment of the chosen details. For what is being created is a mythical landscape, whose details are significant beyond their reality. Even in the first version of 'Patmos' there is a suggestion that, as in 'Brod und Wein' (line 57), the mountains are altars for the worship of the gods. 'Duftend', then, is the smoke and scent of sacrifices. The later versions make this explicit:

> Von tausend Tischen duftend . . .   (line 30, ii,174,180,185)

The enjambement between antistrophe and epode (lines 30-31) to reach the climax of the vision and complete the syntactic unit begun seven lines back is a mark of the technical mastery always controlling this vision. The suspense of increasing vision is exactly matched in syntax; as is the fulfilment: 'Mir Asia auf . . .'

Then follows a description of what the poet has in sight:

> ungewohnt
> War ich der breiten Gassen, wo herab
> Vom Tmolus fährt
> Der goldgeschmükte Pactol
> Und Taurus stehet und Messogis,
> Und voll von Blumen der Garten,
> Ein stilles Feuer; aber im Lichte
> Blüht hoch der silberne Schnee;
> Und Zeug unsterblichen Lebens
> An unzugangbaren Wänden
> Uralt der Epheu wächst und getragen sind
> Von lebenden Säulen, Cedern und Lorbeern
> Die feierlichen,
> Die göttlichgebauten Palläste.

(lines 32-45)

It is a composite picture, like the paragraphs quoted from *Hyperion*, but put together with infinitely greater care and to infinitely greater effect. The component parts are fetched from near and far—it is not possible to say unequivocally from where, nor exactly how they stand in relationship to one another. Again, as in the *Hyperion* passages, this valuable imprecision is deliberately achieved by the equivocal placing of the word 'wo' (line 33); also by the relating syntactically—'*Und* Taurus stehet . . .', '*aber* im Lichte . . .', etc.—of places far apart in reality. Is Sardes intended (lines 33-35) where the Pactolus flows from Tmolus through the streets? 'Die breiten Gassen . . .' seems more to indicate 'the broad streets' (εὐρύάγυιἄ) of Troy. Messogis is to the south of Tmolus, and Taurus still further south. Miletus may be indicated, one of the ports, the gates of Asia Minor (lines 46) and the nearest to Patmos, the goal of the poet's journey; for near Miletus, at the mouth of the Meander, Chandler found an especially fertile area known locally as 'The Gardens', and of Miletus he wrote: 'Miletus ist ein sehr geringer Ort, wird aber noch Palat, oder Palatia, die Palläste genannt'.[23] (Cf. lines 37 and 45 of 'Patmos'). The town was renowned for its palaces in Hellenistic times.

The associations are as various as the localities: of Bacchus in Tmolus and the Pactolus (also in the detail of the ivy); of Homeric heroes in the wide streets and the god-built palaces;[24] of eighteenth-century travellers, and of the author's own novel.

The widespread localities and associations are compressed into the small space the poem can make available. The various elements are bound into a unity by poetic form.

It gives further unity to the vision that the details of locality and landscape are built up and ordered into an overall image. The garden, the sheer, ivy-covered walls,

and the pillars make up an immense and magnificent structure, truly
'göttlichgebaut'. As in 'Friedensfeier' (lines 1-9) and 'Brod und Wein' (lines 55-58)
the natural landscape is seen as a building on an immense scale, a work of divine art.
In 'Patmos' Hölderlin first described the snow-covered peaks as 'ein silbern
Geländer'—which makes the architectural image perhaps more obvious than he
finally wanted it to be. In a later version (ii, 174) the palaces (lines 44-45) instead
of being 'feierlich' are 'felsenhart', which indicates the source of the metaphor in
the natural landscape, the sheer mountain walls.

Within the unifying metaphor the disparate details and localities already
mentioned are all independently effective.

Jung, in elucidating the general, archetypal meaning of the imagery in this
'schizophrenic's' vision,[25] overlooks those meanings that are precisely intended
within a carefully worked-out private mythology. The vision is finally
comprehensible only on Hölderlin's own terms.[26] Certainly the descriptive details
amount to a vision—it is all intensely *seen*—but did this vision well up
uncontrollably out of the poet's subconscious? or was it composed, piece by piece,
with one selected detail after the other?

The latter seems the more likely. The vision was composed, in essentially the
same way as the descriptive passages of *Hyperion* were composed, but with an
intensity and a richness that only the strictest poetic form could hold in check.
After this vision Hölderlin was never again so successful.

A particular quality of these lines in 'Patmos', and of poetic description in
general, is that being themselves compressed and controlled, their effect on the
reader's imagination is evocative and expansive. That is perhaps due to the element
of deliberate imprecision in the composition: options are left open to the
imagination. Prosaic description limits the imagination, invites the reader to
consider and not go beyond certain specific details. But poetic description, in every
detail it offers, widens the imagination's scope. For example:

> Dort an der Ufern, unter den Bäumen
> Ionias, in Ebenen des Kaisters,
> Wo Kraniche, des Aethers froh,
> Umschlossen sind von fernhindämmernden Bergen . . .
> ('Die Wanderung', lines 64-67, ii,140)

The vision is enlarged: from the coast, the river estuaries with their famous cities,
inland among the exotic Ionian vegetation, to the wide plains, the distant
mountains, under the infinite sky. And beyond the landscape, that itself extends
further than the eye can see, is the dimension of meanings, suggestions, and
associations. The associations, both general and peculiar to Hölderlin, of those four
lines are too numerous to list.

The topography is in order, the chosen details are apt—but the lines are more
visionary than descriptive. The eye is led out of and beyond the landscape by the
landscape details themselves.

So far this chapter has been concerned with the landscapes of the ideal Greek world, and it is understandable that Hölderlin's vision of them should be so intense. Having examined how such visions are composed, it may now be worth examining how Hölderlin reacts to and makes use of those landscapes that he saw, not through the medium of a hallowed literary tradition nor through foreign travellers' accounts, but with his own eyes.

Apologizing to Neuffer for his lack of descriptive talent he wrote: 'ich bin meist mit dem Totaleindruk zufrieden' (vi,168). This comment has already been discussed in Chapter 1,[27] but it may be useful again here, under a different aspect. How does Hölderlin's receptiveness to the general, overall effect of a landscape affect his description of it? A passage from 'Emilie' provides an example of his method:

> Wie oft
> Im Abendlichte stand ich auf dem Hügel
> Mit dir, und sah das grüne Thal hinauf,
> Wo zwischen Bergen, da die Rebe wächst,
> An manchem Dorf vorüber, durch die Wiesen
> Zu uns herab, von luft'ger Weid' umkränzt,
> Das goldne ruhige Gewässer wallte!
>
> (lines 170-176, i,282-83)

First, it is a view from a hill. 'Totaleindruk' is most easily experienced from a vantage point. It is significant that the lengthiest and best of the few descriptive passages in Hölderlin's letters are views from hills.[28] Similarly in the poetry, from 'Die Tek' and 'Kanton Schwyz' onwards. Landscape seen from a height and distance loses much of its distracting particularness. It becomes appreciable in its lasting, general, component parts. Looking at the landscape Hölderlin then chooses those of its details by which it can be most permanently characterized. It is not that he snatches up a detail here and there, overlooking all others, but that from his vantage point, experiencing a 'Totaleindruk', he selects the details he considers to be most telling—not the details which would most exactly convey any peculiarities of the particular scene before him, but those which would most lastingly convey what is basic, unchanging, and overall in that landscape. In 'Emilie', to describe the landscape of the Neckar valley Hölderlin selects: the hills with their vineyards, the meadows, the villages, the willows along the river-bank. These few details are hardly a *description* of the landscape—they do no more than stand for it. They are the accepted symbols of it.

This is a relatively long descriptive passage and 'Emilie', a leisurely, not to say long-winded poem, contains others like it, but still none of them has fullness—there is no fullness of detail such as a realistic, prose description would inevitably have. These poetic descriptions are the very reverse of exhaustive: few details are given, as parts for the whole, or reminders.

Perhaps it does not finally matter which details the poet selects, so long as they belong in and can be made to be expressive of the landscape. Hölderlin generally

picks out willows to be the characteristic detail of the Neckar banks, but alders
would perhaps have done as well. In 'Des Morgens' he finally wrote:

> die Buche neigt
> Ihr schwankes Haupt . . .

(lines 2-3, i,302)

having discarded—why?—the poplar and the birch (i,612). But the details are not
quite arbitrary; there is not a wide choice, there are not that many overall typical
details. It would not do to choose anything too particular or recherché. If the hills
are generally flat-topped, then it would not do to pick out the exceptional, pointed
one.

It should be said that certain landscapes can be quite adequately conveyed in
this general, selective way, whilst others demand the fullest and most particular
description. It so happens that the landscapes Hölderlin knew best are naturally
suited to his way of apprehending and communicating them. Swabia, especially, is
a country easily appreciable in its basic component parts. In a typical Swabian
landscape the river, with its willows, alders, and poplars, is central. Flat meadows
are to either side of it, or fields of corn and root-crops. The valley is wide and flat,
bordered by low hills. Hillslopes facing south have vineyards, others have orchards,
and quite distinctly above vineyards or orchards the forest begins. Roads and paths
go over the valley floor in remarkable clarity:

> Holde Landschaft! wo die Straße
> Mitten durch sehr eben geht . . .

('Das fröhliche Leben', lines 33-34, ii,275)

A landscape 'Wo die Natur sehr einfältig', as Hölderlin wrote at a time when the
simple components of the scene were more than ever important to him.[29]

Such a landscape loses nothing by being described in the most general terms—the
river, the meadows, the cornfields, the orchards, the vineyards and the forest. Each
detail is archetypal.

Towns and villages in this landscape, even today, have a distinctiveness, a
separateness, are appreciable as entities in themselves and distinct parts of the
whole. You can still walk comfortably out of Tübingen; the many villages around
are quite distinct from the town and from one another. In 1800 Tübingen was still
walled; there was very little building outside the walls until the 1820s. And pictures
of the time show Frankfurt similarly complete in itself:

> Fernher dämmert die Stadt, wie eine eherne Rüstung
> Gegen die Macht des Gewittergotts und der Menschen geschmiedet,
> Majestätisch herauf, und ringsum ruhen die Dörfchen . . .[30]

In general, Hölderlin's innate sensitivity to all that is archetypal in human
existence was aided by the conditions of the times he lived in, when archetypes
were a good deal more apparent than they are now.

The two areas of Germany that Hölderlin knew best, Swabia and the Rhine-Main plain, are not dissimilar enough to appear very differently in his poetry. Both landscapes are conveyed in more or less the same details: river, vineyards, orchards, etc. The landscape has to be *quite* different, like the Alps, before a different version of it appears in the poetry. Landscapes that are in fact similar become well-nigh indistinguishable from one another when generalized and included in a poem.

This can be further discussed with the help of the GStA. Writing to his sister in the spring of 1799, Hölderlin described his situation in Homburg:

das Städtchen liegt am Gebirg, und Wälder und geschmakvolle Anlagen, liegen rings herum; ich wohne gegen das Feld hinaus, habe Gärten vor dem Fenster und einen Hügel mit Eichbäumen, und kaum ein paar Schritte in ein schönes Wiesthal. Da geh' ich dann hinaus wenn ich von meiner Arbeit müde bin, steige auf den Hügel und seze mich in die Sonne, und sehe über Frankfurt in die weiten Fernen hinaus . . .
(vi,316)

Adolf Beck, editing the letters, notes: 'Das in Nr. 174 geschilderte Bild erscheint *unverkennbar* [my emphasis] in der Ode 'Mein Eigentum' vom Herbst 1799' (vi,891).

In seiner Fülle ruhet der Herbsttag nun,
　Geläutert ist die Traub und der Hain ist roth
　　Vom Obst, wenn schon der holden Blüthen
　　　Manche der Erde zum Danke fielen.

Und rings im Felde, wo ich den Pfad hinaus
　Den stillen wandle, ist den Zufriedenen
　　Ihr Gut gereift und viel der frohen
　　　Muhe gewährer der Reichtum ihnen.

Doch heute laß mich stille, den trauten Pfad
　Zum Haine gehn, dem golden die Wipfel schmükt
　　Sein sterbend Laub, und kränzt auch mir die
　　　Stirne, ihr holden Erinnerungen!
(lines 1-8 and 33-36, i,306-307)

Beck's note is useful in a discussion of Hölderlin's poetic-descriptive method. Of a passage in an earlier letter (vi,240, lines 56-59) he notes: 'Die Umgebung, die Hölderlin schildert, geht dichterisch verwandelt, aber *eindeutig erkennbar* [my emphasis] in den ersten Abschnitt (v.2-7) des Gedichtes "Die Muße" ein' (vi,836). 'Mein Eigentum' is a better poem than 'Die Muße', a better example of Hölderlin's poetic-descriptive art (there is an untypical, excessive amount of not very significant detail in 'Die Muße'—fish, swallows, butterflies, and bees), and, together with the passage from the letter, it will serve to illustrate my argument.

It is amusing but, I think, not very profitable to attempt to recognize particular landscapes in Hölderlin's poems. In a sense it is a perverse exercise because it works directly against the poet's intention. If a particular landscape can be identified that will always be despite the poet.

It happens that the letter and the poem 'Mein Eigentum' were both demonstrably written in Homburg and thus it becomes reasonable to associate them. But if the dates and place of composition were not known, what exactly in the poem would remind a reader of the letter? Nothing in particular—the poem *has* nothing in particular; but, for that matter, neither has the prose passage, except oak-trees and Frankfurt. And it is this imprecise quality of the prose that makes the exercise of deriving the poem from it rather a nonsensical one. Doubtless Hölderlin had a particular scene before his eyes, but in his manner of describing it (even in prose), or even in his manner of seeing it, the particular scene's peculiarities are lost and only general details—woods, gardens, meadows—and a central one—the oak-trees on the hill, a focal point of the scene—are conveyed. The description has neither fullness nor precision. If Frankfurt is named it is with something of that poetic solemnity with which Stuttgart, Tübingen, or Lindau are named in the poems. Of course, such a prose passage easily becomes poetry—its details are chosen as for a poem. But does it become 'unverkennbar' 'Mein Eigentum'? The question can hardly be asked; wrong criteria are being applied. Not that the poem has moved unrecognizably far from the 'original' prose, but that both, poem and prose, are so general as hardly to be descriptions of a particular place. Certainly, the poem cannot be said to derive from a particular, real landscape. The landscape in Hölderlin's poem and (but for Frankfurt) the landscape in the letter might have been almost anywhere in Southern Germany, and if they do resemble one another that is not surprising, because all Hölderlin's South German landscapes turn out more or less like that.

The particular landscape that research has established to be the poem's 'source' is fortuitous and pretty well irrelevant. Wherever it was it merely reminded Hölderlin of the typical South German landscape, of an archetypal image that the peculiarities of particular places never touched.

The landscape of 'Mein Eigentum' is summarized in the usual chosen details: orchard, vineyard, grove of trees, path; and, as usual in Hölderlin's poetry, these details, in their starkness, naturally assume symbolic status. And even in the prose passage the tendency is the same, towards what is typical and symbolic.

Hölderlin poeticized landscape while he looked at it. He naturally saw it in poetic terms—for example, as heroic or idyllic—and he responded immediately to what was general and typical in it. This tendency grew in him. What was at first a normal readiness to interpret and idealize landscape according to contemporary, sentimental conventions (e.g. in 'Die Tek') became an instinctive urge to mythicize it. Having worked out a coherent mythology involving localities he lived in, he then quite naturally interpreted them according to his myths—in poems like 'Heidelberg', 'Stutgard', or 'Heimkunft'.

And the same development (towards, in fact, a total poetic obsession, so that he lived his poetry's myths) is apparent in his letters. The letters from Hauptwyl describing the Alps are the proof that there never was a 'prose-description stage' for Hölderlin: he could not describe prosaically because he never saw the landscape in any but mytho-poetic terms. In the letters from Hauptwyl the mythicizing of landscape is already complete, even before 'Heimkunft', 'Unter den Alpen gesungen', or 'Der Rhein' were written.

Most often, of course, Hölderlin *celebrates* rather than *describes* the places that are important to him. The place, Greek or Hesperian, may simply be named, in a solemn tone that makes the glamorous associations of the name resound throughout the poem:

> Und Ajax liegt
> An den Grotten der See,
> An Bächen, benachbart dem Skamandros.
>
> ('Mnemosyne', lines 37-39, ii,198)

Or:

> Man nennet aber diesen den Ister.
>
> ('Der Ister', line 21, ii,190)

This, the solemn naming of glamorous places, is a common poetic device, and no poet has used it to greater effect than Hölderlin. His personal commitment to the places he names and his unrivalled appreciation of their significance entitle him to celebrate them: they are never trivially used.

But Hölderlin's normal style when celebrating a place is first to name it, and then briefly to characterize it with a chosen detail. It is in the classical tradition to characterize places so. In poetry and tragedy a locality is briefly but often very memorably identified with a short descriptive phrase or simply with an epithet. Places carry with them their chief associations. For example: Parnassus, its twin peaks, sacred to Apollo and Dionysus; Dodona, its sacred oak and priests of Zeus; Mycenae, its gold.

To the Greek places of his world Hölderlin attaches, for the most part, the characteristics and associations that the Greeks themselves established. Thus:

The Maeander	— its endless windings
The Nile	— its mysterious source
Colonus	— its horses
The Cayster	— its cranes [31]

These established characteristics are concisely attached to the place-names. In 'Der Adler' Hölderlin writes:

> Wo den Schatten der Athos wirft,
> Nach Höhlen in Lemnos.
>
> (lines 7-8, ii,229)

From his reading of the classics (perhaps Pliny, Book IV, Chapter 12) or from

Chandler (*Asia Minor*, p. 23) or from the curious inset in the map at the back of Reichard's version of Choiseul, Hölderlin would know that, at the solstice, the Shadow of Mount Athos reached the market-place of Myrina on Lemnos, eighty-seven miles away to the east. In classical style he thus identifies Athos by its most remarkable feature. And similarly Lemnos—by its caves, where the smiths of Hephaestus worked and where Philoctetes suffered.

In the same classical manner, whether there was an exact classical precedent or not, Hölderlin characterises the Cephissus—plane-trees, olives, myrtles, nightingales, and swans; Tivoli—elms on the banks of the Anio; Virgil's grave—laurels; Cithaeron—fir-trees and vines; Ida—woods and clouds.[32] And so on—there are any number of examples.

Also in the classical style, with no sense of its being inappropriate, he characterizes Hesperian places. The significance of this, as a device to bind together the east and west of his poetic world, has already been discussed.[33]

Mount Taunus is 'mit Eichen bekränzt'; Swabia and Lombardy are 'von hundert Bächen durchflossen'; Gascony is remembered as a locality 'wo viel Gärten sind'. The Stuttgart region has its fruit-trees along the road, the Neckar its willows and the red earth of its banks, all Württemberg its cornfields.[34] To characterize these well-known localities thus concisely Hölderlin has selected still further among those details already selected as typical and generally characteristic and used in longer poetic-descriptive passages.

These descriptive phrases may then be further compressed into descriptive epithets.

Applied to Greek places (with or without an exact classical precedent):

Hymettus	— 'der vielgepriesne' ('Die Wanderung', line 71, ii,140)
Cyprus	— 'die quellenreiche' ('Patmos', line 58, ii,166)
Pactolus	— 'der goldgeschmükte' (ibid., line 35)
Castalia	— 'blüthenumduftet' ('Der Archipelagus', line 212, ii,109)

Or to Hesperian places (again in the Greek style, deliberately, as discussed in a previous chapter):

Stuttgart	— 'die gepriesene' ('Stutgard', line 76, ii,88)
Lindau	— 'wellenumrauscht' ('Heimkunft', line 57, ii,98)
Alps	— 'göttlichgebaut' ('Der Rhein', line 5, ii,142)
Heidelberg	— 'ländlichschön' ('Heidelberg', line 4, ii,14)
Heidelberg castle	— 'schiksaalskundig' (Ibid., line 22)
Bohemian hills	— 'wohlgeschmiedet' ('Das Nächste Beste', line 47 ii,238)

Some of these are direct loan-translations of Greek epithets—'wohlgeschmiedet', 'göttlichgebaut', 'wellenumrauscht', and the others are compounds formed in Greek style. It should be noted how apt many of them are, how well they serve their purpose, conveying with maximum economy an essential and typical feature of the locality: the South German roads lined with fruit-trees, the mixed colours of cherry and apple blossom ('weißblühend und röthlich' in 'Die Wanderung', line 5). Less able poets, unhappy unless every noun has its adjective but anxious never to be 'unpoetically' particular or precise, never go beyond what is obvious. Their descriptive epithets are *nichtssagend*. Hills are high, groves are holy, fields are green.[35] Hölderlin at his best manages the difficult task of compressing into an epithet or short phrase details that will strikingly convey what is permanent and typical in the landscape he sees. He grasps what is fundamental and archetypal; his epithets and descriptive phrases are simple, essential and true, in the best tradition of the classical poets who were his models.

CHAPTER 6

THE DISINTEGRATING WORLD, 1802-06

There are important differences between the poetic world of such poems as 'Die Wanderung', 'Germanien', and 'Patmos' ('Widmungsfassung'), and the world of 'Andenken', '. . . der Vatikan . . .' or 'Griechenland'. The poetic world of 1801, coherently composed and expressive of one central idea, becomes something else, something less coherent but, perhaps, richer in the years up to Hölderlin's final mental breakdown in 1806. It can be quite clearly seen when the coherent world comes to an end, or begins to come to an end. The crucial experience is the journey to Bordeaux, the time there and the journey home, the months between December 1801 and July 1802. That is the break in Hölderlin's creative life.

So much happened in that time, some of it inspiring, some of it merely destructive. The journey there, over the Auvergne in winter, was, as I suggested in an earlier chapter, the crisis in Hölderlin's development, when the symbolic, mythical import of his own life became obvious and conclusive. The experience in Bordeaux of the sea and of the most foreign surroundings he was ever faced with was an inspiration that broke open the limited world of 1801, without ever finding—except in 'Andenken'—adequate poetic form. But the odd names and memories of places scattered through half a dozen unfinished poems are an indication of what rich sources Hölderlin would have drawn on had his mind not failed. On the journey home from Bordeaux, after some kind of emotional crisis in his job, he suffered those violent impressions, of mythical significance to him, that he resumed in the letter to Böhlendorff. He arrived in Nürtingen 'mit verwirrten Mienen und tobenden Geberden, im Zustande des verzweifelten Irrsinnes und in einem Aufzug, der die Aussage, daß er unterwegs beraubt worden sey, zu bestätigen schien'.[1]

In Stuttgart, either on his way home from France or after having already been home, he learned of Susette Gontard's death. It is difficult to evaluate what effect this news would have on him. In one sense, at least, it would have little effect. He had left her two years before, and from that date onwards his personal life had been a matter of less and less concern to him. He lived increasingly in the impersonal world of poetic obsession. From their first meeting, or even before it, Susette Gontard, the ideal woman, 'die Athenerin', had a place in Hölderlin's mythology and could never be lost. The myth remained, ineradicable, despite separation and even despite death. In that sense, then, it cannot be said that the final loss of the real woman contributed to the disintegration of Hölderlin's poetic world. It was enough to have known her, to have experienced the truth of the myth. In Hyperion's words:

Ich hab' es Einmal gesehn, das Einzige, das meine Seele suchte, und die Vollendung, die wir über die Sterne hinauf entfernen, die wir hinaufschieben bis an's Ende der Zeit, die hab' ich gegenwärtig gefühlt. Es war da, das Höchste, in diesem Kreise der Menschennatur und der Dinge war es da!
    Ich frage nicht mehr, wo es sey; es war in der Welt, es kann wiederkehren in ihr, es ist jezt nur verborgner in ihr. Ich frage nicht mehr, was es say; ich hab' es gesehn, ich hab' es kennen gelernt.

(iii,52)

It is on that level of passionate idealism that the poet Hölderlin lived his life. At the same time, although Hölderlin increasingly disregarded the fact, there was another self that had to make shift in the everyday world of material want. In the two years' absence from Susette Gontard Hölderlin had known nothing—in real, personal terms—but harassment, disappointment, and incomprehension. In those terms he will have felt her death to be a final and unbearable affliction. Perhaps more than any other poet Hölderlin actually lived his poetic obsessions, so that it is not at all satisfactory in his case to distinguish emphatically between the world of art and the world of everyday life. But the fact remains that he did live and suffer in the real world, and whilst the poet was engaged in translating this experience into lasting, impersonal correlatives, the man himself was being intolerably afflicted.

For a few months the break that Bordeaux had made was not obvious. Hölderlin lived quietly in Nürtingen; the madness calmed down. He took up his old interests. In the autumn he finished 'Patmos' and worked at a first version of 'Der Einzige', both poems begun before he went to Bordeaux, and both, especially 'Patmos', *eminently* poems of the coherent world, as much of that world of 1801 as 'Germanien' or 'Die Wanderung'. Indeed, 'Patmos', in the version that Sinclair handed to Landgraf Friedrich in the spring of 1803, is the best achieved expression of Hölderlin's coherent poetic world, the nearest he came to a satisfactory synthesis of Greece and Hesperia.

To go back to poems begun before Bordeaux and finish them so that they conformed entirely with the ideas of 1801 was relatively easy; perhaps most of the work was already done. But the first new poem, 'Andenken', written in the spring of 1803, shows how the coherent world had begun to disintegrate. Later versions of 'Der Einzige' and 'Patmos', written in the months following, express a world more and more unlike that of 'Germanien'.

Before turning to particular poems of this later period I should like to try to characterize in general terms the world that they express. Compared with the poetic world of 1801 it is a disintegrating world. But this does not mean simply that it is the world of a poet less and less able, because of madness, to control his work. Hölderlin was not conclusively mad when he arrived home in the summer of 1802. His friends and his mother saw him in a fit of madness, brought on by the journey and, possibly, by the news or foreboding of Susette Gontard's death, and this fit passed off. The journey to Regensburg with Sinclair in the autumn of 1802 had a calming effect, at least for a time. It is worth noting that Sinclair maintained a belief in the essential sanity and intellectual capability of his friend until at least as late as August, 1804.[2]

Neither 'Patmos', nor 'Andenken' nor 'Mnemosyne' is the poem of a madman. The coherent world of 1801 began to disintegrate—and 'Andenken' can be said to be the first expression of its disintegration—not because Hölderlin was going mad, but because, for one reason or another, the ideas that made the world of 1801 coherent were altered, developed, or abandoned. The coherent world disintegrated, partly by collapsing inwards as its central ideas were changed, and partly by expanding, by suddenly having to incorporate a hitherto unpermitted richness and variety.

Obviously, madness completes the disintegration. Arbitrariness and incoherence become increasingly the characteristic features of the late, unfinished poems. The loss of intellectual grasp is obvious, the inability to make things cohere.

Two trends are distinguishable in the poetry of 1802 to 1806. The first is the continuation or consequential development of the ideas that established the poetry of 1801. The old mythology remains more or less intact. Poems are rooted in it and either re-state, in the old terms, familiar themes or rationally develop them. The later versions of 'Patmos' and 'Der Einzige', 'Der Ister' and 'Kolomb', for example, all develop a theme already important in 'Germanien' or 'Die Wanderung', namely the assertion of Hesperia against the pull of Greece. In this, the most sustained and coherent theme of the late poetry, places are named as they were in the poetry of 1801, to externalize ideas. In Hölderlin's imaginative world the emphasis shifts from east to west; Hesperian places and their heroes predominate. This widens the earlier poetic world by following up the possibilities inherent in it; and by widening it beyond its former limits the new interests contribute to its final disintegration. Poems developing the new interests are mostly unfinished: the poetic world is no longer capable of a complete coherence.

But a second trend is more obviously destructive: it is the naming of places outside any coherent scheme, a more private, less consequential use of them, one natural to many poets but unprecedented in Hölderlin's work. There are private memories of Bordeaux; places are named that have nothing to do with the old, central theme, the relationship of Greece and Hesperia. And it is this private remembering of places—on the whole still intelligible to the informed reader—that opens the way to the cryptic, confused, or arbitrary naming that is typical of the last fragments. The poetic world—coherently imagined, a deliberate composition of significant places—totally breaks up when places with a purely private meaning are allowed, or when, in a few of the poems of Hölderlin's madness, their meaning, if any, is inaccessible.

Under these general headings: 'Traces of the old coherence and new coherent themes' and 'The private and obscure celebration of places' the world of the later poetry can now be examined in detail.

Traces of the old coherence and new coherent themes

The composition of Hölderlin's coherent poetic world has already been discussed in an earlier chapter and it will be sufficient here to indicate that in such poems as 'Der Adler' (lines 1-23) or 'Der Ister' (especially lines 7-9) the old historical-geographical scheme is maintained and assumed. Even in very late and obscure fragments there are still traces of it. In 'Wenn aber die Himmlischen . . .', for example, the Alps are a landmark to the reader since they appear in their old significance as the throne of the gods; the style of the poem is difficult, but its theme is a familiar one: the trials of the interim age. 'Der Adler' and 'Der Ister', having re-established the mythology in which they are working (in nearly all his hymns Hölderlin re-states the terms of his mythology), then go on to develop ideas already present but not developed in the poetry of 1801. 'Der Adler' examines the important concept of simple existence during the difficult, transitional age.[3] 'Der Ister' defines and asserts Hölderlin's Hesperia. The old mythological framework is intact, and within it (and causing an expansion or alteration of it) these new ideas are developed. Hesperia is the main coherent theme of the late poetry, and the one I shall chiefly concern myself with.

Hölderlin's first concern was always the future of western civilization, and, in particular, the role of his own country. The future was his responsibility, that he upheld despite considerable temptation to be uselessly nostalgic for the Greek past. If this is borne in mind, that he was always concerned about his country, then much of the discussion of a possible 'abendländische Wendung'[4] becomes unnecessary. It is true that for about ten years, from 1790 to 1800, Greece was uppermost in his mind. But contemporary Europe was never forgotten: the preoccupation with Greece gave Hölderlin terms in which to discuss his own country's predicament. What he learned from Greece he applied to Germany, and what he admired in the Greek past he hoped to see realized in a European future. Then in the mature poetry, in the historical-geographical world it creates, there are two poles, Greece and Hesperia, both exerting an attraction. The Greek past is an inspiration and a temptation, the Hesperian future is a responsibility, and all Hölderlin's writings work at reconciling these two demands. In the completed version of 'Patmos' the reconciliation is all but achieved.

In Michel's theory Hölderlin abandoned Greece and came back home to Germania. (And this was his salvation. As Michel has it: '[Es] ist die Rettung

Hölderlins zu seinem eigentlichen Beruf, "Sänger des Volks" zu sein, Wortführer des Nordens, Gesetzsprecher des Deutschtums, Führer zu jeder Art von geistiger deutscher Kultur.')[5] It is misleading to talk of a 'return' to Germania: there is a more intense preoccupation with Hesperian matters. And there is certainly no abandoning of Greece. Hesperia and Greece remained related and their relationship was the main theme of Hölderlin's poetry until he could no longer write intelligibly on anything but the view from his window in Tübingen. They are the two poles of his poetic world for as long as it exists. There is abundant evidence of this, especially in the later years.

The letter to Böhlendorff of December 1801 has been variously interpreted, and I have no new interpretation to offer. What Hölderlin propounds there seems to me a purely intellectual, idealist system, pleasing, perhaps, in its criss-crossing relationships but impossible to make any practical sense of. However, accepting the system, one thing is certain: the two spheres, the Hesperian and the Greek, are dependent on one another. Greeks have naturally a quality not inborn in Hesperians, namely 'das Feuer vom Himmel', 'das heilige Pathos'. Hesperians need this, and turn to the Greeks in search of it. Moreover, the Greeks are an example in a second sense: they have perfected that quality inborn in Hesperians and foreign to themselves, namely 'die abendländische Junonische Nüchternheit'. 'Deßwegen sind uns die Griechen unentbehrlich–', doubly indispensable: we learn from them both 'das Eigene' and 'das Fremde' (vi, 426).

The whole system then applies the other way round and Hesperians (or, presumably, qualities of the Hesperian mind) are doubly important to the Greeks. They would have learned from us (had we co-existed) to make proper use of that passion already naturally theirs, and would also have learned and then excelled in our typical order and clarity. Presumably it is for these latter qualities, in Hölderlin's mythology at least, that Heracles makes his journey north to the banks of the Ister: the Greeks need 'Schatten' and 'Kühlung' to complement their native fire (ii,191).

The important thing here is to indicate that Hesperia was firmly related to and dependent upon Greece. Hölderlin could not turn away from Greece at a time when his greatest concern was the predicament of his own country.

It is well known that in 1803 Hölderlin was still intensely preoccupied with both poles of his world. He was translating Sophocles—and in such a way that the plays would be more comprehensible to the modern Hesperian mind: 'Um es unserer Vorstellungsart mehr zu nähern' (v,268); emphasizing the general truth and relevance of the Greek myths: 'Wir müssen die Mythe nemlich überall beweisbarer darstellen' (v,268).[6] He sent the plays to the Prinzessin Auguste von Hessen-Homburg in the spring of 1804, and in the accompanying letter wrote, according to Gustav Schlesier, 'von dem Werth des Vergleichens der antiken und unserer Zustände' (vi,439). In dedicating these plays to the Princess he wrote: 'Sonst will ich, wenn es die Zeit giebt, die Eltern unsrer Fürsten und ihre Size und die Engel des heiligen Vaterlands singen' (v,119-20). As in earlier letters to Wilmans (vi,435 and 436) the two interests, Greece and Germany, are naturally associated. There is no question of abandoning the one for the sake of the other. Thinking of Germany Hölderlin has Greek terms of reference and comparison in mind:

Die Fabel, poëtische Ansicht der Geschichte, und Architektonik des Himmels beschäfftiget mich gegenwärtig vorzüglich, besonders das Nationelle, sofern es von dem Griechischen verschieden ist.

(vi,437)

That is the main theme of the late poetry: the defining and asserting of Hesperia against Greece, 'den hesperischen/*orbis*, im Gegensaze gegen den/*orbis* der Alten zu bestimmen' (ii,876). Granted that in these last years there is a more mature and intense preoccupation with Germany than ever before—and in so far it may be permissible though not very helpful to speak of an 'abendländische Wendung'—it is nevertheless only with reference to Greece that the predicament of Germany and the whole Hesperian world can be understood. A very late hymn, perhaps the last that Hölderlin attempted, although Hesperian in content has the title 'Griechenland'.

'Ihr sichergebaueten Alpen . . .'

To some extent this new purpose, the defining and asserting of Hesperia, can be pursued without extending the physical limits of the earlier established poetic world. 'Ihr sichergebaueten Alpen . . .', for example, is a hymn in praise of Swabia, like 'Die Wanderung'. And it is more exclusively concerned with Swabia than that earlier poem, more like 'Der Winkel von Hahrdt'. In its unfinished form it is little more than a list of places to be celebrated, some already having, others awaiting a brief characterization in classical style. There are compound epithets: 'sichergebauet', 'sanftblikend', and places are remembered in their characteristic details, here, especially, trees: the sweet-scented firs of the Black Forest (lines 3-7), the limes, willow, and mulberry of a Swabian village (lines 12-15), the apple-trees of the Stuttgart area (lines 32-33).[7] In style the poem relates to the Ancient World. Then 'Römisches tönend' (1.36) is an explicit connexion discovered in the home landscape and the preceding lines 'und Blize fallen/Am hellen Tage' suggest such an intervention of the gods from a clear Greek sky as 'Brod und Wein' celebrates (1.64). Finally, additions to the MS between and next to lines 2 and 3 reinforce the relationship:

Das Wirtemberg	Die Tempel und der Dreifuß und Altar
	Denn immer sind
	Die Himmlischen miteinander . . .

(ii,865)

In the early poem 'Die Muße' a Greek temple was incongruously intruded into a

Germanic landscape. I suggested that this was one of Hölderlin's first, clumsy attempts to relate Greece and Germany as the poles of a coherent world. In the hymns of 1801 every opportunity was taken to intrude Greek elements into the Hesperian sphere, and in the later poetry, when Hesperia is more than ever Hölderlin's concern, the device is still frequently used—rather more emphatically and less subtly than in the finished hymns. It is as though those lines 'Die Tempel und der Dreifuß und Altar . . .' were a sort of stereotyped intrusion that Hölderlin had to hand whenever he wanted to indicate the relatedness of Greece and Hesperia. Lines very reminiscent of them occur in two other poems written between 1803 and 1806. In both versions of 'Dem Fürsten', a poem celebrating Friedrich Wilhelm Karl, Duke of Württemberg—a poem of the kind he had said he would write in the dedication to the Prinzessin von Homburg—Hölderlin included the lines:

> wo sie den Tempel gebaut
> Und Dreifuß und Altar . . .
>
> (lines 13-14, ii,246 and 247)

—unequivocally Greek elements in a Hesperian context. And again, in 'An die Madonna', he concludes his description and interpretation of the Westphalian landscape with the lines:

> . . . das Land, da
> Die Himmlischen all
> Sich Tempel . . .
>
> (lines 113-15, ii,214)

— a final indication of that important Hesperian area's relatedness to Greece.

It is a characteristic of this later poetry that places are named more frequently and willingly than ever before:[8] in 'Ihr sichergebaueten Alpen . . .', for example, to sketch out the physical shape of Swabia, with the names of mountains, rivers, and towns. (It should be noted that in this poem, as in 'Die Wanderung', the old boundaries of Swabia are intended—the Alps are the southern limit. In this geographical framework the mythology of 1801 can be seen to be still intact.)

It is furthermore typical of these late poems that Hölderlin is not only prolific and exact in the naming of places, but also extremely personal. Every place mentioned in 'Ihr sichergebaueten Alpen . . .' was well known to him: he was born and lived much of his life by the Neckar; he lived close under the Alps early in 1801; he crossed the Black Forest on his way to Bordeaux; he had seen the Danube frequently when visiting his sister, also at Regensburg with Sinclair in 1802; he knew Lake Constance, and the towns on its shores,[9] from his journeys to and from Hauptwyl; he had good friends in Stuttgart and was often there (e.g. June-July, 1802) and would know the particular attractiveness, the view, of the 'Weinstaig' (line 29) that leads out of the town southwards to Degerloch; he studied in

Tübingen and walked with his friends along the Spitzberg (doubtless visiting the ruins on the Oedenburg, where the ridge juts out to the south overlooking the course of the old Roman road (line 36)); and with Magenau, in sentimental mood, he roamed along Thill's valley. It happens that these specific and highly personal references are still within the limits of the coherent poetic world (and are, moreover, raised by the act of poetic celebration to more general status). Those in 'Andenken' are outside the limits of that world, and it ceases to matter as the coherent world disintegrates.

The whole poem, for all its personalness, is an act of definition and celebration on behalf of Hesperia, against 'den *orbis* der Alten'.

It was becoming more and more important for Hölderlin to make sense of his own age, of the whole era since the decline of Greece:

> Seit nemlich böser Geist sich
> Bemächtiget des glüklichen Altertums . . .
>
> ('Der Einzige', lines 69-70, ii,159)

He was inclined to call the modern era simply an age of darkness—'gesangsfeind, klanglos' (ibid., line 71)—and put all his hope in the future. But increasingly he felt it his responsibility to evaluate the Christian age and interpret it positively:

> Begreiffen müssen
> Diß wir zuvor. Wie Morgenluft sind nemlich die Nahmen
> Seit Christus. Werden Träume. Fallen, wie Irrtum
> Auf das Herz und tödtend, wenn nicht einer
>
> Erwäget, was sie sind und begreift.
>
> ('Patmos', lines 162-66, ii,182)

It was his responsibility to 'erwägen' and 'begreifen'. This necessarily extended his interests, and so the limits of his poetic world. 'Der Einzige' (2. Fassung, lines 76-80), 'Patmos' (Bruchstücke der späteren Fassung, lines 158-61) and Fragments 46, 47, and 48 all begin to evaluate the period since Christ, especially the Middle Ages, the pilgrims, the crusaders, the deeds of the Emperors. This interest naturally causes new places to be introduced into the poetic world: Jerusalem, Canossa. It alters the significance of others already well established, like the Alps and particularly, in '. . . der Vatikan', the Gotthard pass.

But it is clear, in 'Patmos' and 'Der Einzige' for example, how unalterably this Hesperian world is related to Greece. Both poems still strive towards the synthesis: 'Der Einzige' towards the trefoil Christ, Dionysus, Heracles. In 'Patmos' further links associate the Hesperian god Christ with the antique world: Cos is included in the later versions as a counterpart to Patmos, Peleus as a counterpart to John. The pentecostal thunder is compared to the sowing of the dragon's teeth at Thebes.

Hölderlin's attempts to define the Hesperian *orbis* inevitably involved him in attempts to understand the role and significance of the Hesperian god Christ. 'Der

Einzige' and 'Patmos' in their several versions are the evidence of his final failure to clarify his own relationship with Christ. This failure is outside the scope of my thesis—what concerns me here is how the preoccupation with Christ affected the composition of Hölderlin's poetic world.

The later versions of 'Patmos' become more and more interested in the person of Christ himself, in the details of his life and ministry; and then in the events following his death, in the consequences throughout the following age of darkness. And typically, to sum up this overwhelming mass of new material, place-names and proper names are freely used:

> Vom Jordan fern and Nazareth
> Und fern vom See, an Capernaum, wo sie ihn
> Gesucht und Galiläa die Lüfte, und von Cana.
> ('Patmos', lines 136-38, ii,185)

The device is a useful one, and in these later poems Hölderlin became increasingly dependent on it. Place-names say a good deal, concisely and often powerfully. Hölderlin always knew this, but made judicious, never extravagent use of them. He fell back on them now when there was more than ever to say—all Christian history had to be dealt with—and when his linguistic powers were beginning to fail him. Hölderlin's poetic world expanded at a time when his intelligence was becoming less and less able to control it. He was grateful for place-names and proper-names, as fixed points with which a start could be made, at least. They were concrete instances, relatively easy to grasp. The many late additions of place-names in other poems—e.g. 'Die Wanderung', 'Brod und Wein'—were intended to serve the same purpose: clarification, the establishing of reliable instances. (Definite memories of places, the remembering or composing of simple landscapes have the same function. This will be discussed in the following chapter.)

Clearly, the near perfect unity of the finished version of 'Patmos' is destroyed by the emphasis on the places of Christ's life, and by the referring to other later events and outside places: the crusades to Jerusalem and the penitential journey to Canossa. The poem disintegrates into little more than an overwhelming list of poetic jobs to be done. It is as far from final poetic form as are the Fragments 47 and 48:

> Johannes. Christus. Diesen, ein
> Lastträger möcht ich singen . . .
> ('Patmos', Ansätze zur letzten Fassung, ll.151-52, ii,186)

Together with Heracles, Cos, and Peleus. And more besides:

> Und auch möcht
> Ich die Fahrt der Edelleute nach
> Jerusalem, und wie Schwanen der Schiffe Gang und das
> Leiden irrend in Canossa, brennendheiß
> Und den Heinrich singen.   (ibid., lines 158-61)

And in this way, as he realizes the vast amount to be done, Hölderlin's coherent world is broken apart. He saw that the near-perfection of the early 'Patmos' was no longer permissible, and, totally honest as he was, he set about dissolving that world in an incoherent mass of possibilities.

'An die Madonna'

The mother of Christ receives Hölderlin's attention too, although as a Protestant he was a stranger to her cult. 'An die Madonna', in Pindaric style, recounts and interprets her myth; she takes her place in Hölderlin's mythology as the Hesperian goddess of patient love. Her love endures throughout the age of darkness that began at the death of her son. Though different in nature she is the equal of any Greek deity: this Hölderlin indicates again and again in the poem by deliberately relating her and her Hesperian sphere to the antique world.

Moving from a direct celebration of the Madonna herself to a more general consideration of the Hesperian predicament Hölderlin remembers and interprets places he visited with Susette Gontard and Heinse in the summer of 1796 (lines 108-15). The interpretation has already been discussed in an earlier chapter;[10] the important thing here is to note that in this poem, as in 'Ihr sichergebaueten Alpen . . .', the places are not being remembered in an act of private gratitude and tribute, not for the many personal associations they hold, but for the general cultural significance that can be imposed on them. Personal sympathies will have led Hölderlin to name them initially, but then at once they are enhanced, in the terms of the well-established coherent mythical world. Frankfurt is similarly enhanced in 'Vom Abgrund nemlich . . .' (lines 13-16). These places are being used in the service of a fixed idea—sometimes obscurely and not always very convincingly at this late stage of Hölderlin's creative life, but the imaginative process is the same as that which composed a coherent world of disparate places in 1801. The one theme of 1801 is being developed—there is more concern than ever for Hesperia—and the technique, the naming and interpretation of places, has not altered.

All these interests—the Madonna, Christ, European history since his death—can be seen as aspects of the new emphasis in the late poems, as attempts at the definition of Hesperia. They derive directly from the interests that composed the poetic world of 1801. (It can be seen in 'Der Einzige' and 'Patmos' how they *grow out of* poems that almost perfectly express that coherent world.) This development was inevitable, largely because of Hölderlin's absolute honesty, and it takes place for the most part within the old boundaries of his poetic world. New places are introduced, for example, Cana, Westphalia, but in the poems discussed so far no completely new horizons have been opened up.

It is under the influence of Bordeaux and the sight of the Atlantic that the old world of Hölderlin's poetry truly expands. The voyages of discovery are an even more 'expanding' theme than the crusades or the deeds of the German emperors.

Even this theme is not entirely new. Hölderlin's fondness for imagery of sea-travel has already been noted, [11] and 'Der Wanderer' (1797) is proof that early in life he was inspired by the accounts of the great voyages to the South Seas. But then in 'Der Wanderer' he omitted from final versions of the poem precisely those lines which testified to his enthusiasm, because, as I suggested, South Sea islands had no place in the simple mythical world the poem was creating. For the sake of coherence he left out Tinian and Tahiti, and during the next six years there is no hint of such places in his finished poetry. Yet it need not be assumed that his interest had vanished; occasional notes among his manuscripts indicate that it had not. There was simply no justification for the inclusion of far-away islands in the world of 1801.

How, then, in the following years did he come to write 'Andenken' and 'Kolomb' and why did he entitle a poem concerned with the usual one theme 'Tinian'?

The inspiration was almost certainly the personal experience of an Atlantic port. Hölderlin had looked forward to his first sight of the sea, exotically distant from his Swabian homeland: 'Ich werde den Kopf ziemlich beisammen halten müssen, in Frankreich . . . auf den Anblik des Meeres . . . freue ich mich auch' (vi,427). For once his reading was complemented with real experience. Doubtless his old interest revived, and memories of the accounts he had already read. Later he must have read more, as the poem 'Kolomb' shows.

He could justify the inclusion of the new theme—the sea-voyages—(if at this late stage he felt its inclusion had to be justified), as being, like the interest in the Middle Ages, a further definition of the Hesperian *orbis*. It is in the notes for 'Kolomb' that that important phrase occurs. The new theme, then, is only the extension of older ones, but its expression involves an immeasurable expansion of his world. It may also be assumed that Hölderlin no longer saw any point in resisting the attraction of this exotic subject. His poetry gains a great deal in the last two or three years of his creative life, when his ideas were no longer so rigid. He wrote much after 1802 of a greater richness and variety than anything in the earlier, more finished work.

'Andenken'

'Andenken', written in the spring of 1803, must be discussed from two angles: as a private act of memory, and as another attempt to define the Hesperian age. The second aspect is relevant here.

The voyage to India, that 'the friends' have undertaken, is a Hesperian myth, remembered at the sight of the Atlantic; a Hesperian equivalent of the Greeks' voyage beyond the Pillars of Hercules. It helps in defining the Hesperian age if this myth, one of the age's most important, can be interpreted and understood. The last two strophes of the poem are an attempt at interpretation.

There are two possibilities: the sea-voyage, years of deprivation, warfare and hardship,[12] or the inland journey to the source. But of this latter course Hölderlin says:

> Mancher
> Trägt Scheue, an die Quelle zu gehn . . .
>
> (lines 38-39, ii,189)

He does not say that it is impossible, merely that some are reluctant to attempt it, preferring the obvious difficulties of the voyage. This is the typical course, already discussed in an earlier chapter: a period of trial and wandering abroad must be gone through before the ideal mythical homeland can be settled in.

India is not simply a distant, exotic goal, a farthest point, from which the sailors will return the way they went when the period of wandering is over. India, in Hölderlin's mythology; is itself the source.[13] Bellarmin and his companion, sailing downstream, away from the source, to the confluence of the Dordogne and the Garonne, to the estuary and into the Atlantic, they also, sailing westwards, have the source as their ultimate goal. Their course seems to be an alternative: the sea-route west, rather than the land-route east.

Obviously all this has very little in common with the historical facts. Only in Hölderlin's mythology can European mariners setting out for India be thought of as returning to the source. It is a personal reading of history, and, in the terms of a private mythology, a fully convincing one.

Alternative ways of living are being suggested, alternative ways of getting through the difficult interim period until the dawning of that ideal age in which life will be lived in the peace and harmony of an ideal homeland, itself close to the source. And one is the way of action, perhaps Sinclair's way (if, as in the variants of 'An Eduard', Bellarmin is Sinclair); and the other is the poet's way, Hölderlin's own, the way of patience and introspection.

The general Hesperian predicament is considered in personal terms: what are the ways of life open to Hölderlin and his friends? How are the times to be lived through: in action, to bring about the ideal age? or in patient waiting, reflection and faith? Increasingly Hölderlin preferred the latter course. His poetry becomes less and less a confident annunciation of a future age, more and more an anxious evaluation of the Hesperian one, and finally an attempt simply to hold out, hoping that better times will come.

'Tinian'

Voyages of discovery are considered again in the unfinished poem 'Tinian'. There are three stages of Hölderlin's interest in this island (excluding tne early reference in 'Der Wanderer', 1797), not necessarily the three stages of work on one and the same poem.

On a folded sheet of paper containing the beginnings of 'Der Archipelagus' Hölderlin noted the one word 'Tinian', as the title or nucleus of a poem to be written. This note (H^1, ii,873) was probably made before 1800.

Next are a few words on page 52^r of the *Stuttgarter Foliobuch*:

	Tinian. Der Schiffer.
Der Sturm am Vorgebirge.	Dort
	der Palme Frucht.
Tinian.	(H^2, ii,873)

Over these, obliterating them, Hölderlin wrote the poem 'Thränen', probably in 1802. The note before 1800 ('Tinian') and these jottings before 1802 show that Hölderlin's interest in the voyages of discovery had not entirely lapsed since his work on 'Der Wanderer' in 1797. But he did not complete a poem on the subject because in 1800 to 1801 his ideas clarified and simplified, a definite poetic world was created to contain and express them, and irrelevant topics and places were not admitted. Other interesting possibilities, sketched out on the same sheet as 'Tinian' (H^2)—for example Fragment 19, 'An meine Schwester'—were not followed up, probably for the same reason.

The poem 'Tinian' finally got under way rather later. It is not possible to say exactly when (H^3 is a single, separate sheet having nothing on it but 'Tinian') but in style it belongs with poems of 1803 and beyond. Certainly after the return from Bordeaux—it will have been the sight of the sea and perhaps the subsequent reading or re-reading about Anson's voyage that caused Hölderlin to work on a poem of which the sea-voyage was to be an important part.

Tinian is a small island in the Pacific, one of the Mariana group, where Anson and his fleet sheltered in 1742. In eighteenth-century literature it was often used simply as an exotic place-name. For example, by Wieland: 'ein Sitz der Frühlingsgötter, ein Zaubergrund, ein wahres Tinian'.[14] Hölderlin stopped using place-names in this way about 1797 when working on 'Der Wanderer'. Tinian, like India in 'Andenken', is a place in Hesperian mythology, and the poem, by making use of it, shows what significance the South Sea voyages had in Hölderlin's Hesperian terms.

The poem is unfinished; there are gaps that make understanding it difficult, and the language of completed parts is sometimes obscure. Nor can Beißner's text be thought of as definitive; he has compiled it after his understanding of Hölderlin's intentions.

Tinian, the island, is where the poem starts. It could be expected that, as in 'Der Rhein' or 'Patmos', the place would initiate the theme, and then, having been interpreted, be left behind. But it seems, at first, that precisely this introductory consideration of the place itself is lacking. Hölderlin wrote:

Süß ists, zu irren
In heiliger Wildniß . . .

(lines 1-2, ii,240)

The wilderness is both the island Tinian itself and the voyage there: a far-away place come upon in the course of those wanderings abroad that characterize the Hesperian age. ('Wilderness' and 'wanderings' are very similar—in the period of wilderness the paths are overgrown and travellers lose their way.) But then when Hölderlin should further consider the island, 'die heilige Wildniß', and what the journey there means, he wrote only dashes, between what Beißner prints as lines 2 and 4, lines normally spaced in the MS, to indicate that more had to be written to lead into the next phase of the poem. Were these necessary lines never composed? I would suggest that lines 22-37 in Beißner's text should be inserted where the dashes are, between lines 2 and 4. These lines are all overleaf on the MS page (Marbach 2163v) in two blocks (23-28, 29-37) and where they belong and in what order is by no means certain. Hellingrath and Beißner disagree. If my reorganization be accepted the poem would open thus:

Süß ists zu irren
In heiliger Wildniß
Und lustzuwandeln, zeitlos . . .

That would be an opening like 'Nah ist/ Und schwer zu fassen der Gott'—a paradoxical composition, an honest reflection of faith and doubt. 'Süß' and 'irren', 'heilig' and 'Wildniß' are precariously balanced; and that tension is there in the third line too, for in Hölderlin's thinking it is not a good thing to be 'zeitlos' and the word qualifies the pleasurable and leisurely connotations of 'lustzuwandeln.' (Compare 'An die Madonna', line 100: also a wandering in a god-ordained wilderness.)

The argument of the poem would then be as follows: It is sweet (and right) for us to wander abroad. That is our proper fate. The Greeks had their chariot-races, the Romans their circuses, but our hallmark (our birthmark and distinction), what we need as a necessary spur and what we have as our destiny, is wandering. (Compare Hellingrath, iv,398; GStA, ii,876, ll.4-8 and ii,855, ll.7-16.) Then lines 29-37 depict the luxuriant flora on the South Sea island of Tinian,[15] and so, metaphorically, the confusion of the interim age. Lines 32-33:

nicht ist
Es ziemend, diese zu pflüken . . .

may be compared with lines 96-98 of 'An die Madonna':

Vor allem, daß man schone
Der Wildniß göttlichgebaut
Im reinen Geseze . . .

Since the wilderness is God's work it is unseemly to react against it.

The Hesperian significance of Tinian is revealed: the island is an illustration of the wilderness and journeying typical of the age. The next phase of the poem is the return home, illustrated in an image Hölderlin was fond of—migratory birds returning:

> Des Frühlings, wenn im warmen Grunde
> Des Haines wiederkehrend fremde Fittige . . .
>
> (lines 10-11)

Being home, to drink from the home-country's rivers, just as Romulus and Remus, abandoned in the wilderness, drank from their foster-mother the wolf. The wanderer, coming back to his homeland after the necessary time abroad, will be almost a stranger there, a foster-child in his own mother-land. It may be difficult for him to come into his own again: 'das eigene muß so gut gelernt seyn, wie das Fremde' (vi,426).

The homeland is then epitomized in one simple picture: bees and butterflies on willow-branches in flower.

The poem has moved from abroad (Tinian) to the simplest home landscape, and for the rest of its course begins further to define the Hesperian area.

The Alps are the dividing line between Hesperia and the old Greek world: 'Von Gott getheilet . . . Der Welttheil . . .' (lines 18-19). This was their significance in 'Germanien'. They are moreover a stronghold: 'zwar sie stehen/ Gewapnet . . .' (lines 20-21). A stronghold of the gods as in 'Der Rhein' and 'Wenn aber die Himmlischen . . .'? Or rather the protective frontier of Hesperia? Their significance is ambiguous. In these later poems, including 'Mnemosyne', the Alps are interpreted otherwise than in 'Der Rhein'. They are more of a barrier to be crossed only with great difficulty, over a high pass ('Mnemosyne') or they themselves are the wilderness ('Das Nächste Beste', line 54, ii,238) set against the Hesperian renaissance. The mythical world in which they are so important is losing its coherence, and they are liable to be interpreted again and differently. In other poems—'. . . der Vatikan . . .', 'Griechenland', Fragment 48—they have simply the historical significance they have had since the Middle Ages.

'Tinian' is a definition of the Hesperian age. The island is interpreted to illustrate an idea. This idea is familiar from the coherent world of 1801—wilderness, journeying, and return home—but now in the later poetry Hölderlin takes his illustrative example, the island, from outside the old boundaries of that world. He allows himself more variety of expression, his world gets wider and richer, but too late for him to control it.

Kolomb

Hölderlin worked at a poem on Columbus as early as 1789 (ii,315 and 928). Like 'Andenken' and 'Tinian' the later poem will have been inspired by the months in Bordeaux. The purpose of 'Kolomb' is made clear in Hölderlin's marginal note on the manuscript. He wrote out a first version of the poem, leaving large gaps; Beißner prints this as the text (ii,242-245). Later Hölderlin wrote Fragment 48 in the right-hand margin of the first page. This fragment is a list of great historical characters, all, loosely, Hesperian except Demetrius Poliorcetes, King of Macedonia (337-283 B.C.), who is named immediately after the lines:

> Wir bringen aber die Zeiten
> untereinander
>
> (lines 4-5, ii,329)

as though to illustrate that intention. Greek and Hesperian heroes were to be deliberately confused and related.

Below this fragment in the right-hand margin Hölderlin later noted: 'Flibustiers, Entdeckungsreisen/als Versuche den hesperischen/*orbis*, im Gegensaze gegen den/*orbis* der Alten zu bestimmen' (ii,876). This seems unconnected with Fragment 48; most probably it is a note on the poem 'Kolomb'.

Later still Hölderlin began the expansion of the poem's first draft. Line 15, for example, 'Anson und Gama . . .' is expanded so:

> . . . und Flibustier, und Äneas
> Und Doria, Jason, Chirons
> Schüler, in Megaras Felsenhöhlen und
> Im zitternden Reegen der Grotte bildete sich
> Als auf dem wohlgestimmten Saitenspiel ein Menschenbild
> Aus Eindrüken des Walds, und die Tempelherren die gefahren
> Nach Jerusalem Bouillon, Rinaldo,
> Bougainville . . .
>
> (lines 15-21a, ii,877-878)

The list illustrates the note previously made in the margin, actually obliterating a part of it, and carries out the intention of Fragment 48 (lines 4-5) in confusing the Greek and the Hesperian ages.[16]

The course of the poem is roughly as follows:
Lines 2-10, ii,242 and 877

Great praise is due to the heroes of the sea. Expanding the opening lines Hölderlin defines the value of journeying. This would be an important section, but only one or two phrases stand out recognizably from the obscurity:

> Thätigkeit zu gewinnen . . .
> . . . und Ordnung, durchaus bündig
> Heimische Wohnung kurzgefaßt
> zu lernen . . .
> . . . hohe Bildung, nemlich für das Leben

This sounds like the familiar theme: the journey abroad as necessary preliminary to the return home, experience abroad being necessary before the homeland can be appreciated. The desert seems suggested in lines 7-8 ('dürre Schönheit/In den Sand') and the ocean in line 10 (in the detail of the telescope). Those fragments make sense, but removing them out of their more difficult context is a dubious exercise.

Lines 14-26, ii,242 and 877-78

Examples of sea-heroes, classical and Hesperian. As in the later versions of 'Patmos' and 'Der Einzige' Hölderlin presents himself with an overwhelming list of subjects, all clamouring for attention. There is a baroque excessiveness in these later poems—but it is less a matter of style than of the poet's realizing how impossibly much he has to do. There are many sea-heroes, they are all great men, and it is the poet's responsibility to pay them their due.

Lines 27-32, ii,242-43

But Columbus is to be the subject of this poem. Visionary journey in Pindaric style to his birthplace in Genoa.

The central part of the poem is an account of Columbus's life. The details seem to have been taken from a French biography. First his youth in Genoa. He is inspired by pictures of foreign lands (lines 34e-34g, ii,878), by stories or ballads of great men and travel (lines 34h-34i), and by the study of maps (lines 51-52). It was his vocation to expand the old world: 'Das Erdreich, griechisch, kindlich gestaltet' (line 65r) beyond the simple, comprehensible form in which the Greeks had known it.

The voyage is described, particularly Columbus's difficulties with his mutinous crew (lines 60-65u, ii,878-79), but here the details are too specific to be understood by a reader ignorant of which biography Hölderlin was drawing on. But lines 66-73 (ii,244) are clear enough: the sea-god intervenes on Columbus's behalf. Hölderlin's Hesperian hero gets the kind of assistance that Greek heroes often had from the gods, Ulysses from Athene, for example.

In its next phase (lines 117-25, ii,244) the poem would have dealt with Columbus's discoveries. His was an age of discovery, and many maritime powers, like Genoa (line 125) but particularly Portugal (line 123) and Spain, by whom Columbus's expedition was financed, were busy acquiring territories overseas. Perhaps Hölderlin is saying, with a curious innocence, that there were enough islands for all comers. Possibly he had in mind the Papal Bulls of 1493 which divided up the Atlantic between Spain and Portugal. Genoa, not itself at that time a major power outside the Mediterranean, might be thought of as being represented in the person of Columbus himself.

In conclusion (lines 127-55, ii,244-45) the poem moves from the particular hero Columbus to a general consideration of the hero type in the whole hierarchy of gods and men.

The obscurity of 'Kolomb' is largely due not to its being unfinished but to the particularness, the privateness of the references and details. In his use of place-names the confusion of the general and obvious with the private and obscure is very striking. Lisbon and Genoa, for example, are clear in their associations: Columbus was born in Genoa (probably); Portugal was Spain's great maritime rival (Columbus served the Portuguese Crown in 1481-82, and only went to Spain after patronage had been refused him in Lisbon). Hölderlin names, and so celebrates these places, as Pindar names Syracuse or Agrigento, before an audience to whom their associations are clear. Similarly Jerusalem (line 21, ii,878). Line 34a (ii,878) is more difficult: 'Vorm Kornhaus sizend, von Sicilien her . . .'. In the fifteenth century, as in classical times, Sicily supplied grain to the Mediterranean cities. The young Columbus, watching the grain ships unload at Genoa, was inspired to make voyages of his own. The associations of the place-name Sicily are of a general kind and Hölderlin expected his readers to appreciate them.

But the opening lines of the poem are expanded in a strangely private fashion:

Wünscht' ich der Helden einer zu seyn
                    des Schäfers, oder eines Hessen, (dessen eingeborner Sprach
Und dürfte frei mit der Stimme es bekennen
So wär' es ein Seeheld.

(lines 1-3, ii,242 and 877)

Why 'eines Hessen'? In 'Das Nächste Beste' the starlings' unlikely route from south-western France is over 'der Katten Land' (line 40, ii,235), which is Hesse. Hölderlin travelled through Hesse in 1796 with Heinse and Susette Gontard, and several times in late poems, written after her death, he refers to places they lived in or visited together. Perhaps most important though, Hölderlin's close friend Sinclair was from Hesse. 'Mit der Stimme . . . eines Hessen' probably means no more than 'honestly', 'forthrightly', honesty and forthrightness in speech and action being Sinclair's characteristic qualities. It may be that Hesse's chief hero, Hermann, should be remembered, as an embodiment of the same virtues (cf. vii,2, 78). Shepherds, too, as Hölderlin conceived of them (Swiss ones, for example), would be expected to speak their minds boldly and plainly.

But whatever it means the reference is in itself a small indication of Hölderlin's increasing unsureness of touch. The imaginative process is the same as it always was: a place is simply made to stand for an abstract quality, just as Arcadia stood for innocence and Lesbos for poetic inspiration in the very early poetry. But the chosen place is not so widely recognized as holding the associations that the poet wants to evoke. Hölderlin's choice is governed by entirely personal loyalties; in his world the place clearly does mean something definite, and in his poem he makes no concessions to the reader's ignorance. That indicates a loss of poetic tact.

The main theme of 'Kolomb', like that of 'Andenken' and 'Tinian', can still be seen as a development of themes that formed the coherent world of 1801; and the new places that these poems add—Lisbon, India, the South Seas—can be seen as reasonable, consequential extensions of the old world's frontiers. In that respect it can be said that the world of 1801 has not disintegrated, but expanded. The expansion, however, is not under control; the poems thus expanding the world of

1801 are for the most part unfinished. They widen the world by revealing new possibilities, but do not establish a new form and new boundaries. The old world loses its coherence and shape.

A second trend in the poetry of 1803 to 1806 works more obviously against the whole idea of a coherent poetic world, and that is the remembering of places for their own sakes, or the naming of places with so private an involvement in them that when they should, in the poem, have a general significance accessible to the reader, their effect is only enigmatic or baffling. 'Kolomb' has already provided a small example of this latter aspect, but the whole trend can now be discussed in detail under the heading:

The private and obscure celebration of places
Bordeaux was the impulse to write such poetry. The experience was so intense that in poems afterwards purely personal memories had to be admitted. Beginning with 'Andenken':

> Der Nordost wehet,
> Der liebste unter den Winden
> Mir, weil er feurigen Geist
> Und gute Fahrt verheißet den Schiffern.
> Geh aber nun und grüße
> Die schöne Garonne,
> Und die Gärten von Bourdeaux
> Dort, wo am scharfen Ufer
> Hingehet der Steg und in den Strom
> Tief fällt der Bach, darüber aber
> Hinschauet ein edel Paar
> Von Eichen und Silberpappeln . . .

(lines 1-12, ii,188)

This is a personal tribute to place, quite private; the poet simply remembers places important to him. And a device often used by Hölderlin to link the east and west of his coherent poetic world is here used for purely private ends. He finds a means of transmitting his imagination through space and time. In 'Die Wanderung' the swallows' migratory route associates Swabia with Asia Minor; here the north-east wind, blowing to the south-west, links Swabia, where Hölderlin is, with Bordeaux and the Atlantic coast, where he was.

This personal tribute to place, common in other poets, is new in Hölderlin's work. Formerly he could not allow it. Only when a place having private significance could be enhanced to general significance in the context of the coherent world would he permit himself to celebrate it. Now personal memories have their own rights. The poplars and oaks overhanging the stream are a preview of that clinging to personally experienced visible things that characterizes the last poems Hölderlin wrote.[17]

'Andenken' is a finished poem. It achieves a harmony between the personal memories (mostly in the first two strophes) and the more general Hesperian theme already discussed. It is in no way a poem of Hölderlin's madness, nor is it obscure (it is difficult), but in allowing such a personal due to place to be paid it makes possible the obscure privacy and arbitrariness of references to places in later poems.

The French places are not forgotten. In 'Das Nächste Beste' an attempt is made to give them more general significance by putting them into the context of an established Hölderlin theme. The starlings' return from their wintering places in south-western France to their homeland in Germany is used as an image or indication of the imminent coming of the Hesperian gods. That is the old process: the raising of the personal to a general significance. In the same poem the hills around Regensburg, that Hölderlin saw in the autumn of 1802, are similarly enhanced. The process is the same, but the initial choice was too personal and particular, or simply not apposite. Hölderlin cannot make the hills convincing, not to his audience, at least. To himself the meaning of the hills was obvious. There never was a time when his ideas were as evident to his audience as they were to himself, he never enjoyed the sympathy that Pindar or Homer had; but in his best poetry he was able to find clear, generally comprehensible correlatives of those ideas, so that his audience could, if they chose, understand and be persuaded. But in the late poems he completely loses touch; he loses all sense of what will serve as a convincing correlative. The poem ' . . . der Vatikan . . . ' shows Hölderlin withdrawing further into his own private world.[18]

'. . . der Vatikan . . .'
The theme of ' . . . der Vatikan . . . ' (ii,252-53) is a familiar one: how shall the difficult interim age be lived through? The theme emerges, just enough to be recognizable, out of the poem's obscurity. The present is a time of confusion and error: 'gehet izt viel Irrsaal' (line 7), of impious questions (lines 7-8). The poet's responsibility is, as always:

> Gott rein und mit Unterscheidung
> Bewahren . . .
>
> (lines 12-13)

The poet keeps his faith in God, keeps the image of him clear, and steadfastly announces his coming, as John announced the coming of Christ. In these times of confusion, of 'Sprachverwirrung' (line 36), spokesmen, men of faith, are needed to maintain sense and hope: 'Die erhalten den Sinn' (line 35). The poem concludes with the familiar vision of harmony and peace:

> Dann kommt das Brautlied des Himmels.
> Vollendruhe. Goldroth.
>
> (lines 44-45)

That is the outline; the details are often obscure, but it is interesting, having recognized the theme, to see how Hölderlin chooses to illustrate it at this late stage of his creative life.

He juxtaposes private memories and references of general, historical significance: thus Julius Caesar, 'welcher Calender gemachet' (lines 9-10) rubs shoulders with Hölderlin's friend and mentor Heinse; and Rome, about which Heinse wrote extensively in his *Ardinghello*, is associated with Westphalia. Heinse is one of the few who remain clear-sighted and full of faith during the interim age of darkness and exclusion from God. It was in recognition of this that Hölderlin addressed 'Brod und Wein' to him. The clear statement of responsibility (lines 12-13) could equally well be his or Hölderlin's. He appears quite appropriately in the company of Julius Caesar and John the Baptist—both, in Hölderlin's mythology, figures who foretell the end of the old classical age of light, and the onset of the Hesperian darkness, in which Hölderlin and Heinse now find themselves. Heinse's book is at the back of this poem. Hölderlin remembers the places already associated with the hero Ardinghello. Here, as in 'Griechenland', Hölderlin celebrates the Gotthard for its true European-historical significance (rather than for its mythical significance in a poetic world of his own creation). He refers to the old pilgrimage route: 'Über Tyrol, Lombarda, Loretto . . .' (line 24) and to the Capucine hostelry that served the pilgrims:

> . . . wo des Pilgrims Heimath
> auf dem Gotthard, gezäunt, nachlässig, unter Gletschern
> Karg wohnt jener . . .
>
> (lines 24-26)

('Jener' is possibly the pilgrim; or it may refer to the Gotthard itself, where the hostelry was—'wohnt' is then a Graecism, one that Hölderlin was particularly fond of.)

Remembering these places, perhaps through *Ardinghello*, Hölderlin is in fact doing what he proposed in the later versions of 'Patmos' and 'Der Einzige', namely attempting to understand the times since Christ.

There follows a curious list of birds. First, in the Alps, the eider-duck and the eagle. The eider really belongs in Arctic or sub-Arctic conditions and not in the Alps, but perhaps the glaciers of the Gotthard seemed a suitable habitat. These two birds, and the two following, the crane and the owl, all have the same significance—they are reminders of divinity, of the ideal. The eider and the eagle in the Alps are close to God—'vor Gott, wo das Feuer läuft der Menschen wegen' (line 28), close to the sources of elemental life. Hölderlin allows the idea—that in the age of darkness the faithful remember the age of light—to assume another form: 'Des Wächters Horn tönt aber über den Garden . . .' (line 29). The significance is obvious—the watchman, awake and faithful to the ideal, during the age of darkness[19]—but where is he? Still in the Alps? The idea overrides; the context is lost.

Then, perhaps only by thinking of significant birds, Hölderlin shifts to Greece:

> Der Kranich hält die Gestalt aufrecht
> Die Majestätische, keusche, drüben
> In Patmos, Morea, in der Pestluft.
> Türkisch.

(lines 30-33)

This is fairly familiar ground. The solitary crane, among ruins ('Griechenland', line 44, i,180), or left behind by its brother cranes (*Hyperion*, iii,16), is a favourite image. The bird is a reminder of better times; here it holds itself upright, is majestic and chaste in a time of servitude. The passage is curiously full of familiar and typical details:

'Drüben'—cf. 'Drüben sind der Trümmer genug im Griechenland. . .' (ii,645), a very late addition to 'Der Archipelagus'.

'Patmos'—cf. Hölderlin's own poem. He would scarcely have chosen such an un-Greek island to stand for Asia Minor had he not spent years on a poem of that name.

'Morea'—is the medieval name for the Peloponnese, used frequently by Chandler, and by Hölderlin in 'Der Rhein' (line 15) and *Hyperion* (iii, 171). Like 'Patmos' it is an echo within the world of his own work.

The phrase 'in der Pestluft' may be taken literally. It would then be the only mention in Hölderlin of what Chandler repeatedly referred to in both volumes of his work: the plague. Leaving the mainland of Greece, at the end of his travels, Chandler spoke of 'the badness of the air, which was now almost pestilential on this side of the Morea'.[20] In Zakynthos he and his party were quarantined for fourteen days before being allowed to sail home. Typically, Hölderlin makes no mention of plagues in his ideal world of 1801. Once that world disintegrated a mass of hitherto unusable material overwhelmed him. 'In der Pestluft' is then secondly an image of the Turkish occupation: 'Türkisch' (line 33). This, too, a matter of historical fact, is a theme that was not admitted in the coherent poetic world of 1801. Together with other details of the passage—cranes, plague, Morea—it relates back to the years of Chandler, of *Hyperion*, 'Der Main', and 'Der Nekar'. The details are memories within Hölderlin's own world.

After the crane comes the owl (line 33), a bird with a similar symbolic significance. In 'Gesang des Deutschen' the rough draft:

> und auf den
> Säulen ein einsamer Kranich trauert . . .

(ii, 387)

becomes:

> und scheu der
> Vogel der Nacht auf der Säule trauert.

(lines 31-32, ii,4)

The crane becomes an owl. There are several biblical passages in which an owl is the spirit of desolation and destruction: Isaiah 13, 21 and Psalm 102, 6 for example. Hölderlin's line, 'die Eule, wohlbekannt der Schriften', seems biblical rather than Greek (which the crane is).

In all these cases: in the loneliness of the Gotthard, in Turkish-occupied, plague-ridden Greece and in the destroyed cities the birds are reminders of better times: 'Aber/Die erhalten den Sinn'.

Familiar themes emerge from the obscurity, and often it is place-names, Hölderlin's easiest means of saying things, that give the clues.

It is obvious how enclosed his world has become. His main concern is still a general cultural one, but it is the private world of his own life, of his own reading and work, that he draws on for the illustrative details of his theme.

'Griechenland' (ii,254-58)

In this poem, too, familiar themes are discernible. It helps to know the manuscripts. One version (Beißner's H^1, pp.254-55) was written on both sides of a single sheet of paper; another (H^{2a}, p.256) on one side of a double sheet, and what Beißner prints as the third version (H^{2b}, pp.257-58) are the alterations and expansions of this—between lines, in the margins and over the page. The third version complicates the second without adding much to the theme. Its last lines, 46-51, lead back to what Beißner prints as the first, and a more or less coherent argument can be discovered if H^1 is seen as the intended continuation of H^{2b}.

The theme of the second and third versions is roughly as follows. There are certain signs—bird-song, thunder—that after a long period of chaos divine order is about to return. Nature has survived all the upheaval: 'fest ist der Erde/Nabel' (H^{2b} lines 16-17). The elements have survived; God is present in them, appearing to human beings in forms they can bear to experience, obscure, beyond their intelligence. But present all the same, in nature.

It is always God's way, even in times of chaos, to restrain human beings, protecting them from themselves. It is their responsibility to live securely on earth.

At this point (line 45 of H^{2b}) connexion is made with H^1. The question is how to live on earth, how human beings are to live and preserve themselves. There are two choices, as there were in 'Andenken'. The first is to live in peace and restriction, content with a simple life in simple, earthly, day-to-day surroundings:

> Süß ists, dann unter hohen Schatten von Bäumen
> Und Hügeln zu wohnen, sonnig, wo der Weg ist
> Gepflastert zur Kirche.

$$(H^{2b}, \text{lines } 46\text{-}48; \text{cf. } H^1, \text{lines } 2\text{-}14)$$

This may be compared with a setting in 'Mnemosyne' (lines 18-24, ii,197). This maintaining of life in the simplest surroundings will be discussed in the next chapter. More relevant here, because of the places it involves, is the alternative way of life in the interim period, the journey:

> Reisenden aber, wem,
> Aus Lebensliebe, messend immerhin,
> Die Füße gehorchen, blühn
> Schöner die Wege, wo das Land . . .

(H^{2b}, lines 48-51)

This joins on to H^1 at line 16.

H^1 goes on to exemplify the poem's opening lines—'ihr Wege des Wanderers!'

> Avignon waldig über den Gotthardt
> Tastet das Roß . . .

(lines 17-18)

How are the places to be understood? There are two areas, possibly two separate journeys are implied. The first is a southern one, from Avignon over the Alps, and through Italy to Virgil's grave, on the road from Naples to Puteoli. Not a pilgrimage like the journey in '. . . der Vatikan . . .', nor a historical undertaking like 'Heinrichs Alpenübergang', but more of an amateur's trip to Italy, such as Hölderlin's contemporaries, Heinse for example, undertook. Virgil's grave was a site that literary travellers visited. Heinse describes it in his *Ardinghello*: 'Ein Lorbeer steigt in der Mitte stolz hervor . . .'.[21] The journey is really outside Hölderlin's sphere— outside his own experience, and not of historical-religious Hesperian significance (except in so far as sentimental journeys to Italy were typical of the times). Probably it derives from his reading, especially of *Ardinghello*, and from what Heinse himself had recounted of his Italian journey.

Each place is briefly characterized. Avignon (or perhaps the area before the climb up to the pass begins) is 'well-wooded' (line 17); moss-roses grow on the Alps (lines 21-22); laurels grow around Virgil's grave (lines 18-19). Only the laurels are really appropriate; neither woods nor moss-roses are distinctive features—they might be anywhere, they are not what the places are renowned for. Flowers, like the birds in '. . . der Vatikan . . .', make a curious leitmotiv. Three times the laburnum is mentioned (lines 6,11,14); the traveller's roads are said to blossom; the Alps have moss-roses and the grave laurels. And flowers are a motif in the second sphere or journey, growing along the roads, untended, like crystals in the ocean,[22] immediately outside the town. And as if to give an instance of this the next line reads: 'Gärten wachsen um Windsor' (line 26). And finally along the coast:

> Schöne Gärten sparen die Jahrzeit.
> Am Canal.

(lines 29-30)

It is as though the important thing were the flowers. Where might flowers be? On the Alps, around Windsor, along the English Channel. There is a sort of baroque insistence on and amplification of one idea.

I have no explanation of this last, mysterious area. England did not feature in Hölderlin's coherent world. Beißner suggests that the lines might refer to the wedding in May 1797 of Württemberg's Erbprinz Friedrich with the English Princess Charlotte. The ceremony was in London, the celebration in Windsor:

> Gärten wachsen um Windsor. Hoch
> Ziehet, aus London, '
> Der Wagen des Königs.
>
> (lines 26-28)

That may be so. Other memories surfacing in these late poems do belong to that important time in Hölderlin's life—memories of Heinse, Westphalia, Susette Gontard, Frankfurt, *Hyperion*. Or it may be simply that Hölderlin read an account of how the English royal family lived, how Windsor was their out-of-town residence.

An important theme in the poem—journeying as a way of living through the interim age—needed to be illustrated. To make up a typical journey Hölderlin chose places out of his own private world, and either could not see or did not care that what was self-evident to him would be a problem to his reader. The poem becomes inscrutable, and, in a way, suspect. The emphasis on flowers and gardens rather suggests that Hölderlin, instead of cogently developing and illustrating his argument, is allowing himself to be led from one loose association to the next.

But the poem ends with a memory that *can* be recognized, although its significance in the context is unclear:

> Tief aber liegt
> Das ebene Weltmeer, glühend.
>
> (lines 30-31)

Such lines are an indication of what was lost when Hölderlin went mad. After Bordeaux he was open to such impressions. Perhaps he had always been so sensitive, but it was only after Bordeaux, when the coherent world of 1801 began to disintegrate, that he allowed his poetry to be thus enriched.

It *is* an enriching, this disintegration of Hölderlin's world—even though, because of his failing intellect, it leads to incompleteness and obscurity. For not only are the old themes developed and illustrated with more variety than before, but also, most liberating of all, irrelevance is permitted. Not every line of every poem has to be part of the poet's one great theme. Unfortunately this freedom comes too late, and often its product is arbitrariness; Hölderlin's mind wanders among private associations and the reader is no longer helped in understanding them by the certainty that they are related, however obscurely, to one central, familiar theme. Rather it becomes impossible to tell. Are the following lines a new illustration of the old theme, only more obscure than would formerly have been permitted, or are they a quite private and irrelevant fantasy?

Die Aegypterin aber, offnen Busens sizt
Immer singend wegen Mühe gichtisch das Gelenk
Im Wald, am Feuer. Recht Gewissen bedeutend
Der Wolken und der Seen des Gestirns
Rauscht in Schottland wie an dem See
Lombardas dann ein Bach vorüber.

          ('Und mitzufühlen das Leben . . .', lines 10-15, ii,249)

CHAPTER 7

TÜBINGEN, 1806-43

In Hölderlin's poetry of 1800 to 1801 there are occasional moments of total
simplicity. They are moments when the poem's tension and questioning suddenly
ends, and its complexity is resolved:

> Und ausgeglichen
> Ist eine Weile das Schiksaal.
> Und die Flüchtlinge suchen die Heerberg,
> Und süßen Schlummer die Tapfern,
> Die Liebenden aber
> Sind, was sie waren, sie sind
> Zu Hauße, wo die Blume sich freuet
> Unschädlicher Gluth und die finsteren Bäume
> Der Geist umsäuselt . . .
>
> ('Der Rhein', lines 182-90, ii,147-48)

The simplicity is in earthly terms, in human needs and relationships, in the terms of
'die heutige Erde' (ibid., line 179).

> Und vor der Thüre des Haußes
> Sizt Mutter und Kind,
> Und schauet den Frieden . . .
>
> ('Friedensfeier', lines 123-25, iii,537)

Such simplicity is an interlude, the poem returns to its complexity, its
metaphysical questioning, and its awareness of chaos. And, typically, these
moments are never in the present. They are either the memory of an ideal past, of
the time with Susette Gontard, for example:

> Ruhig lächelten wir, fühlten den eigenen Gott
> Unter trautem Gespräch; in Einem Seelengesange,
> Ganz in Frieden mit uns kindlich und freudig allein.
>
> ('Menons Klagen um Diotima', lines 50-52, ii,76)[1]

Or they are an anticipation of the ideal future, as is the passage quoted from 'Der
Rhein', as is almost the whole poem 'Friedensfeier'. Probably in 'Friedensfeier',
after the Peace of Lunéville, Hölderlin was most confident of the imminence of the
ideal age in which all dissonances would be resolved; but even so the poem ends
with a reminder of chaos.

The moments of simplicity are the brief periods of respite that Hölderlin very occasionally allows himself: they are encouraging glimpses of the ideal, as achieved once before in the past and to be achieved again in the future. It is generally true of Hölderlin's mature poems that they are backward- or forward-looking. They oscillate, even within one poem, between the ideal past, Greece, and the ideal future, the new Hesperia. At the height of his powers it was this concern for the ideal future (based on the ideal past) that Hölderlin felt to be his prime responsibility. Before the journey to Bordeaux he believed in the *effectiveness* of his poetry; that he, as a poet, could not only announce but also help to bring about the coming of the ideal age, by interpreting events and by sustaining the faith of ordinary people. Because of this belief an attachment to the immediate present was not to be thought of. The present was not ideal; to be content with it would be the greatest irresponsibility and a betrayal of the hope for the future. There are no instances in the poems of 1800 to 1801 of Hölderlin's being content with the immediate present, with the real circumstances of his own life and his times.

But he lost faith in the religious effectiveness of his poetry. The conclusion of 'Patmos', as Gottschalk says,[2] is a confession of failure: the hymnic poet admits his hubris. He cannot deal directly with the gods, nor do anything to influence them; he sets himself a more modest goal in the interpretation of already established texts. It is interesting, and typical of his total honesty, that Hölderlin should doubt his poetic-prophetic powers at the conclusion of a poem which is certainly the most coherent and convincing expression of his mythic world that he ever achieved. Hölderlin's mythology was never better formulated than in the 'Widmungsfassung' of 'Patmos', yet immediately he doubted the validity of his myths, or, at least, the efficacy of expounding them. He felt he could not do much more about the future he believed in than hope it would come about. And it seems likely that in the years after Lunéville, as troubled and materialistic as those before the Peace, even his hope was less. What bolder affirmation could he make than 'Friedensfeier'? Surely then the discrepancy between the good faith of that poem and political reality seriously distressed him, determined optimist though he was.

The increasing interest in Hesperian history, discussed in the previous chapter, can perhaps be seen as a consequence of this 'Bescheidung des Dichters' (Gottschalk). Unable to precipitate the ideal future or even to talk confidently about it, Hölderlin could at least attempt to understand the more readily ascertainable facts of the past. He then saw it as his responsibility to interpret the legends, the scriptures, and the history of his own Hesperian world,[3] and it is significant that he undertook this at once in the later versions of 'Patmos' and 'Der Einzige'. It did not mean that all hopes of the ideal future had been abandoned, only that the poet's part in bringing it about had become a more modest one. Coming to a better understanding of his own cultural history he was preparing for a future ideal time which would, he hoped, finally dawn without any greater intervention by him.

It happened that this re-appraisal of the poet's role was undergone at a time when Hölderlin's poetic powers—his intellectual grasp and skill with words—were beginning to fail. Thus, not only did he feel himself less qualified to prophesy and announce, but also, simply, he became less able. It is true that among the late fragments there are attempts in the confident, prophetic style of 1801, and the great theme of all Hölderlin's mature poetry is by no means forgotten. But for the most part these attempts fail: they lack the old faith, and they never achieve convincing poetic form. It is generally true of Hölderlin that linguistic, formal difficulties and spiritual difficulties in the writing of a poem are inextricably mixed. Poems remain unfinished—a form of words cannot be found—precisely because a spiritual crisis cannot be resolved.[4] The high, prophetic attempts in the late poems are in this way doubly unsuccessful.

They are the work of a mind struggling against fatigue. Everything written in the later years, up to 1806, was written despite a growing tiredness. It tired Hölderlin's mind to write at all, as his mother reported to Sinclair in 1804 concerning a poem Hölderlin wanted to send to the Prinzessin von Homburg: '. . . und quält sich schon 3 Wochen so sehr, daß er gegenwärtig ganz geschwächt ist und beynahe seine Besinnungskraft verlohren hat'.[5]

The threat, or temptation, of this fatigue is dealt with in two poems, 'Andenken' and 'Mnemosyne', written at a time when Hölderlin was becoming aware of the need to defend himself. Both poems, as their titles indicate, are concerned with memory.

In 'Andenken' the asking for wine is a mark of dangerous relaxation:

> Damit ich ruhen möge; den süß
> Wär' unter Schatten der Schlummer.
>
> (lines 28-29, ii,189)

In 'Mnemosyne':

> Vorwärts aber und rükwärts wollen wir
> Nicht sehn. Uns wiegen lassen, wie
> Auf schwankem Kahne der See.
>
> (lines 15-17, 3.Fassung, ii,197)

Which is a lapsing from the old responsibilities to past and future. The poet's wakefulness and integrity are threatened. It is a mindless state he is tempted to allow himself, a giving way to fatigue. It would be spiritual death. In both poems he resists. How can he counter the temptation? There are two ways open to the poet. The first is the affirmative act of memory, either remembering the great deeds of the past:

> zu hören viel
> Von Tagen der Lieb',
> Und Thaten, welche geschehen.
>
> ('Andenken', lines 34-36).

the heroes of Troy, for example. Or personal memories: the trees, paths, and gardens of Bordeaux. The second way is the way of attachment to the real, present world, to his fellow human beings, to what Hölderlin calls 'die Tageszeichen' ('Mnemosyne', 3.Fassung, line 24).

In all the obscurity, incoherence, and incompleteness of the late poems these two themes—Hölderlin's two ways of self-affirmation—find perfect, clear poetic expression.

I want first to discuss the theme of private memory, in the poetry up to 1806. Then the theme of attachment to the simple details of the real, present world, in the poetry up to 1806 and in the final Tübingen poems.

Hölderlin wrote 'Andenken' early in 1803; his memories go back twelve months to Bordeaux:

> Dort, wo am scharfen Ufer
> Hingehet der Steg und in den Strom
> Tief fällt der Bach, darüber aber
> Hinschauet ein edel Paar
> Von Eichen und Silberpappeln . . .
>
> (lines 8-12)

The scene is exactly remembered: river-bank, path, stream, river, and trees were so a year before. Hölderlin recomposes the scene and fixes its relationships in words. He is not saying anything *about* the scene's details; he is merely saying, as exactly as he can, how they were. The 'aber', for example, in line 10, does not express any opposing or antithetical development in the thought (there is no 'thought', no 'argument'); its syntactic function is adversative only in that it introduces a further and contrasting detail of landscape: the stream falls, the trees rise above it. The memory is fixed in the syntax of the poem, and the success he has in wording it is a measure of the actuality of the memory in the poet's mind, and thus of lasting contact with his own past: 'Noch denket das mir wohl . . .' ('Andenken', line 13).

Such memories, rare in the earlier work, are frequent in the later poems, especially of the time in France. They are extraordinarily vivid, the more so when, in the fragments, they stand out from obscure and unfinished contexts:

> wo
> Bis zu Schmerzen aber der Nase steigt
> Citronengeruch auf und das Öl, aus der Provence, und es haben diese
> Dankbarkeit mir die Gascognischen Lande
> Gegeben.
>
> ('Vom Abgrund nemlich . . .', lines 27-31, ii,250-251)

Such sensuousness, rare in the poetry of 1801, is characteristic of the fragmentary visions and memories of these late poems. It is as though Hölderlin's senses were keener than ever before. The smell of the lemons and olives (probably brought in

from Provence to Bordeaux for export) is an irrepressible memory, almost
physically re-experienced. And it is this experience that Hölderlin calls 'diese
Dankbarkeit'. The past makes demands on the poet; it wants remembering. The
poet owes his past its due of memory. He is both obligated, and grateful; the
memories and the putting of them into words are what he needs to maintain
himself. The very act of remembering and writing is in itself affirmative: what he
remembers and writes hardly matters. Thus the quite innocent oaks and poplars
overhanging the stream served Hölderlin's private needs, and he owed them
gratitude and paid the debt by giving them a form of words. He remembered them
out of the mass of things experienced; and out of the indistinctness in which things
naturally occur he remembered a clear grouping and satisfying relationships. In
themselves the details were non-commital and quite without meaning: only the act
of remembering made them matter.

It is remarkable how often in the late poems Hölderlin remembers similar scenes.
'Heimath' and 'Griechenland' both contain memories of particular trees. And in
these lines, for example:

> Wunderbar
> Aber über Quellen beuget schlank
> Ein Nußbaum und   sich. Beere, wie Korall
> Hängen an dem Strauche über Röhren von Holz . . .
> ('Vom Abgrund nemlich . . .', lines 21-24, ii,250)

It is intensely seen: the nuts like coral (they will be walnuts, pinkish when ripe and
growing in clusters) and the strikingly particular detail of the wooden pipes. The
tree in itself is non-committal. The poet's sense of it is expressed in one word:
'wunderbar'. What amazes him is the completeness, the self-possessedness of the
tree. It is so definite.

Obvious but, I think, useful comparisons can be made here with the poetry of
Georg Trakl. Michael Hamburger has discussed Trakl's use of 'bare phenomena in
the form of images'.[6] For example, in the poem 'Verfall': 'Es schwankt der rote
Wein an rostigen Gittern' or: 'Im Wind sich fröstelnd blaue Astern neigen'.[7] Or the
poem 'De Profundis':

> Es ist ein Stoppelfeld, in das ein schwarzer Regen fällt.
> Es ist ein brauner Baum, der einsam dasteht.
>
> (page 63)

In imagist poetry the image comes close to being an end in itself; the mere fact that
phenomena exist is their own justification, and justifies their inclusion in a poem.
'The poetic image, then, becomes autonomous and "autotelic", or as nearly as the
medium of words allows'.[8] It has no meaning other than itself. The poet merely
notes things as they are.

But, in practice, however innocent things themselves may be, the poet's use of
them will almost always be tendentious. He may do no more than acknowledge

their existential integrity, their apartness from himself. But often awareness of their separate identity fills him with horror; they affront him with their self-possessedness, they seem so much more solid than himself. This is a basic matter in the existentialist philosophy of the absurd:

s'apercevoir que le monde est 'épais', entrevoir à quel point une pierre est étrangère, nous est irréductible, avec quelle intensité la nature, un paysage peut nous nier.[9]

Sartre's hero Roquentin suffers it:

Tous ces objets . . . comment dire? Ils m'incommodaient; j'aurais souhaité qu'ils existassent moins fort, d'une façon plus sèche, plus abstraite, avec plus de retenue. Le marronier se pressait contre mes yeux.[10]

The independent life that asserts itself in Van Gogh's chairs, cornfields, and trees could be felt to be similarly disturbing.

There are many other examples, of course. The disquieting 'otherness' of things is a theme that recent literature has treated at length.

Trakl sometimes lets things be, and is slightly appalled by their independence: 'Ein brauner Baum steht abgeschieden da' ('Elis', page 93). But more often the bare phenomena clearly lose their innocence and become expressive images, generally of anxiety and decay. In the lines already quoted from Trakl's poems words like 'rostig', 'sich fröstelnd', even 'neigen' are tendentious, and the emotional tenor of such a line: 'Im Abendgarten morsche Bäume sausen' (page 56) in a poem entitled 'Menschliche Trauer' is obvious.

Hölderlin, in some of his late work, is a precursor of such poetry. Trakl learned a lot from him, particularly the recording of bare, existential images, something which Hölderlin did almost unwillingly in his late poetry, as a necessary *pis aller* when the great prophetic themes could no longer be dealt with. Innocent phenomena make up a threatening landscape in 'Hälfte des Lebens':

> Die Mauern stehn
> Sprachlos und kalt, im Winde
> Klirren die Fahnen.

> (lines 12-14, ii,117)

Like Trakl's:

> Die Mauern starren kahl und grauverdreckt
> Ins kühle Dunkel.

> ('im Dorf', page 76)

The walls are the visible correlative of a state of mind; things as they are aptly express a private horror. Are the walls in themselves horrifying? This would be the existentialist view. Or do they suddenly correspond to and make visible an entirely human, private state? The human being sinking into the anxious state suddenly sees the inherent horror of the walls. His more susceptible mind discovers the horror latent in other things.

I know of only one further example in Hölderlin's work of this sensitivity to the inherent horror of things that was Trakl's particular gift. It is a strophe of a late Tübingen poem, 'Der Kirchhof':

> Wie still ist's nicht an jener grauen Mauer,
> Wo drüber her ein Baum mit Früchten hängt;
> Mit schwarzen thauigen, und Laub voll Trauer,
> Die Früchte aber sind sehr schön gedrängt.

(lines 9-12, ii,277)

That makes a disquieting scene, although the last line rather attenuates it. Very like poems by Trakl:

> Die Apfelbäume sinken kahl und stad
> Ins Farbige ihrer Frucht, die schwarz verdarb.

('Im Dorf' (2), page 75)

However, after discussing at such length the latent appallingness of all phenomena, it must be said that in general, apart from in the two poems 'Hälfte des Lebens' and 'Der Kirchhof', bare phenomena do not appal Hölderlin as they do Trakl and the existentialist writers of this century; and that when he pays them their due and remembers them exactly and records them as they are, he gains in self-assurance from being confronted by them. They are firm and he attaches himself to them; he keeps his place in the world by relating himself to them. The otherness of the nut-tree in 'Vom Abgrund nämlich . . .' is a wonder to Hölderlin, and a strength to him, not a horror.

In 'Mnemosyne' the temptation of vagueness and non-participation is countered thus:

> Wie aber liebes? Sonnenschein
> Am Boden sehen wir und trokenen Staub
> Und heimatlich die Schatten der Wälder und es blühet
> An Dächern der Rauch, bei alter Krone
> Der Thürme, friedsam . . .

(3.Fassung, lines 18-22, ii,197)

I take the opening phrase to mean: but what of the things we love, will they not help? (Beißner takes it to be a critical self-apostrophe: 'what *do* you think you're doing?')

The details make up a comfortingly real scene—of sunlight and shadow, familiar ('heimatlich') and, above all, human. The two earlier versions of the poem had in addition larks and clouds, but the scene is complete without them, less idyllic, more human. It is not an idyll—dry dust is not an idyllic detail—but a composition of secure and familiar facts. Its meaning is then made explicit:

> gut sind nemlich
> Hat gegenredend die Seele
> Ein Himmlisches verwundet, die Tageszeichen.
>
> (lines 22-24)

The variants help to clarify these lines:

> es gefallen nemlich
> die Lebenszeichen / Tageszeichen / Jahreszeichen / hat ein Himmlisches
> Die Sinne betäubt / die Seele getroffen / genommen / betroffen
>
> (ii,822-823)

The scene, earthly and human, is a comfort to one who has suffered from his dealings with the gods. How had Hölderlin suffered? By 1803 his personal life was in ruins, his mind was unstable and his poetic genius was failing. The gods had inflicted suffering on him—at least, that was how he understood it: struck down by Apollo, or suffering the fate of Tantalus. One of the 'Mnemosyne' variants—'die Sinne betäubt'—aptly describes the physical and mental state that Hölderlin was sinking into after the return from Bordeaux. He had suffered directly at the hands of the gods, through the fate they had laid on him, through his hubris in approaching too close.

But also, paradoxically, he had suffered through the obstinate absence of his gods, through their refusal to make themselves manifest, through the total failure of his poetry to induce them to appear. The paradox—one that Erich Heller and Anthony Thorlby have illuminated[11]—is that Hölderlin's gods, in whom he believed passionately, remained absent, that his religious intensity, his suffering 'at the hand of' the gods, derives from his painful awareness of their absence. The failing confidence in the years after 'Friedensfeier', the more modest work he assigns himself at the conclusion of 'Patmos' are indications of what he suffered through the gods, or because of them, because of their absence.

This suffering and disappointment can be resisted and refuge found against it in an attachment to the simplest facts of human life on earth. 'Die Tageszeichen' are a comfort, and, even more important, attachment to them offers a means of self-preservation against the threat of total uncommittedness, the attractive drowsiness of the boat rocking to and fro. At least the poet's wakefulness is preserved. Something is salvaged, for the time being. But this is a long way from the confident prophecies of the great hymns, and it is far, also, from the moments of ideal peace and harmony occasionally and briefly imagined in those hymns. The simple landscapes of 'Mnemosyne' or the fragments of the last Tübingen poems do not represent the ideal age that Hölderlin always hoped for: they are not the moment of final reconciliation, the 'Brautfest' ('Der Rhein', line 180), the peace of 'Friedensfeier', not 'Vollendruhe. Goldroth' (. . . 'der Vatikan' . . ., line 45). They are less than all that, they are a solace here and now to a desperately disappointed man, what he most needed and all he was capable of.

Another danger, the opposite extreme to fatigue and total relaxation of the will, can also be countered by a deliberate attachment to earthly things. It is the temptation of unrestraint. This, too, is a metaphysical matter, a danger men are prone to in their lives and in their dealings with the gods. It is a form of hubris; in effect a death-wish. The streams are an expression of it in 'Stimme des Volks'. The heroes give way to it, and however impressive their ending, they nevertheless incur the censure of the gods ('Mnemosyne'). The people of Xanthus are a warning example. This proneness to unrestraint is a basic human characteristic; but it must nevertheless be countered. The gods intervene wisely:

> Und hemmen öfters, daß er lang im
> Lichte sich freue, die Bahn des Menschen.
> > ('Stimme des.Volks', 2.Fassung, lines 31-32, ii,52)[12]

But human beings must also help themselves:

> Nemlich immer jauchzet die Welt
> Hinweg von dieser Erde, daß sie die
> Entblößet; wo das Menschliche sie nicht hält.
> > ('Der Einzige', 3.Fassung, lines 71-73, ii,163)

'The earth' is the indestructible planet on which 'the world'—the human race and its civilization—exists. The ecstatic, transcendental, self-destructive tendency in human beings threatens life on earth; in extreme terms, it threatens to depopulate the earth, just as the town of Xanthus was depopulated by the mass suicide of its inhabitants. The temptation must be countered by 'das Menschliche', by an attachment to human earthly life:

> Und es bieten tauschend die Menschen
> Die Händ' einander, sinnig ist es
> Auf Erden und es sind nicht umsonst
> Die Augen an den Boden geheftet.
> > ('Die Titanen', lines 58-61, ii,219)

Concisely put: 'Wohl thut/Die Erde. Zu kühlen' ('Der Einzige', 3.Fassung, lines 97-98).

In much earlier poems Hölderlin, living and wandering abroad, had prayed for some kind of permanent centre to his life:

> Und daß mir auch zu retten mein sterblich Herz,
> Wie andern eine bleibende Stätte sei,
> Und heimathlos die Seele mir nicht
> Über das Leben hinweg sich sehne . . .
> > ('Mein Eigenthum', lines 37-40, i,307)

The need increased as his years of wandering showed no signs of coming to an end; and as his awareness of the symbolic value of his life grew stronger, the need, like the journeying, was enhanced to mythical status. Unrestraint, dissolution, and never-ending homelessness were a part of the human condition; 'ein Bleiben im Leben' ('Der Frieden', line 44) was the hoped-for remedy.

After Bordeaux, as his mental health deteriorated, the need became more imperative than ever before, although he was living at home, in the ideal homeland he had always celebrated and longed to return to. The two extremes of his illness were the state of torpor described by his mother in letters to Sinclair, and the violent outbreaks which, Schwab records,[13] occasionally drove the family from the house in Nürtingen, or, as Sinclair wrote, aroused the anger of the common people in Homburg;[14] these outbreaks grew less frequent in later years and he sank into docile weak-mindedness. Against both states—the torpor of the wine in 'Andenken', of the rocking boat in 'Mnemosyne', and the wild temptation 'hinweg von dieser Erde'—the clinging to simple present reality is an attempted defence.

An aspect of this increasing undemandingness is, in several late poems, the offering of an alternative to the journeying that had previously seemed unavoidable. In 'Mnemosyne' there is first the mindless relaxation tantamount to extinction; second, better than the first but still modest, is the simple maintaining of life in comfortingly familiar surroundings; and third is the journey, over the pass into the new age. Only the first is unacceptable; life in the simple everyday setting is in itself an achievement, the journey may be done by others ('ein Wandersmann' not 'wir'). Hölderlin had reached a stage where his demands were very modest. In Rilke's words:[15] 'Wer spricht von Siegen? Uberstehn ist alles'. And in Hölderlin's:

> Und was du hast, ist
> Athem zu hohlen.
>
> ('Der Adler', lines 31-32, ii,230)

Yet life is not quite so bare. The poet, even if he does not put out to sea with his friends (in 'Andenken') or himself climb the pass into the new age (in 'Mnemosyne') still has a duty to fulfil. If he cannot prophesy, he can at least remember. He must remain mindful of the past, both his own and that of the culture to which he belongs.

It is not surprising that Swabian critics looking for descriptions of Swabia in Hölderlin's poems choose many of their examples from the late fragments. In half a dozen of these poems there are descriptive passages as satisfying, in their novelty, as anything Hölderlin ever wrote. They do, of course, show up in a rather false light by being the only parts of a poem that Hölderlin managed to put successfully into words. But still they are novel, since previously Hölderlin had never allowed himself to write at such length in that way:

> . . . und Rosendornen
> Und süße Linden duften neben
> Den Buchen, des Mittags, wenn im falben Kornfeld
> Das Wachstum rauscht, an geradem Halm,
> Und den Naken die Ähre seitwärts beugt

Dem Herbste gleich, jezt aber unter hohem
Gewölbe der Eichen, da ich sinn
Und aufwärts frage, der Glokenschlag
Mir wohlbekannt
Fernher tönt, goldenklingend, um die Stunde, wenn
Der Vogel wieder wacht. So gehet es wohl.

('Heimath', lines 7-17, ii,206)

Two things are remarkable about this and other, similar descriptive passages in 'Griechenland', 'Ihr sichergebaueten Alpen . . .', or 'Wenn nemlich der Rebe Saft . . .': they are detailed and visual; they are Germanic, or even definitely Swabian, 'heimatlich'. As an alternative to journeying the staying at home in such simple landscapes is offered:

Süß ist, dans unter hohen Schatten von Bäumen
Und Hügeln zu wohnen, sonnig, wo der Weg ist
Gepflastert zur Kirche.

('Griechenland', 3.Fassung, lines 46-48, ii,258)

(This instead of the journey: 'Reisenden aber . . .', line 48)

Even in the final Tübingen poems there are occasional reminders of the possibility of journeying:

der Ebnen sanfte Wege
Sind in den Feldern fern, und über Wasser gehet
Der Mensch zu Örtern dort die kühn erhöhten Stege.

('Aussicht', lines 6-8, ii,281)

Paths and bridges are frequently noted, as parts of the landscape:

So hat der Mensch das Feld geräumiger und Wege
Sind weit hinaus, daß Einer um sich schauet,
Und über einen Bach gehen wohlgebaute Stege.

('Der Frühling', lines 14-16, ii,283)

But Hölderlin notes them as the details of the simple landscape that has become his entire world. The paths do not lead out of it, at least not for him, observing them, but come and go within it.

The world of the last Tübingen poems is no wider than the view from Hölderlin's tower. One poem is entitled 'Griechenland' (ii,306), but the title is as arbitrary as are the dates and signatures of many of the others:

Mit Unterthänigkeit

d: 3$\underset{=}{\text{ten}}$ März 1648.   Scardanelli.

(ii,286)

No places are named; the landscape is always the one immediately in sight. The hymns of 1801 are sited in a coherently imagined world that stretches from India to Swabia; the hymns and fragments until 1806 sketch out a world of greater scope and richness, and of less coherence, in which many exotic places, as far as the South Seas, briefly feature. After that not a place-name is mentioned, and the world shrinks back to a few graspable details in the immediate vicinity.

The poems celebrating this world are simple and rhymed: rhyme binds, and achieves a simple harmony; within its small scope the world is comfortingly whole.

There is scarcely a sad or jarring note, almost no uneasiness. Hölderlin is pleased and comforted by what he sees. His pleasure in the view, and in being taken for walks as far as Waiblinger's summer-house on the Österberg is attested by Schwab and others.[16] But this does not mean that for thirty-five years he had peace of mind; rather the opposite; he had constant need of the natural world, outside himself:

> Wenn ich auf die Wiese komme,
> Wenn ich auf dem Felde jezt,
> Bin ich noch der Zahme, Fromme
> Wie von Dornen unverlezt.

> Und Betrachtung giebt dem Herzen
> Frieden . . .
> ('Das Fröhliche Leben', lines 1-4 and 29-30, ii,274-75)

The landscape, and the recording it in rhyme serves a comforting, recuperative function. It should not be supposed that Hölderlin's weak-mindedness was in any way an enviable state. Although not dramatically terrible like the violent paroxysms from which he first suffered it was nevertheless an unpleasant condition to be in—one of perpetual restlessness and nervous, fussy anxiety. It is reported that Hölderlin spent hours in the garden below his room obsessively plucking up grass and earth.[17] Such repetitive actions, like those of autistic children, are attempts to maintain or even to create a world in which to live.

Repetitiveness is the most obvious characteristic of the last poems. Repetitiveness in their themes: the recurring seasons, which he describes (not always at the appropriate time of year: some poems celebrating summer were demonstrably written in winter),[18] or simply notes (in the titles of poems that themselves have little to do with the season). Their recurrence is pleasing, or comforting: 'Es gefallen nemlich/Die Jahreszeichen, hat ein Himmlisches/Die Sinne betäubt' (ii,822). And the same landscape is repeatedly conveyed, in the same representative details—fruit-trees, river, path, bridge, vineyards—so perfecting a process of simplification that had always been typical of his art. All this in one style—repeating the verse form, the rhymes, even the fictitious dates affixed to the poems.

Hölderlin never quite gave up abstract thought. There are, even in these last poems, attempts, all unsuccessful, to intrude metaphysical, or at least abstract meanings into the physical, earthly context of things simply seen and recorded, even to write poems on abstract subjects: 'Höheres Leben', 'Des Geistes Werden';

abstract nouns abound. But the expression of the abstract is beyond his powers. The letters written in these years are so confused because they attempt to be more than the simplest relating of things seen. Hölderlin seems to have realized this:

Mein Briefschreiben wird Ihnen nicht immer viel seyn können, da ich das, was ich sage, so sehr, wie möglich, mit wenigen Worten sagen muß, und da ich jezt keine andere Art zu sagen habe.

(vi,464)

He could record what he saw in a very few words:

> Die Berge stehn bedeket mit den Bäumen . . .
> ('Der Frühling', line 5, ii,292)

> Zwar gehn die Treppen unter den Reben hoch
> Herunter, wo der Obstbaum blühend darüber steht . . .
> ('Wenn aus dem Himmel', lines 21-22, ii,269)

This is very little, but it is essential and enough.

NOTES AND REFERENCES

CHAPTER 1

1. Further discussion of Hölderlin's love for his homeland occurs in Chapter 4, pp.72 ff.
2. See Chapter 2, pp.21-29; Chapter 5, pp.98 ff. and Chapter 7, pp.140 ff.
3. See Chapter 2, pp.21-24.
4. Journeying and homecoming are the subject of Chapter 4.
5. See Chapter 3, pp.60-61.
6. See Chapter 3.
7. See Chapter 3, pp.54 ff.
8. See Chapter 4, pp.82 ff.
9. This development is traced in Chapters 2, 3, and 6.
10. But what happens is that the poetry asserts itself: as a more complicated and ambiguous thing than the man, his nature and his ideas. These ideas, for all their simplicity as ideas, are nothing like so simple in poetic practice; nor are they ever more than one among many constituents of the poem's total meaning. Cf. my article 'The Meaning of a Hölderlin Poem', *Oxford German Studies*, 9(1978), 45-67.
11. With the exception of 'Der Winkel von Hahrdt'—and even this is less an independent poem about a particular place than a small contribution towards Hölderlin's overall poetic purpose in the years after Bordeaux, which was to define and assert the Hesperian sphere against the Greek. (Fully discussed in Chapter 6.)
12. Unless after 1803, when Hölderlin's sense of what private details might serve as illustrations of general themes was failing him. Cf. discussion of 'Kolomb', '. . . der Vatikan' and 'Griechenland' in Chapter 6, pp.119 ff.
13. See Chapter 5, pp.98 ff.
14. Cf. Wolfgang Binder, 'Sprache und Wirklichkeit in Hölderlin Dichtung', *HJB* (1955-56), 183-200. Cf. Novalis: 'Die Welt hat eine ursprüngliche Fähigkeit durch mich belebt zu werden—Sie ist überhaupt a priori von mir belebt—Eins mit mir. Ich habe eine ursp [rüngliche] Tendenz und Fähigkeit die Welt zu beleben—Nun kann ich aber mit nichts in Verhältniß treten—was sich nicht nach meinem Willen richtet, oder ihm gemäß ist— Mithin muß die Welt die ursp[rüngliche] Anlage haben sich nach mir zu richten— meinem Willen gemäß zu seyn.' (*Schriften*, edited by Richard Samuel, second edition, Vol. II, (Stuttgart, 1965), p.554).
15. (Tübingen, 1946), pp.41-44.
16. Cf. discussion of 'Der Ister' and 'Das Nächste Beste' in Chapter 3, pp.61-65.

CHAPTER 2

1. Switzerland was also frequently compared with the Vale of Tempe in Thessaly—again, not inappropriately. Cf. Friedrich von Matthisson, 'Der Genfer See', ll.57-58, or 'Die Kinderjahre', l.170.
2. Cf. Lothar Kempter, *Hölderlin und die Mythologie* (Horgen, 1929), p.15.
3. GStA vi, 623. And cf. pp.36-37 of this chapter.
4. Examples of similar usages in the poetry of Hölderlin's contemporaries:
Karl Philipp Conz, 'Hymne an die Phantasie':
> . . . wenn jetzt in Alzinous Gärten
> Oder Hesperiens Land . . .

Christian Ludwig Neuffer, 'Auf den Frieden 1801':
> Den Krieg, den schändenden, laß den Barbaren,
> Den Tygern Libyens laß ihn . . .

Albrecht von Haller, *Die Alpen* (Bern, 1732), ll.315-16:
> Wahr ists, daß Lybien uns noch mehr neues giebet,

Und jeden Tag sein Sand ein frisches Unthier sieht . . .
5. 'Der Genfer See', ll.78, 85, 87; 'Der Alpenwandrer', l.54 (Etna), l.71 (Greenland); 'Die Kinderjahre', l.194((Peru), l.196 (Golonda); 'Abendgemälde', l.70 (Indus). 'An Agathon', l.5 (Paestum).
6. Cf. Neuffer, 'Elegie an Magenau', ll.59-62:
    . . . und riefen Homeros,
    Marons und Juvenals heilige Zeiten zurük,
    Träumten uns ganz in die glüklichen Tage der grauenden Vorwelt,
    Izt auf Hellas Gefild, izt auf Ausonischer Flur . . .
             (GStA vii,1,217).
7. Cf. Gotthold Friedrich Stäudlin's poem 'An die Jünglinge meines Vaterlands'.
8. 'Die Landschaft', in *Taschenbuch von der Donau*, 1825 (edited by Neuffer), pp.343 ff. Similar setting in Conz's 'Winterfantasie':
    Da, wo gotisch von den starren Höhen
    Blikt die alte Heldenburg herab . . .
9. 'Schloß Württemberg'. Similar settings in Johann Jakob Thill's 'Stauffen' and, of course, Matthisson's 'Elegie in den Ruinen eines alten Bergschlosses geschrieben'.
10. Thill, 'Stauffen', ll.23-24.
11. Matthisson, 'Elegie', ll.57-58.
12. K.P. Conz, 'Schloß Württemberg'.
13. Thill, 'Stauffen', ll.41-44.
    Most of the poems referred to on pp.21-22 are to be found in Paul Böckmann's useful anthology *Hymnische Dichtung im Umkreis Hölderlins* (Tübingen, 1965).
14. *Schwab*, ii,267.
15. Cf. 'Am Tage der Freundschaftsfeier', ll.99-116, i,61.
16. 'Emilie' was written (to order) in 1799 but is close to these early poems in sentiment, much closer to 'Burg Tübingen', than to 'Germanien'. 'Emilie' is a curious regression into the Germanic idiom—by 1799 Hölderlin was already committed to Greece as the ideal land.
17. Lothar Kempter, *Hölderlin und die Mythologie*, p.107.
18. In his *Musenalmanach* of 1782: in the foreword, and in his own poem 'An die Jünglinge meines Vaterlands'.
19. 'An die Ruhe', ll.31-32, i,93. Cf. Stäudlin, 'Elegie am Grabe des J.J. Rousseau':
    Zu der heiligen Stätte, wo, rings von Pappeln umsäuselt,
    Galliens Sokrates schläft . . .
20. Carl Vietor, *Die Lyrik Hölderlins* (Frankfurt, 1921), pp.28-29.
21. Discussed in Chapter 4.
22. See Chapter 4, pp.69-72.
23. 2 Vols. (Zürich, 1793).
24. Sir Gavin de Beer, *Travellers in Switzerland* (London, 1949), gives a useful list of journeys and dates.
25. He described his journey in a letter of 6 and 16 September 1790 to Dorothy Wordsworth, in *Descriptive Sketches* (1791-92) and in Book 6 of *The Prelude*.
26. 19 June 1775, Cf. *Schriften der Goethe-Gesellschaft*, 22, p.30.
27. Cf. vi, 39 ll.249-251. Also 'Die Tek', ll.3-6, i,55.
28. Matthisson, 'Der Alpenwandrer'; Stäudlin, 'Die Gletscher bei Grindelwald'; Stolberg, 'Hymne an die Erde'.
29. Cf. Sir Kenneth Clark, *Landscape into Art*, Pelican Books reprint (London, 1961), pp.97-98—the degeneration of landscape painting into an 'art of recognition' giving 'the popular taste . . . ready-made equivalents for its favourite themes'.
30. Cf. J.G. Ebel, *Über den Bau der Erde in dem Alpen-Gebirge*. (Zürich, 1808), p.4.
31. p.34. The Rhine, important in the rough drafts (ii,391, 1.18; ii,392, 1.28), is omitted from the final version. Cf. the notes for 'Dem Albekannten' (ii,832).
32. i,549, 1.6 and i,237, 1.39. Cf. p.40 of this chapter.
33. ii,713-15. Additions to lines 18,20,22,65, and 90 of the poem.
34. Added to the MS above the dedication 'An Vater Heinze', ii,722.
35. Discussed in Chapter 4, pp.82 ff.
36. Richard Chandler, *Travels in Greece* (Oxford, 1776), p.110.
37. Ibid., p.85.
38. Ibid., p.79.

39.   Hölderlin's poetic-descriptive method is discussed in Chapter 5.
40.   Richard Chandler, *Travels in Asia Minor* (Oxford, 1775), p.74.
41.   Wilhelm Heinse, *Ardinghello und die glückseeligen Inseln* (Leipzig, 1924), pp.166,212,366.
42.   Matthisson, 'Der Genfer See', ll.93-96.
43.   *Schwab*, ii,290.
44.   Cf. vi,232,235,263. iii,76. Also 'Diotima', 61-64 (i,214).
45.   *Schwab*, ii,280.

CHAPTER 3

1.   Cf. Herder: 'Immer verjüngt in seinen Gestalten, blüht der Genius der Humanität auf und ziehet palingenetisch in Völkern, Generationen und Geschlechtern weiter' in *Sämtliche Werke* (reprinted Hildesheim, 1967), xiii, 353. All Herder references are to this edition. Cf. also Hölderlin's fragment 'Palingenesie' (ii,317) which was written in his own copy of the *Musenalmanach* for 1792, next to his poem 'Hymne an die Freiheit', certainly after November 1796 (when he asked his brother to return the copy), almost certainly after 1797 (when Herder's essay *Palingenesie* appeared) and possibly as late as June 1799 (when a letter to his brother contains reminiscences of the Herder text). Cf. vi, 935 and *HJB* (1944), pp.76-87.
2.   I should like to acknowledge my debt to Peter Nickel. His dissertation *Die Bedeutung von Herders Verjüngungsgedanken und Geschichtsphilosophie für die Werke Hölderlins* (Kiel, 1963) has been of particular help to me–Chapters 9 and 10 especially.
3.   'Am Quell der Donau', l.80, ii,128. Cf. ii,687,688,690,691.
4.   Herder, xiii, 411.
5.   Herder, xiii, 431-33.
6.   'Der Einzige', ll.53-59, ii,154. 'Dichterberuf', ll.1-4, ii,46.
7.   Cf. 'Der Ister', ll.7-8, ii,190.
8.   Herder, xiii, 402.
9.   Cf. 'Die Wanderung', ll.64-72, ii,140.
10.   Cf. Herder, v, 497: 'Harmonie der Griechischen Leyer!'
11.   An encouraging comparison might perhaps be drawn between the German *Kleinstaaterei* and the Greek system of small, independent city-states.
12.   These Greek places celebrated and made use of by Hölderlin (only the most important references are given here):

Olympia	'Brod und Wein', ll.100-101, ii,93.
	'Der Einzige', l.19, ii,153.
Delphi	'Brod und Wein', l.62, ii,92.
	'Der Archipelagus', l.211, ii,109.
Corinth	'Am Quell der Donau', l.75, ii,128.
	'Der Einzige', l.21, ii,153.
	'Der Ister', l.31, ii,191.
Delos	'Der Archipelagus', ii.13-15, ii,103.
	'Gesang des Deutschen', l.57, ii,5.
Dodona	'Der Archipelagus', l.227, ii,110.
Thebes	Ibid., ll.229-30.
Olympus	'Der Adler', l.6, ii,229.
	'Der Ister', l.29, i,191.
	'Mnemosyne', variant of l.46, ii,823.
Parnassus	'Am Quell der Donau', l.37, ii,126.
	'Die Wanderung', l.73, ii,140.
	'Germanien', l.43, ii,150.
Tmolus	'Die Wanderung', l.73, ii,140.
	'Patmos', l.34, ii,166.
Cithaeron	'Am Quell der Donau', l.37, ii,126.
	'Brod und Wein', l.51, ii,91.
Colonus	'Der Archipelagus', l.177, ii,108.
Cos	'Patmos', l.153, ii,181.
Troy	'Mnemosyne', l.39, ii,198.

               'Die Wanderung', l.90, ii,140.
    Pindus   'An die Deutschen', l.37, ii,10.
    Helicon   Ibid., l.37.
    Haemus 'Der Adler', l.6, ii,229.
13. 'Der Archipelagus', ll.104-35,282,285-86, ii,106 ff.
14. Cf. 'Andenken', ll.40-43, ii,189.
15. 'Der Archipelagus', ll.65-66, ii,105.
16. Cf. Herder, v, 496: 'ein rechtes Zwischenland der Kultur!'
17. Cf. Herder, xiv, 96: 'Klein-Asien also ist die Mutter Griechlandes'.
18.   *Ephesus:*   'Der Einzige', l.24, ii,153.
     Smyrna: Ibid., l.23.
     Tenedos: 'Die Wanderung', addition to l.65, ii,714.
      Chios: 'Der Archipelagus', l.15, ii,103.
19. Jung, *Symbols of Transformation*, Vol. V of *Collected Works*, (translated by R.F.C. Hull), pp.407-11 (London, 1953-68).
20. See Chapter 5, pp.95-97.
21. *Taurus and Messogis:* 'Patmos'. l.36, ii,166.
            Cayster: Ibid., l.49. Also 'Die Wanderung', l.65, ii,140.
           Pactolus: 'Patmos', l.35, ii,166.
22. See Chapter 5, pp.88 ff.
23. The predicament of the modern Greeks is, of course, a theme that Hölderlin was concerned with in his novel, scarcely at all in his poetry. 'Der Main' (ll.19-24) and 'Der Nekar' (ll.27-32) are the only poems in which the theme is treated, and in style and mood they are poems of the *Hyperion* years. (Cf. Chapter 5, pp.92-93). There is one curious, direct reference in the late fragment '. . . der Vatikan . . .' (ll.32-33)—discussed in Chapter 6, pp.126-27.
24. 'Tuskisch'—adjective from the Latin *Tusci*.
25. Herder, xiv, pp.153 ff.
26. Cf. *Empedokles*, ll.1559-60, iv,66. '—wie auf schlanken Säulen, ruh/Auf richt'gen Ordnungen das neue Leben'.
27. Cf. 'Der Frieden', 'Dem Allbekannten'. But also Fragment 21. Rome begins to matter in the later poetry as a centre of the *orbis ecclesiae* (ii,941).
28. Similar imagery in Herder, xiii, 412-13.
29. In 'Die Wanderung', ll.72-75, ii,140. Cf. 'Germanien', ll.43-48, ii,150 and 'Der Adler', ll.1-8, ii,229.
30. 'Die Wanderung', l.71.
31. Cf. 'Das Nächste Beste'; Herder, xiii, pp.33 ff.
32. Much of what follows, concerning the Pietists Bengel and Oetinger, derives from Nickel's dissertation, particularly Chapter 9.
33. The title of a work by Friedrich Christoph Oetinger (1702-82). Johann Albrecht Bengel (1687-1752) forecast the millenium for 1836.
34. *Die güldene Zeit*, p.50. See Nickel, op.cit., pp.183 ff.
35. Title of a work by Oetinger (Frankfurt and Leipzig, 1762).
36. vi, 413. Cf. ll.17-18 of the same letter. The Peace and the Alpine landscape are again associated.
    For an excellent appraisal of Hölderlin's months in Hauptwyl see Lothar Kempter, *Hölderlin in Hauptwyl* (St Gallen, 1946).
37. 'Die Wanderung', ll.7-8, ii,138. The same geography in 'Ihr sichergebaueten Alpen . . .'.
38. Cf. p.68.
39. Cf. 'Der Rhein', 'Der Adler', '. . . der Vatikan . . .', 'Griechenland', Fragment 28.
40. 'Die Wanderung', ll.8-19, ii,138.
41. Herder, v,504-05.
42. See Chapter 4.
43. Cf. 'Hymne an den Genius Griechenlands', ll.30 and 35, i,126. Also especially 'Thränen', ii,58.
44. *Iliad*, viii, 519.
45. 'Die Wanderung', l.4, ii,138. *Iliad*, viii,47.
46. 'Der Main', l.37, i,304.
47. 'Heimkunft', ll.57 and 59, ii,98.
48. Ibid., l.62. Pindar, 'Pythian IV', l.211.

49. 'Stutgard', l.76, ii,88. 'Die Wanderung', l.71, ii,140. Pindar, 'Pythian IV', ll.77. 'Nemean II', l.5.
50. 'Das Nächste Beste', l.47, ii,238. Cf. Homer, *Iliad*, xxiv, 396.
51. 'Heidelberg', l.22, ii,14.
52. 'Die Wanderung', l.5, ii,138.
53. See pp.42-43.
54. See the rough drafts of the lost opening strophe of 'Am Quell der Donau', ii,687 ff.
55. Herder, xiii, 33 ff.
56. Cf. 'Tinian', ll.10-11, ii,240. 'Die Wanderung', ll.83-85, ii,140.
57. Cf. J.G. Ebel, *Über den Bau der Erde in dem Alpen-Gebirge*, p.14: 'Eine auffallende Erscheinung ist es, daß die längsten und bedeutendsten Thäler in der Richtung oder Streichung des Alpengebirges liegen'.
58. 'An die Madonna', ll.108-11, ii,214. See Chapter 6, p.111 and p.114 for further comment on this passage.
59. ll. 80,82,83, ii,140. Cf. Herder, xiii, 410.
60. Cf. 'Der Adler', ll.7-8, ii,229.
     'Wenn aber die Himmlischen . . .', l.85, ii,224.
     Pindar, 'Pythian I', ll.93-104 − translated by Hölderlin, v,66.
61. In Emil Staiger's translation. Cf. also ll.201-10, 936-39.
62. For example, by Ernst Müller in *Hölderlin: Studien zur Geschichte seines Geistes* (Stuttgart, 1944), pp. 391 ff.
63. Wilhelm Michel, *Hölderlins Abendländische Wendung* (Jena, 1923), p.39.

CHAPTER 4

1.   'Emilie vor ihrem Brauttag' and 'Das Nächste Beste', for example.
2.   Switzerland: vi, 94,149,401; also vii,1,154.
     Frankfurt: vi,173.
     Heilbronn: vii,1,125.
     Copenhagen: vi,158.
     Pomerania: vi,312. Travelling-companion: vi,149.
3.   *Anleitung auf die nützlichste und genußvollste Art in der Schweitz zu reisen*, Volume 1, 31-32.
4.   *Schwab*, ii,277.
5.   vi, 408 and 1051.
6.   vi,167 and 737.
7.   Cf. especially vi, 362.
8.   Cf. Friedrich Beißner, *Hölderlins Übersetzungen aus dem Griechischen* (Stuttgart, 1933), pp.147-84.
9.   Cf. 'Mnemosyne', ll.8-9, ii,197.
10. 'Der Einzige', l.78, ii,159.
     'Patmos', ll.159-60, ii,186.
11. 'Mnemosyne', ll.29-34, ii,198.
     'Abendphantasie', ll.3-4, i,301.
     'Der Wanderer', especially ll.89 ff., ii,82-83.
12. 'Heidelberg', variants ll.11-12, ii,410.
     'Heimkunft', l.52, ii,97.
13. 'Mnemosyne', ll.29-34, ii,198.
14. 'Der Wanderer', rough draft l.76, i,520.
     'Die Heimath', l.10, ii,19.
     'Der Nekar', ll.9-13, ii,17.
15. Cf. vi,232, especially ll.29-32; also 'Rükkehr in die Heimath', ll.15-20, ii,29.
16. Cf. vi,362, especially ll.58-60.
17. Discussed in Chapter 5, pp.92-93.
18. Cf. 'Germanien', especially ll.1-16, ii,149.
19. Cf. 'Die Wanderung', l.91, ii,141.
     'Am Quell der Donau', ll.74 and 86, ii,127-28.
     'Germanien', ll.1-16, ii,149.
20. Cf. Emil Petzold, *Hölderlins Brod und Wein* (Darmstadt, 1967), p.95. Also Lothar Kempter, *Hölderlin und die Mythologie*, (Horgen, 1929), note 34.

CHAPTER 5

1. vi,123 and 129-30.
2. Cf. 'Die beschreibende Poësie' (i,229). For comment on the early Swabian poems see Chapter 2, pp.21-29, on the late 'descriptive' fragments see Chapter 7, pp.140 ff.
3. Richard Chandler, *Travels in Asia Minor* (Oxford, 1775). *Travels in Greece* (Oxford, 1776). German editions, Leipzig, 1776 and 1777. References are to the English editions unless otherwise stated. I shall quote from the German editions only when it is important to show exactly what Hölderlin read.
4. Choiseul-Gouffier, *Voyage pittoresque de la Grèce*, Vol.I. (Paris, 1782). Translated into German by Heinrich August Ottokar Reichard, in two parts, Gotha, 1780 and 1782. Probably Reichard translated no further than p.164 of the French original. References are to the French edition unless otherwise stated.
5. This same passage is commented on, for a different purpose, by Ernst Müller in *Hölderlin: Studien zur Geschichte seines Geistes* (Stuttgart, 1944), p.263.
6. Chandler, *Greece*, German edition, p.329 (English edn., p.230).
7. Ibid., p.331 (English edn., p.232).
8. Ibid., p.419 (English edn., p.294).
9. Ibid., p.331 (English edn., p.232).
10. German edn., p.38 (English edn., pp.27-28).
11. Chandler, *Asia Minor* – Myrtles : p.80, p.110.
    Laudanum: p.246.
    Swans : p.258 (Also Homer, *Iliad*, ii,460).
12. Ibid., p.255 and p.261.
13. Ibid., pp.255-56.
14. E.g. 'Die Tek', 'Kanton Schwyz', 'Emilie vor ihrem Brauttag'. These are the metres Haller and Neuffer favour.
15. Choiseul, *Voyage pittoresque*, p.68.
16. *Sarcophagi* Chandler, *Asia Minor*, p.43.
    Choiseul, *Voyage pittoresque*, Plate 7, p.13.
    The plate shows a white marble sarcophagus used as a cistern. Choiseul comments: 'Fait pour consacrer peut-être, la mémoire d'un héros, la barbarie des habitants l'a dévoué aux usages les plus vils'.
    Pillars, altars: Chandler, *Asia Minor*, p.16, p.43.
    Jackals: Ibid., p.35, p.115, p.171.
    Hölderlin, iii,7.
    Cranes: Chandler, *Asia Minor*, p.22.
    Hölderlin, iii,16.
17. iii,86.
18. Chandler, *Asia Minor*, p.208.
19. *The Poetical Works of William Wordsworth* (Oxford, 1940), i,58. Cf. the variants of 'Dichtermuth', ii,530-31.
20. Homer, *Iliad*, xviii, 11.
21. See Chapter 3, pp.49-51.
22. See Chapter 3, pp.44 ff.
23. Chandler, *Asia Minor*, German edition, p.206 (English edn., p.146 'The Gardens': Ibid., p.179 (German edn., p.253).
24. 'Der goldgeschmükte Pactol . . .': cf. Sophocles, *Philoctetes*, l.394. Euripides, *Bacchae*, l.154.
25. Jung, *Symbols of Transformation*, pp.407-11.
26. Discussed in Chapter 3.
27. p.8.
28. E.g. vi,132 and 239. Cf. iii,21.
29. 'Das Fröhliche Leben', l.37, ii,275.
30. 'Die Muße', ll.21-23, i,236, and cf. vi,239.
31. *Maeander:* 'Der Archipelagus', ll.48-49, ii,104.
    Nile: Ibid., ll.51-52.
    Colonus: Ibid., ll.177-78.
    Cayster: 'Die Wanderung', ll.65-66, ii,140.
32. *Cephissus:* 'Der Gott der Jugend', ll.33-40, i,190.
    Tivoli: Ibid., ll.25-32.
    Virgil's grave: 'Griechenland', ll.18-19, ii,254.
    Cithaeron: 'Brod und Wein', ll.51-52, ii,91.

	Ida:	'Die Wanderung', l.90, ii,140.
33.	Chapter 3, pp.60-61.	
34.	*Taunus:*	'Der Wanderer', l.54, ii,81.
	Swabia:	'Die Wanderung', l.4, ii,138.
	Gascony:	'Das Nächste Beste', l.10, ii,237.
	Stuttgart:	'Stugard', ll.71-72, ii,88.
	Neckar:	'Der Gang aufs Land', l.37, ii,85.
		'Heimkunft', variant of l.69, ii,624.
	Württemberg:	'Das Nächste Beste', ll.41-42, ii,235.

35. Neuffer in his long poem 'Die Landschaft' (quoted p.21) provides examples enough of this emptiness. At the same time he attempts to be exhaustive; he feels compelled to list everything he sees. The result is a surfeit of insignificant detail.

CHAPTER 6

1. *Schwab*, ii,308.
2. Though he may have had his own—political—reasons for doing so. See the correspondence of Sinclair and Hölderlin's mother, especially 20 December 1802 (Hellingrath, vi,347), 17 June 1803 (ibid., vi,349) and August 1804 (ibid, vi,367); GStA, vii,2, 241-43, 254-56, 299.
3. Discussed in Chapter 7.
4. The theory put forward by Wilhelm Michel in an essay of 1919—later published in a collection of essays entitled *Hölderlins abendländische Wendung* (Jena, 1923). References are to this edition.
5. Michel, op.cit., p.13.
6. Cf. Michel's phrase 'abendländisch erlebbar zu machen' (op.cit., p.33).
7. The poem was sketched out down the lefthand side of the MS page. Lines 24-32 occur in the wide margin on the right, by the gap Hölderlin left between 'Wann aber . . .' and 'Des Tübingens . . .'. Beißner inserts them into that gap as his text. But Hölderlin's own insertion between l.2 and l.3, 'Das Wirtemberg' and the marginal lines 'Die Tempel und der Dreifuß etc.', these Beißner prints among the *Lesarten*.
8. See Chapter 2, p.35.
9. The following interpretation of lines 17-22 was suggested to me by Fr. Prof. Schulz of Tübingen University: 'Ihr guten Städte!' are the towns on the shores of Lake Constance. Lines 18-22 refer to the Rhine which flows through and leaves the lake with its identity intact: 'Nicht ungestalt, mit dem Feinde/Gemischet unmächtig . . .', 'Und siehet den Tod nicht'.
10. Chapter 3, p.65. Cf. p.111 of this chapter and Erich Hock's commentary on ll.108-115 (in *Dort drüben in Westfalen* (Münster, 1949), pp.33-38, 68-72).
11. Chapter 2, p.38.
12. The details may derive from the account of Anson's voyage. The phrase 'der geflügelte Krieg', for example (l.44): Anson's mission was to harass the Spaniards in their South American colonies, and to prey on Spanish merchant shipping. 'Geflügelt', as Beißner suggests, will refer to the sails, the 'wings' of the men-of-war. (Significantly, this usage is something of a Graecism—see Beißner's notes, ii,805-06). 'Zu wohnen einsam, jahrlang, unter/Dem entlaubten Mast . . .'—Anson's squadron was repeatedly scattered by storms; the ships were out of sight of one another for weeks at a time. And in all the sailors were three years and nine months away from home. In storms the masts were stripped of their sails: 'and [we] were some sometimes reduced to lie at the mercy of the waves under our bare poles' (*A Voyage round the World* (London, 1748, pp.77; cf. pp.78-79).
13. See Chapter 3, pp.44-46.
14. Quoted by Beißner, i, 523.
15. Not, however, the Tinian that Anson found: 'For the prospect of the country did by no means resemble that of an uninhabited and uncultivated place, but had much more the air of a magnificent plantation, where large lawns and stately woods had been laid out together with great skill . . .' (op.cit., p.306; cf. p.337). Rousseau, drawing on Anson, made a paradise of it in *La Nouvelle Héloise* (edited by René Pomeau, Garnier (Paris, 1960), 394, 396, 454, 455). It is Rüdiger Stéphan's view (in his article 'Le "Tinian" de

Hölderlin') that Hölderlin followed Rousseau. That is a view I do not share. Hölderlin had a mythology of his own and in it Tinian stood not for paradise but for wandering abroad.

16. Cf. a similar mixing of the two spheres in *Ardinghello* (Leipzig, 1924), p.92.
17. Discussed in Chapter 7.
18. Cf. Karl Jaspers, *Strindberg und Van Gogh* (Bremen, 1949), p.134: 'Man beobachtet bei Schizophrenen, wie sie ihren eigenen Mythos bilden, der für sie selbstverständlich, fraglos besteht . . .'.
19. Cf. 'Brod und Wein', l.12, ii,90. Also Fr. 48, ii,329: 'Höret das Horn des Wächters bei Nacht . . .'
20. Chandler, *Greece*, p.297. On the same page he speaks of 'the annual unhealthiness of the Morea'. Cf. p.298: 'my companions and two of our servants being ill of a fever, which was ascribed to the bad air of the Morea' (German edition, p.424: '. . . welche der schlimmen Luft von Morea zugeschrieben wurde'.)
21. Ed.cit., p.375. The passage continues: '. . . der nur nicht lange dauern wird, weil alle Reisenden, Dichter, Prinzen und Damen davon abbrechen, um Antheil an dem Ruhme des Unsterblichen zu haben'.
22. Cf. 'Olympian 2', ll.51-53 (v,46): 'im Meer auch/Mit den Mädchen des Nereus/Den kristallenen . . .'

CHAPTER 7

1. Cf. the much later poem 'Wenn aus der Ferne . . .' (ii,262-3), especially ll.21-32.
2. Hans Gottschalk: *Das Mythische in der Dichtung Hölderlins* (Stuttgart, 1943).
3 Cf. 'Stimme des Volks' (2. Fassung), ll.69-72, ii,53,
   'Patmos', ll.222-26, ii,172,
   also ll.165-66, ii,182.
4. Cf. Robert Graves, 'Harp, Anvil, Oar', in *The Crowning Privilege* (London, 1959), p.99: 'It is an axiom among poets that if one trusts whole-heartedly to poetic magic, one will be sure to solve any merely verbal problem or else discover that the verbal problem is hiding an imprecision in poetic thought'.
5. Hellingrath, vi,357. GStA, vii,2,271.
6. Michael Hamburger, *Reason and Energy* (London, 1970), p.292.
7. Georg Trakl, *Die Dichtungen*, twelfth edition (Otto Müller Verlag, Salzburg), p.9. All subsequent references are to this edition.
8. Hamburger, op.cit., p.292.
9. Albert Camus, *Le Mythe de Sisyphe*, ed. Gallimard, p.28.
10. Jean-Paul Sartre, *La Nausée*, ed. Gallimard, p.163.
11. In 'Idealism and Religious Vision in Hölderlin', *Quarterly Review of Literature* (1959), pp.23-40.
12. Cf. *Anmerkungen zur Antigonä*, v,268, ll.8-11.
13. Schwab, ii,308. And cf. Wilhelm Michel, *Das Leben Friedrich Hölderlins* (Darmstadt, 1963), pp.459-61.
14. In a letter to Hölderlin's mother, 3 August 1806. Hellingrath, vi,369, GStA, vii,2,352.
15. 'Requiem für Wolf Graf von Kalckreuth',
16. Schwab, ii,p.325.
    Wilhelm Waiblinger, *Friedrich Hölderlins Leben, Dichtung and Wahnsinn* (Marbach, 1951), pp.31-32; GStA, vii,3, 66-67.
17. Waiblinger, p.27; GStA, vii,3,64.
18. 'Der Sommer' ('Das Erndtefeld erscheint . . .', ii,285) was written in December 1837. Cf. Friedrich Beißner, 'Zu den Gedichten der letzten Lebenszeit', *HJB* (1947), pp.6-10.

BIBLIOGRAPHY

A. EDITIONS OF HÖLDERLIN'S WORKS AND LETTERS

Sämtliche Werke, Hg. von Christoph Theodor Schwab, 2 Bde. (Stuttgart and Tübingen, 1846)
Sämtliche Werke. Historisch-kritische Ausgabe. Begonnen durch Norbert von Hellingrath, fortgeführt durch Friedrich Seebaß und Ludwig von Pigenot, 6 Bde. (München, 1913-23)
Sämtliche Werke (Große Stuttgarter Ausgabe), Hg. von Friedrich Beißner und Adolf Beck, 8 Bde. (Stuttgart, 1943 ff.)

B. CONTEMPORARY WORKS OF TOPOGRAPHY AND TRAVEL

Anson, George (Baron), *A Voyage round the World in the Years 1740-44*, (London, 1748). German translation by Eobald Toze (Leipzig and Göttingen, 1749)
Barthélemy, Jean Jacques (Abbé), *Voyage du jeune Anarcharsis en Grèce*, 5 vols (Paris, 1788). German translation (Berlin and Libau, 1789)
Chandler, Richard, *Travels in Asia Minor* (Oxford, 1775)
—— *Travels in Greece* (Oxford, 1776). German translations (Leipzig, 1776 and 1777)
Choiseul-Gouffier, Marie Gabriel (Comte de), *Voyage pittoresque de la Grèce*, 2 vols (Paris, 1782 and 1809). German translation (probably only as far as p.164 of vol. 1) by Heinrich August Ottokar Reichard (Gotha, 1780 and 1782)
Conz, Carl P., *Schildereyen aus Griechenland* (Reutlingen, 1784)
Ebel, Johann G., *Anleitung auf die nützlichste und genußvoliste Art in der Schweitz zu reisen*, 2 vols (Zürich, 1793)
—— *Über den Bau der Erde in dem Alpen-Gebirge* (Zürich, 1808)
Forster, Johann G.A., *J.R. Forsters . . . Reise um die Welt während den Jahren 1772 bis 1775 . . .* 3 vols (Berlin, 1784)

C. BOOKS AND ARTICLES ON HÖLDERLIN

Beck, Adolf, 'Aus den letzten Lebensjahren Hölderlins', *HJB* (1948-49), 15-47
—— 'Zu Hölderlins Rückkehr von Bordeaux', *HJB* (1950), 72 ff.; (1951), 50-67
—— 'Zu Hölderlins Aufenthalt in Bordeaux', *HJB* (1953), 67-73
—— 'Eine Personalbescriebung Hölderlins und die Frage seines Weges nach Bordeaux'. *HJB* (1957), 67 ff.
—— 'Hölderlin im Juni 1802 in Frankfurt?' *HJB* (1975-77), 458-75
Beißner, Friedrich, *Hölderlins Übersetzungen aus dem Griechischen* (Stuttgart, 1933)
—— 'Über die Realien des *Hyperion*', *HJB* (1954), 93-109
—— *Individualität in Hölderlins Dichtung* (Winterthur, 1965)
Benn, Maurice B., *Hölderlin and Pindar* (The Hague, 1962)
Bertaux, Pierre, *Hölderlin. Essai de biographie intérieure* (Paris, 1936)
—— *Hölderlin und die Französische Revolution* (Frankfurt/M., 1969)
—— 'Hölderlin in und nach Bordeaux', *HJB* (1975-77), 94-111
Binder, Wolfgang, 'Sinn und Gestalt der Heimat in Hölderlins Dichtung', *HJB* (1954), 46-78
—— 'Sprache und Wirklichkeit in Hölderlins Dichtung', *HJB* (1955-56), 183-200
Boeckh, Joachim G., *Die deutsche Landschaft bei Hölderlin* (Gießen, 1941)

153

Böckmann, Paul, *Hölderlin und seine Götter* (Munich, 1935)
Böhm, Wilhelm, *Hölderlin*, 2 vols (Halle, 1928-30)
— — *Hölderlin und die Schweiz* (Frauenfeld, 1935)
Böschenstein, Bernhard, *Hölderlins Rheinhymne* (Freiburg/Brsg., 1959)
— — 'Hölderlins späteste Gedichte', *HJB* (1965-66), 35-36
— — *Konkordanz zu Hölderlins Gedichten nach 1800* (Göttingen, 1964)
Gottschalk, Hans, *Das Mythische in der Dichtung Hölderlins* (Stuttgart, 1943)
Guardini, Romano, *Form und Sinn der Landschaft in den Dichtungen Hölderlins*
    (Tübingen, 1946)
— — *Hölderlin, Weltbild und Frömmigkeit*, second edition (Munich, 1955)
Gundolf, Friedrich, *Hölderlins Archipelagus* (Heidelberg, 1911)
Harrison, Robin B., *Hölderlin and Greek Literature* (Oxford, 1975)
Häussermann, Ulrich, *Hölderlin in Selbstzeugnissen und Bilddokumenten* (Reinbek,
    1961)
Heller, Erich (with Anthony Thorlby), 'Idealism and Religious Vision in Hölderlin',
    Quarterly Review of Literature (1959)
Hellingrath, Norbert von, *Hölderlin-Vermächtnis* (Munich, 1936)
Hock, Erich, *Dort drüben in Westfalen* (Münster, 1949)
— — 'Zu Hölderlins Reise nach Kassel und Dribourg', *HJB* (1969-70), 254-90
Kempter, Lothar, *Hölderlin und die Mythologie* (Horgen, 1929)
— — *Hölderlin in Hauptwyl* (St Gallen, 1946)
Kirchner, Werner, 'Hölderlin und das Meer', *HJB* (1961-62), 74-94
Lerch, Karl, ' "Zu euch, ihr Inseln!"': Hölderlin und die schwäbische Landschaft',
    Revaler Zeitung (21 June 1944)
Lüders, Detlev, *Die Welt im verringerten Maasstab* (Tübingen, 1968)
Michel, Wilhelm, *Das Leben Friedrich Hölderlins* (Darmstadt, 1963)
— — *Hölderlins abendländische Wendung* (Jena, 1923)
Müller, Andreas, 'Die beiden Fassungen von Hölderlins 'Wanderer' ', *HJB*
    (1948-49), 103-31
Müller, Ernst, *Hölderlin, Studien zur Geschichte seines Geistes* (Stuttgart, 1944)
Nickel, Peter, *Die Bedeutung von Herders Verjüngungsgedanken und
    Geschichtsphilosophie für die Werke Hölderlins* (Diss. Kiel, 1963)
Niethammer, Hermann, 'Des Seminaristen Friedrich Hölderlin Reise von Maulbronn
    nach der Pfalz', *Tübinger Blätter*, 38 (1951), 24-34
Otto, Walter F., *Der griechische Göttermythos bei Goethe und Hölderlin* (Berlin,
    1939)
— — *Hölderlin und die Griechen*', *HJB* (1948-49), 48-65
Pannwitz, Rudolf, 'Hölderlins Erdkarte' in *Hölderlin: Beiträge zu seinem
    Verständnis in unserem Jahrhundert,* edited by Alfred Kelletat (Tübingen, 1961)
Peacock, Ronald, *Hölderlin* (London, 1938)
Petzold, Emil, *Hölderlins Brod und Wein*, new edition (Darmstadt, 1967)
Raabe, Paul, *Die Briefe Hölderlins* (Stuttgart, 1963)
Riedel, Ingrid (Ed.), *Hölderlin ohne Mythos* (Göttingen, 1973)
Rosteutscher, J., *Hölderlin, der Künder der großen Natur* (Bern, 1962)
Ryan, Lawrence J., *Friedrich Hölderlin* (Stuttgart, 1962)
Schmidt, Jochen (Ed.), *Über Hölderlin* (Frankfurt, 1970)
Schuffels, Klaus, 'Griechenlandbild und Schöneitsideal als Ausdruck
    demokratischen Denkens'; *Etudes Germaniques* (1973), 304-17
Stahl, Ernst L., *Hölderlin's Symbolism* (Oxford, 1945)
— — 'Hölderlin's "Friedensfeier" and the Structure of Mythic Poetry', *Oxford
    German Studies* (1967), 55-74.
Staiger, Emil, 'Hölderlin und die Schweiz', *Atlantis* (1943), 289-94
Stéphan, Rüdiger, 'Le "Tinian" de Hölderlin', *Les Pharaons (La Voix des Poètes, 38)*
    (1970), 26-33
Szondi, Peter, *Hölderlin-Studien* (Frankfurt/M., 1967)
Vietor, Carl, *Die Lyrik Hölderlins* (Frankfurt/M., 1921)

Volker, Werner, *Hölderlin 1770-1970* (Schiller-Nationalmuseum, Katalog Nr. 21) Stuttgart 1970)
Wailblinger, Wilhelm, *Friedrich Hölderlins Leben, Dichtung und Wahnsinn*, new edition (Marbach, 1951)

D. GENERALLY RELEVANT READING

Anderle, Martin, 'Das gefährdete Idyll', *German Quarterly*, xxxv,4
de Beer, Sir Gavin R., *Early Travellers in the Alps* (London, 1930)
— — *Travellers in Switzerland* (London, 1949)
Bowra, Sir Cecil M., 'The Meaning of a Heroic Age' (Earl Grey Lecture, 1951)
— — *The Greek Experience* (London, 1957)
Butler, Eliza M., *The Tyranny of Greece over Germany* (Cambridge, 1935)
Cary, Max, *Geographic Background of Greek and Roman History* (Oxford, 1949)
Clark, Sir Kenneth, *Landscape into Art*, Pelican reprint (London, 1961)
Hamburger, Michael, *Reason and Energy* (London, 1970)
Heller, Erich, *Studien zur modernen Literatur* (Frankfurt/M., 1963)
Jaspers, Karl, *Strindberg und Van Gogh* (Bremen, 1949)
Jung, Carl F., *Symbols of Transformation* (Vol. 5 of the *Collected Works*, trans. by R.F.C. Hull, London, 1953-68)
Müller, Andreas, *Landschaftserlebnis und Landschaftsbild* (Stuttgart, 1955)
Otto, Walter F., *The Homeric Gods* (London, 1955)
Parry, J.H., *The Age of Reconnaissance* (New York, 1964)
Rehm, Walther, *Griechentum und Goethezeit*, second edition (Leipzig, 1938)
Rose, John H., *The Mediterranean in the Ancient World* (Cambridge, 1934)
Seymour, T.D., *Life in the Homeric Age* (New York, 1907)
Zweig, Stefan, *Der Kampf mit dem Dämon* (Leipzig, 1925)

INDEX OF PLACES

INDEX OF PERSONS AND MYTHOLOGICAL FIGURES

MODERN HUMANITIES RESEARCH ASSOCIATION

TEXTS AND DISSERTATIONS
(formerly Dissertation Series)

VOLUME 12

Editor
H. B. Nisbet
(Germanic)

The Significance of Locality
in the Poetry
of Friedrich Hölderlin